Environment and Aging Theory

Recent Titles in
Contributions to the Study of Aging

Senior Centers in America
John A. Krout

Shared Housing for the Elderly
Dale J. Jaffe, editor

Who Cares for Them? Workers in the Home Care Industry
Penny Hollander Feldman with Alice M. Sapienza and Nancy M. Kane

Aiding and Aging: The Coming Crisis in Support for the Elderly by Kin and State
John Mogey, editor

Population Aging in the United States
William J. Serow, David F. Sly, and J. Michael Wrigley

Suicide Among the Elderly in Long-Term Care Facilities
Nancy J. Osgood, Barbara A. Brant, and Aaron Lipman

Social Policies for the Elderly in the Third World
Martin B. Tracy

Elder Mistreatment: Deciding Who Is at Risk
Tanya Fusco Johnson

Centenarians: The New Generation
Belle Boone Beard
Nera K. Wilson, Albert J. E. Wilson III, and Belle Boone Beard
Gerontology Center, Lynchburg College, editors

Passages of Retirement: Personal Histories of Struggle and Success
Richard S. Prentis

The Chronically Disabled Elderly in Society
Merna J. Alpert

Uprooted in Old Age: Soviet Jews and Their Social Networks in Israel
Howard Litwin

Environment and Aging Theory

A FOCUS ON HOUSING

EDITED BY
Rick J. Scheidt
and Paul G. Windley

Contributions to the Study of Aging, Number 26

GREENWOOD PRESS
Westport, Connecticut • London

Library of Congress Cataloging-in-Publication Data

Environment and aging theory : a focus on housing / edited by Rick J.
  Scheidt and Paul G. Windley.
      p. cm.—(Contributions to the study of aging, ISSN
  0732–085X ; no. 26)
    Includes bibliographical references and index.
    ISBN 0–313–28389–3 (alk. paper)
    1. Aged—Housing—United States. 2. Aged—United States—
  Psychology. 3. Housing—United States—Psychological aspects.
  4. Environmental psychology—United States. I. Scheidt, Rick J.,
  1944– . II. Windley, Paul G., 1941– . III. Series.
  HD7287.92.U54E58 1998
  363.5'946'0973—dc21   97–37968

British Library Cataloguing in Publication Data is available.

Library of Congress Catalog Card Number: 97–37968
ISBN: 0–313–28389–3
ISSN: 0732–085X

First published in 1998

Greenwood Press, 88 Post Road West, Westport, CT 06881
An imprint of Greenwood Publishing Group, Inc.

Printed in the United States of America

The paper used in this book complies with the
Permanent Paper Standard issued by the National
Information Standards Organization (Z39.48–1984).

10 9 8 7 6 5 4 3 2 1

Copyright Acknowledgments

The authors and publisher are grateful for permission to reproduce the
following copyrighted material.

Figure 1.1, ''Lawton and Nahemow's Competence-Press Model.''
Copyright © 1998 by the American Psychological Association. Reprinted with
permission.

Figure 5.1, ''A Model of the Relationship between Environmental and Personal
Factors and Resident Stability and Change,'' and Figure 5.2, ''A Model of the
Determinants of Social Climate in Group Residential Facilities.'' From *Group
Residences for Older Adults: Physical Features, Policies, and Social Climate*,
by Rudolf H. Moos and Sonne Lemke. Copyright © 1994 by Oxford
University Press, Inc. Reprinted by permission.

To M. Powell Lawton:

mentor, visionary, scientist, and genuinely nice guy.

Contents

Preface   ix

1. Environment and Aging: Theory Revisited
   M. Powell Lawton   1

2. Changing an Older Person's Shelter and Care Setting: A Model to Explain Personal and Environmental Outcomes
   Stephen M. Golant   33

3. Gender and Housing for the Elderly: Sorting Through the Accumulations of a Lifetime
   Susan Saegert and Dolores E. McCarthy   61

4. The Phenomenology of Housing for Older People
   Robert L. Rubinstein   89

5. The Social Ecological Approach of Rudolf Moos
   Rick J. Scheidt   111

6. The Evolving Concept of Behavior Settings: Implications for Housing Older Adults
   Carolyn Norris-Baker   141

7. Theory and Research on Housing for the Elderly: The Legacy of Kurt Lewin
   Patricia A. Parmelee   161

Index   187
About the Contributors   191

Preface

Since its inception, environmental gerontology has shown a mission-oriented focus for creating and enhancing the residential environments of older populations. Theory-driven research has been a key engine pushing the field of environment-aging relations toward this goal. Much research in the housing field was launched and enhanced by major theoretical contributions made during the past 25 years. During the past 15 years, however, a perceptible decrease in formal theoretical advances in this area has become apparent. The purpose of this volume is to examine seven new, existing, or classic environment-aging perspectives with exciting promise for stimulating innovative thinking, research, and intervention on housing older adults.

In Chapter 1, M. Powell Lawton revisits environment-aging theory with a new twist. Concluding at the outset that the "person" component has been underrepresented in most major theories of environmental gerontology, Lawton carefully articulates heretofore missing (from environment-aging models) "terms of the organism"—including motivation, cognitive-attentional mechanisms, affect or emotion, and components of temperament and personality. He discusses the interactional significance of these components to the environment. Lawton specifically focuses on the relevance of these person attributes to housing and environmental theory, including their relevance for maximizing the congruence between older residents and diverse housing environments. Lawton considers factors that indicate when and why it may be more feasible to change older individuals in some circumstances while changing their host environments in others.

In Chapter 2, Stephen M. Golant tackles the complex task of explaining differences in the ways that older persons adjust to residential changes. He seeks answers to two critical questions: Why do older persons view some aspects of residential change more positively than other aspects? and, Why, despite bearing personal similarities to other residents and relatively uniform changes in housing environments, do older persons offer differing evaluations of these changes? Dissatisfied with existing models, Golant presents an original interactionalist model for assessing both subjective and objective residential change. He offers guidelines for assessing the strengths and weaknesses of studies attempting to measure the influences of environmental change. His careful attention to practical measurement of key concepts makes the model immediately applicable to the study of residential change in diverse shelter and care settings for elderly populations.

Working with the framework of environmental psychology, Susan Saegert and Dolores E. McCarthy apply a feminist perspective to issues of gender, housing, and the elderly in Chapter 3. They explore several "structured social inequalities" associated with gender. These include poverty, illness, longevity, and living conditions; the role of gender in discussions about housing needs for the elderly; gender-related assumptions affecting conceptions of the life course, especially those related to appropriate housing; and how gender and housing are intertwined throughout life. The authors offer a thoughtful analysis, illustrating how housing decisions and residential changes are inextricably bound to personal changes (both gains and losses) in social roles, social identity, and place attachment and why it is important for housing professionals to consider the dialectic among these issues in women's lives. Issuing a call for gender-specific considerations in housing design for elderly populations, they illustrate the often unheralded leadership of older women working within local communities to secure access and enhance housing development.

In Chapter 4, Robert L. Rubinstein, an anthropologist, offers an overview of a phenomenological or experiential perspective on housing for older adults. He traces the origins and outlines the theoretical underpinnings of this approach, which requires an understanding of the "construed world" in collective and personal domains. Rubinstein presents the contrasts that emerge almost immediately when the experiential perspective is applied to housing issues, including distinctions between "housing" and "home" and between traditional environment-aging measurement approaches and qualitatively oriented experiential approaches that take an accounting of the environmental associations made by older persons in their multilayered environments. These theoretical and methodological distinctions are made clearer in a case study (an older widow who lives alone) that illustrates the rich, complex relationship she has with her home and her neighborhood.

For the past 20 years, the social ecological approach of Rudolf Moos has increased our understanding of how the social environment affects the well-being of inhabitants in diverse settings, including older residents of sheltered care settings. In Chapter 5, after tracing its roots and describing its defining features, Rick J. Scheidt offers an overview of the integrative model and measurement procedure (Multiphasic Environmental Assessment Procedure, or

MEAP) Moos uses to study the interaction of physical environmental, policy, and program factors and social climate variables as they affect the adaptation and well-being of older residents of sheltered care settings. The usefulness of the social ecological approach is illustrated by two theoretical applications addressing determinants of social climates ("environmental personalities") and means to improve the adaptive fit between elders and their residential settings. Scheidt reviews the practical uses of the MEAP and its separate components, including evaluation of purposeful environmental change and assessment of resident design and program preferences. Finally, Scheidt examines potential applications of the social ecological model to housing issues beyond special living environments, including naturally developing or planned retirement communities, neighborhoods, housing tracts, and small communities, and for assessment of differences between social climate features of past versus present housing environments.

The final two chapters are rather distinct from those that precede them. Each revisits an influential environment-behavior perspective to examine its specific potential for enhancing research and practice relative to elder housing.

In this regard, in Chapter 6, Carolyn Norris-Baker examines the value of the "behavior setting" theory of Roger Barker and colleagues, an approach that has rarely been considered as a conceptual or methodological approach for examining housing issues for older adults. Norris-Baker defines and illustrates the concept of behavior settings—units consisting of an interaction between behaving persons and things, time, and the immediate environment—using a case study scenario of a typical day in the life of an older resident of a continuing care retirement community. She critiques several new ways to use behavior setting theory for "ecological diagnosis and intervention," including dealing with boundary problems between settings, designing "focal points" among settings that will coordinate and enhance resident interaction, and determining "optimal size" guidelines for setting that healthful challenge to older participants.

Finally, in Chapter 7, Patricia A. Parmelee revisits the field theory of Kurt Lewin, whose thinking, captured in his now-classic formula $B = f(P, E)$, inserted environment as a requisite feature for understanding the "psychological life space" of the individual. Parmelee introduces readers to Lewinian field theory and to the broader assumptions of the transactional perspective it helped to shape. Central elements and assumptions of the "life space," that is, the psychological field where behavior occurs, are discussed in relation to their implications for housing. Parmelee calls for greater attention to the social life space in gerontological housing research and discusses how this concept may enrich understanding of immediate interpersonal, as well as larger sociocultural, processes construed by older adults. She examines implications of the bedrock Lewinian assumption that all environments are ultimately subjective and why the construed past and future are important factors for understanding the reactions older adults offer to the "immediate situation." She offers several examples to illustrate how Lewinian field theory can improve our understanding of housing issues for the elderly, including understanding how the social life space of older residents influences interaction within their environments, how cultural diversity influences person-environment transactions in old age, and how our own cultural values and biases shape the direction of theory and research on housing for the aged.

We believe there is much in these perspectives to inform and stimulate research on environmental gerontology, with direct implications not only for theorists and researchers but also for environmental managers, housing specialists, regional and community planners, policy shapers, family life educators, health-care providers, and design professionals. Each chapter represents something of a "note in a bottle," containing considerations that hopefully will be applied by gerontological housing professionals "around river's bend" in the new millennium.

Rick J. Scheidt
Paul G. Windley

Environment and Aging Theory

1

Environment and Aging: Theory Revisited

M. POWELL LAWTON

Although environmental psychology and social ecology are well established as branches of their parent disciplines, they are relative newcomers to the behavioral and social sciences. Incorporating the physical environment into the behavioral system seemed like a novel idea at the time, despite the clear importance of architecture, nature, social institutions, and the like. It is thus less than a grand insight to admit environment into the human behavioral system, as Lewin (1951) did in his ecological equation: B = f (P, E). All too often, however, environment is either simply assumed and kept unspecified or omitted totally because the content areas studied by psychology are frequently so narrowed as to require only conceptions of the interior of the person.

Despite the intent of the classic theories of person and environment (Helson, 1964; Lewin, 1951; Murray, 1938) to account for the juncture of these two elements, there continues to be tension between holistic (Altman & Rogoff, 1987; Wapner, 1987) and separatist (Magnusson and Endler, 1977) views of this interface. As will be seen later in this chapter, most of the environmental theory applied to gerontological problems has been the separatist variety. Similarly, the point of view taken in this chapter, that although person and environment form a unified system where what is inside is philosophically inseparable from what is outside, for heuristic purposes, it is necessary to speak of, and attempt to measure, them separately.

The core issue of environmental psychology, and the one considered in this chapter in relation to older people, is that of the relationship between what is outside and what is inside the skin of the individual: How does the person utilize the environment in the service of his or her needs? Pursuit of the answer to this question will go beyond earlier writings of the author to deal more completely with personality as it relates to person-environment relations. In the process, emotion will be discussed as an essential element of person-environment trans-actions. In brief, temperamental factors (with implied genetic, biological, and environmental determinants) will be suggested as an additional major element in the process by which personal competence and environmental press (Lawton & Nahemow, 1973) affect outcomes.

This discussion begins with a backward look, tinged with disappointment, at the progression of theory development in environment and aging over the past two decades. Policy and practice seemed to benefit early from the person-environment perspective, but succeeding years failed to provide validation for the continued success of theory in directing practice. A hypothesis will be advanced to account for the plateau in theory development and subsequent action: Advances in environmental knowledge have *not* been matched by advances in knowledge regarding the person and individual differences in the person-environment transaction.

THREE EARLY THEORETICAL FRAMEWORKS IN ENVIRONMENT AND AGING

For this brief historical review, the term *theoretical frameworks* has been used advisedly, because none of the conceptions to be discussed have been worked out in sufficient detail and with requisite vigor to qualify as formal theories. Nonetheless, they attempt to depict dynamic processes in abstract but broadly specifiable relationships to one another. They fall short as theoretical statements, however, because none of them makes a systematic attempt to account for all the major examples of each concept or to make sufficiently clear how to operationalize the concepts.

Lawton and Nahemow's Competence-Press Model

In this model, the major constructs used to predict outcomes are environmental press and personal competence. *Environmental press* was Murray's (1938) term to represent the demand some aspect of the environment made on the person in conjunction with a matched personal need. As used by Lawton and Nahemow (1973), environmental press does not require a collateral need. Rather, press is a statistical construct expressing the probability that a specified environmental stimulus or context would elicit some response among all people. Whether such a response might occur is determined by the level of personal competence of the target individual. Personal competence is conceived in terms of intrinsic performance potential, the maximal expectable performance in biological, sensorimotor, perceptual, and cognitive domains. The outcomes of trans-actions between environment and person are conceived in evaluative terms. The outcome is evaluated in either the external aspect of behavioral competence or the internal aspect of psychological well-being.

A primary postulate associated with the model is that the effect of an envi-

Figure 1.1
Lawton and Nahemow's Competence-Press Model

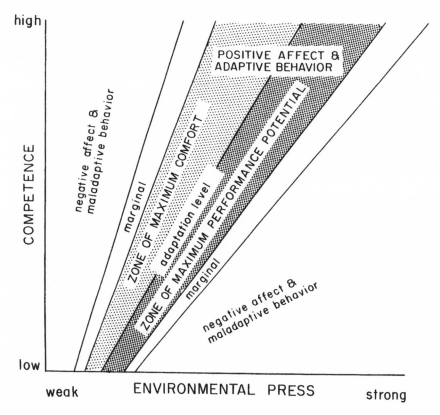

Source: Lawton & Nahemow, 1973, p. 661. Reprinted with permission.

ronmental press of a given magnitude on outcome is greater as personal competence diminishes—the "environmental docility hypothesis." Stated another way, less competent people experience a greater degree of environmental determination than more competent people.

These features are portrayed in Figure 1.1, with personal competence depicted on the *y* axis and press level on the *x* axis. Differential outcomes are schematized on the surface of the figure, depending on the match between press and competence. Small mismatches between competence and press are associated with positive outcomes, and larger mismatches are associated with negative outcomes. Asymmetry between the effects of excess press and a deficiency of press is hypothesized to be mediated by adaptation level with respect to incoming environmental demand. Adaptation level (Helson, 1964) represents the "indifference" point, the value of the external stimulus that is perceived as neither strong nor weak. In terms of posited outcomes, it is the balance point where behavior is relatively automatic, but competence and affect is neither positive nor negative. Press levels incrementally above adaptation level are hypothesized to be associated with learning, novel behavior, and mobilized energy, as well as positive affect ("zone of maximum performance potential"). Press levels incrementally below adaptation level are associated with reduced energy output and competent, but perhaps barely competent, behavior and affect. These outcomes are positive because of the state of relaxation ("zone of maximum comfort") and lack of demand accompanying this low-press state.

The model was subsequently elaborated to account for the central processing by which the external environment is given meaning by the person (Lawton, 1982). Although both objective and subjective environment are included in the press dimension of Figure 1.1, Lewin's ecological equation was modified as $B = f (P, E, PXE)$. That is, the additional interactive term PXE signifies that the central appraisal of E by P has a causal effect on behavior (or in this case, affect) that may be independent of the purely physical attributes of the environment.

Another addition was made in response to growing concern over the effect of the competence-press model in portraying an environmental-deterministic position, with the person in a passive-receptive mode. Following Carp and Carp (1984; see below), the "environmental proactivity" hypothesis was framed (Lawton, 1989). Environment was reconceived in dimensions characterized as both demands and opportunities, or resources. The proactivity hypothesis states that as competence increases, a greater proportion of environmental resources becomes available with which the person may interact. Thus, a differential, interactional hypothesis is set up whereby the less competent are controlled by, and the more competent are in control of, the environment (clearly an overstatement made for emphasis).

Kahana's Person-Environment Congruence Model

Kahana's (1982) hypothesis states that a favorable outcome from a person-environment transaction is most likely to occur when the characteristics of the person are congruent with what the environment has to offer. This conception flows directly from Murray's need-press theory in that the basic components are personal needs for some goal object matched with estimates of the environment's ability to satisfy those needs.

It is important to note that person-environment congruence does not represent a desired outcome in and of itself. Congruence is a person-environment condition that is likely to lead to psychological well-being. Incongruence, in turn, leads to adaptive strategies to restore congruence, which, if unsuccessful, lead to impaired psychological health. The indicators of personal need may be estimates of traitlike needs of the person such as affiliation, autonomy, or achievement. The indicators of environmental attributes are estimates of what may be called "psychosocial contexts." The items measuring environment may sometimes be physical in nature (e.g., percentage of cognitively impaired residents in a care area), or "alpha press" (Murray, 1938). Measurement of the psychosocial context is more usually accomplished by averaging behaviors or attitudes of the multiplicity of other people in physical proximity to the person ("beta press"), for example, "change versus sameness," "amount of deviance tolerated," or "amount of affective stimulation."

Kahana made the basic important distinction between two types of incongruence. The first type is oversupply of the environmental attribute as compared to the second type, an undersupply. Kahana noted the usual deprivation that accompanies an undersupply but also the possibility that some behaviors could remain unexercised and possibly eroded by an oversupply of an environmental response. The possibility of differential outcomes being associated with an optimal degree of incongruence, versus lack of or excess of incongruence, is also included.

Although there have been a number of reports on research utilizing the concept of person-environment congruence (reviewed in Kahana, 1982), the basic nature of the theory has not been elaborated on since its several early statements.

The Stress-Theoretical Model of Person and Environment

Schooler (1982) formulated a third person-environment (P-E) model based on Lazarus's (Lazarus, 1966) stress theory. Lazarus (1990) continued to elaborate his model and has applied it specifically to the environment (1990). However, Schooler's original statement specific to environment and aging was never extended beyond this original statement. Like person-environment congruence theory, stress P-E theory is primarily a cognitive theory. Although Schooler's empirical research (1969, 1982) demonstrated the independent effects of environment in physical terms, Lazarus considers environment only as appraised by the behaving person. In Lazarus's system, the person first appraises an environmental context to assess whether it constitutes a potential threat (primary appraisal). If there is a potential threat, then the person's own resources for coping with the threat are appraised (secondary appraisal). The dynamic process of appraisal, coping, and reappraisal constitutes the person-environment transaction.

Rowles's Transactional View of Older Person in Environment

Although never laying out an explicit statement of a full theory, Rowles has taken an ethnographic, qualitative research approach to the study of person in environment in a number of publications (Rowles, 1978, 1980, 1984). Without asserting the extreme transactionalist position that person and environment are coterminous and inseparable (Altman & Rogoff, 1987), Rowles makes the person-environment gap as minuscule as possible in his concept of "insideness." Insideness is a cognition of a connection between the present self and the physical environment ("physical intimacy with space"; Rowles, 1980, p. 158), the social environment of other individuals and the social order, and the "autobiographical self," the continuity that links the person with the environments of a life span ("a series of remembered places"; Rowles, 1980, p. 160). Rowles sees adaptation to old age as a series of accommodations to changing biology and external circumstances. The adaptation may be either in behavior (e.g., in limiting behavior to progressively smaller physical zones, such as the "surveillance zone" or home) or in cognitive processes, such as environmental fantasy whose end point is the maintenance of insideness. Insideness, in linking the person to environment, compensates for losses in direct interactions with the environment. The ability of autobiographical insideness to transcend the changes of old age and frailty makes this an increasingly salient accommodating mechanism in older people. Unlike other approaches, Rowles's transactional view is descriptive and attempts to explain the meanings that link person and environment, as contrasted with the mental health teleology of other approaches. Although his approach takes into account the physical environment, it is the cognitive connections to environment provided by the person that are of primary importance.

THE PERSON IN PERSON-ENVIRONMENT RELATIONSHIPS

Despite accounting for the person in either behavior or intrapsychic terms, none of the approaches reviewed above went into depth regarding the person, certainly not the depth appropriate to the large amount of research on personality and related topics.

Environmental Dispositions

Occasional reminders of the need to define the person have been seen in the literature, but they went surprisingly unheeded. For example, the same book in which the models of Lawton, Kahana, and Schooler were described (Lawton, Windley, & Byerts, 1982) contained a chapter by Windley (1982) whose focus was the shared area between personality and environment. Building on earlier investigations including his own (1973), Windley suggested that cognitive-behavioral orientations toward specific aspects of the environment (in his own research, needs for privacy, complexity, environmental stability, and environmental manipulation) constituted one such link. Although these orientations had been referred to as "environmental dispositions" (McKechnie, 1970) or preferences, Windley suggested that because such preferences required competent task performance (i.e., *adequate* performance of sensory, motor, cognitive, or behavioral tasks), they were better viewed as abilities rather than traits.

The Complementary/Congruence Model of Well-Being

The most detailed advance in theory development since the 1982 book was the complementary/congruence (C/C) model developed by Carp and Carp (1984). The C/C model carefully separates and details objective and subjective aspects of environment. Although related to both the Lawton and Nahemow (1973) competence-press model and the Kahana congruence model, the C/C model further elaborates the person portion of Lewin's ecological equation by separating lower-order and higher-order needs. For life maintenance (e.g., health or activities of daily living [ADL]) needs, favorable outcomes are associated with environmental functions that complement existing skills when they begin to decline. The environment adds to or acts prosthetically on failing personal competencies.

Higher-order needs, by contrast, are best served by environmental attributes that enhance the match between environmental resources and personal needs. Congruence thus heightens the possibility of growth, enrichment, and positive satisfactions emerging from person-environment transactions. Lawton's (1989) environmental proactivity hypothesis is based directly on the Carps' reasoning regarding congruence.

Well-being is enhanced directly in the complementarity portion of the model either by positive person features or by positive environment features. In the congruence portion of the model, however, person features and environment features have only minor direct effects on outcome, if any. The crucial determinant is the confluence of a personal need with a congruent environmental resource. "The P and E variables are, in themselves, neither positive nor negative from an adaptational viewpoint; for example, it is no better for a person to have high or low need for privacy, or for an environment to provide much or little. The salient issue is the match between individual and environment" (Carp & Carp, 1984, p. 282).

The details of the model are further elaborated, and various empirical tests of portions of the model have appeared in the literature (Carp & Carp, 1982a, 1982b). For the present purpose, the Carps' conception of the personal-need variables is most relevant. For complementarity, lower-order functions are evaluated in terms of competence of performance in the major domains suggested by Lawton and Nahemow (1973): physical health, sensation and perception, motor functions, and cognition.

For the congruence portion of the model, the Carps selected from the universe of Murray-defined (and-named!) needs a subset that appeared to have clear cognates in environmental resources: Harm avoidance, nox avoidance, order, affiliation, similarity, privacy, and aesthetic experience. Two personality traits, extroversion and "nosiness-gossip," were also included.

Independent of the lower-order and higher-order needs is a set of intrapersonal moderating variables, that is, processes that are not linked with an environmental cognate but that transform or condition the effect of the P-E and especially the complementing or congruence variables. These are personal competence (related to perceived control, personal mastery, and ego strength), cognitive coping style, and attitude toward own health.

In overview, then, the Carps' conception posited an important discontinuity between basic and higher-level needs. The person-environment relationship was given greater depth in accounting for the active, positive motivations of people in attaining positive states of mental health. Specifically, some intrapsychic phenomena such as needs and traits were incorporated into this system. The details of intrapsychic structure and some of the mechanisms connecting person and environment were incompletely specified, however.

Missing Components of the Person Construct

The major purpose of this chapter is to draw from knowledge in general psychology to fill in gaps in the aspect of the ecological system that involves the person. Carp and Carp's (1984) reasoning will be the starting point for defining what aspects of the person ought to be accounted for: intrapersonal processes that bear some reasonable relationship to the environment. The search for relevant aspects will encompass the traditional domains of the person, that is, motivation, cognition, affect, and behavior.

In order to do justice to the person side, better use of recent research and theory in general psychology will be made, particularly approaches that have emphasized individual differences. The past decade has seen renewed interest in personality and in emotion, an aspect of personality that was neglected for several decades during the dominance of cognitively oriented views of human functioning. Part of the purpose of this chapter will be to argue that personality consists of inseparable processes in the motivational, cognitive, affective, and temperamental realms and that environment is also an essential member of the transactional processes that relate personality to behavior.

Motivation

Although classic conceptions of motivation have posited universal instincts (McDougall, 1926), and more recent conceptions, drives (Mowrer, 1950) and needs (Murray, 1938), another perspective is offered by considering motivation as the energy behind the organism's attempt to establish and maintain its place in the environment. In this conception, all mental activity and behavior represent an interchange between person and environment with the primary goal being that of incorporating and using those aspects of the environment that produce positive states and minimize negative states and exclude from this transactional world those aspects of the environment that are irrelevant to positive and negative states. Olds and Milner (1954) and later Tucker (1981) reported research that affirmed the presence of neural processes dedicated to the enhancement of positive affect and reduction of negative affect.

These streams of research have been directed toward comprehending the perceptual, cognitive, and affective mechanisms that appear to account for the directions in which human activity is directed. At the present time, despite the convergence of knowledge suggesting that there are differentiable channels of such activity, it is clear that such knowledge is far from definitive. We must thus acknowledge the speculative nature of much of the theory that attempts to account for such knowledge. Such theoretical orientations may be designated as those emphasizing cognitive-attentional mechanisms, affective experience, and temperament. The criterion that will be used to differentiate the scope of this discussion from all that could be said about human behavior from these three perspectives is whether there is a clear link between environment and the person implied by the processes under discussion.

Cognitive-Attentional Mechanisms

Environmental cognition has perhaps constituted the most active research area within environmental psychology (Garling & Evans, 1991; Golledge, 1987). The purposive, proactive nature of people's attempts to comprehend the environment has been an important focus of much theory in general psychology. Gibson (1979), for example, in asserting the unity of the person as knower and the environment as the knowable, emphasizes the active effort that must be made by the person to comprehend what is already encoded in the environment.

On a neuropsychological level, Pribram and McGuiness (1975) describe two neural processes—the activation and arousal systems—linked by negative feedback mechanisms by which people negotiate the external world. The *activation* system utilizes environmental information to maintain a state of motor readiness to engage in behavior relevant to the person's needs. Activation is thus the primary neural system focused on sustained attention, linear processing, and purposeful pursuit of goals. Such focused activity depends on memory, on the recall of schemata from past experience; in short, the activation system is driven by internal processes and motivations to keep attention focused and behavior directed. Redundancy and the exclusion of irrelevant stimuli foster the person's ability to analyze the environmental situation into its component units.

The *arousal* system, by contrast with the attentive vigilance of the activation system, is highly focused on the external environment, with the primary function of detecting change in the environment. Being attuned to novelty, the arousal system quickly habituates in the face of steady stimulation. Efficiency in identifying novel input is enhanced by loose attentional control that maximizes the overall scope of what is attended. To some extent, parallel and relatively global processing characterizes the arousal system. Sensory-perceptual functions directly controlled by the environment are the primary sources of stimulation, as contrasted with the internal, memory-driven motivation of the activation system. The arousal system thus increases the potential for reward by quickly habituating to background stimulation that proves to be nonrewarding and by readiness for novel, potentially rewarding signals.

The foregoing summary has emphasized the separate contributions of the activation and arousal systems. Together they constitute a unitary, jointly acting self-regulatory system where each system is self-limiting through negative feedback. Increased habituation leads to greater sensitivity to novel input, while increased attention and motor control channel goal-directed activity. The two systems work synergistically. When vigilance is high and motor behavior focused, a novel stimulus must be very strong to command attention. When vigilance is low and the need for sequential goal-directed behavior small, the attention span for external novel events is very broadly directed. Among other benefits, this openness increases the opportunity for affective experience, to be discussed later.

This admittedly still-speculative attempt to relate neural function to human behavior seems relevant to understanding environment and aging. These two systems, in a dialectical relationship to one another, describe much more specifically than does classic environmental psychology how environment and the person interact. There is a rough correspondence between the activation system and behavioral motivation that arises from within the person. Similarly, the correspondence between the arousal system and environmental control is clear. Yet each of these generalizations represents a simplistic overstatement of the situation. Environment is involved in both systems, as the object of sustained, goal-directed motor behavior and as the source of potentially rewarding novel stimulation.

These two processes, one of which maximizes attentiveness and the other the search for novelty, are active at all chronological ages. The purpose of this chapter is not to review neuropsychological data bearing on the age relatedness of the basic processes. Nonetheless, on the behavioral level, some age- and/or health-related variation has been established in areas that represent outcomes of the two mechanisms. The literature documents, for example, decreased levels of sensory sensitivity, memory, and incidental learning as age increases. To the extent that external stimulation penetrates less easily, or the formation of new cognitive-affective schemata is impeded, aging may well add its own contribution to changes in the way environment is understood or acted upon.

Affect and the Environment

Affect (used synonymously with "emotion") can no longer be thought of as one of several mental processes. Ample research is at hand to demonstrate the inseparability of emotion and cognition. For example, the endless attempts to argue the primacy of emotion or cognition (Lazarus, 1990; Zajonc, 1980) invoke the response of most psychologists that they constitute a single process, where identifying which is primary is in most instances a subjective judgment. Emotion may serve as a motivation to understand on a cognitive level or, alternatively, knowing may at times lead to emotion. Most often, emotion constitutes one element of an overall schema, or mental representation, composed of memories of earlier similar situations, learned conditioned psychophysiological and motor behavior, and responses to the immediate context. Environment has affective stimulus value, detailed in depth by Russell and Snodgrass (1987). The argument of this chapter goes further, to the effect that people search for emotional experiences, whether for enjoyment, security, or relief from pain, and that synchrony of personal need and environmental resources is the condition associated with favorable affective outcomes. This section will discuss the structure of affect and then relate such structure to aspects of the environment.

The major emotion research relevant to person-environment transactions is the stream of the past decade that has elaborated the distinction between negative affect and positive affect originally made by Bradburn (1969). He developed separate measures of these two types of affect and found that they were unrelated to one another while being correlated with happiness. Recent research has repeatedly confirmed that the major portion of variance in both language-based and self-rated emotion is accounted for by two factors (Lawton, Kleban, Rajagopal, & Dean, 1992; Russell & Steiger, 1982; Watson & Tellegen, 1985). The naming of the two dimensions depends on statistical decisions made by the researcher regarding the orientation of the axes. An unrotated solution typically identifies a large bipolar factor containing pleasant affect terms at one extreme and unpleasant terms on the other. The second factor is a unipolar activation factor (i.e., terms like *aroused, energetic, enthusiastic*). Some (Diener, Larsen, Levine, & Emmons, 1985) have gone so far as to call this second factor an affect intensity factor, with affective meaning being measured by the pleasantness-unpleasantness factor. Watson and Tellegen (1985), however, demonstrated that the difference between this bipolar conception of affective quality and the frequently observed zero correlation between negative and positive affect was primarily a matter of where the reference points were placed. These authors showed that negatively correlated measures of generalized happiness (content, happy, satisfied) and sadness (sad, depressed, lonely, unhappy) were different in the affect terms that defined them from the terms used in research that produced zero-correlated factors of positive affect (active, elated, excited) and negative affect (distress, fearful, nervous).

One may thus easily determine by choice of the terms sampled how narrow or how broad an affective range to represent in a measure of emotion. One conclusion from this research is that there is a relative degree of independence between happy and sad feelings. Second, there are differences between the antecedents of the two types of emotion: Physical health and self-sentiments are more strongly related to negative affect, while social, leisure-time, and environmental attributes are more strongly related to positive affect (Beck & Page, 1988; Bradburn, 1969; Lawton, 1983, 1994b).

Analogous findings have appeared in the neuropsychological literature. Although later complexities have forced modification of the interpretations made from such research, the existence of "pleasure" and "pain" areas in the brain, identified through direct stimulation of these centers, provides an indication that there is some structural basis for the relative independence of positive and negative affect (Olds & Olds, 1965).

In discussing the differential antecedents of positive affect and negative affect, Lawton (1983) suggested that making the distinction between internal and external antecedents provided an explanation that fit the data. That is, negative affect did not appear to be affected by the amount of social interaction with friends or the amount of participation in activities of various types. These externally oriented activities, however, enhanced positive affect. More recent research replicated the differential relationship of leisure-time activity to positive affect (Lawton, 1994b).

On a neuropsychological level, Tucker (1981) has reviewed a large amount of research that appears to support the idea of central nervous system specialization in positive and negative affective functions, varying with hemispheric location of presumed central processes. There is no simple allocation of emotion to the right brain and reason to the left brain, as popularized in the media, nor can one argue that the left and the right brains are the seat of positive and negative affect, respectively. Rather, Tucker suggests that the hemispheric functions represent balancing cognitive-affective processes. The right hemisphere, specializing in processing of affective signals from many sources (viscera, end organs, environment), is necessary for the integration of such signals into emotional meaning, especially of a nonverbal type. The left brain in its focal, differentiated cognitive style, acts as a control system on emotion and a factor in planning and sequential motoria action but still is affected by the holistic emotion processing of the right hemisphere.

These data from study of the neuropsychology of emotion and the subjective experience of emotion are relevant to environmental transactions. The analogy between the brain-process specialization of affective functions and the differential subjective functions of negative affect and positive affect is notable. It will be suggested later that such subjective specialization is even more complex, with "internal" stimuli being internal primarily in the sense of depending more on stored memories and well-practiced cognitive-affective schemata, many of whose origins may well have been in the environment.

TEMPERAMENT AND PERSONALITY

Temperament is a term that has perhaps the longest pedigree of any in psychology, one early version being the four temperaments (sanguine, melancholic, choleric, and phlegmatic). This construct has ebbed and flowed in psychological fashion, now having been reinstated to a high point of contemporary concern. This section begins with a definition of temperament: the most enduring and pervasive cognitive, affective, and behavioral attributes of the person, attributes that also have the strongest genetic and biological components.

It seems especially important to differentiate temperament from personality, which may be defined as the relatively enduring aspects of the person's cognitive, affective, attitudinal, and behavioral responses. Temperament is more strongly biologically determined and less modifiable than is personality. In different terms, genotypes are the major ingredients of temperament, whereas both genotypes and phenotypes (manifestations conditioned by experience as well as by genetic traits) contribute to the definition of personality.

Perhaps because there is no way to disentangle hereditary and experiential factors definitively, research in this area is notable for its failure to attempt to distinguish between temperament and personality. Much of the classic theory and research in personality leans heavily on measuring characteristics that have been shown to be genetically determined. This eliding of temperamental and personality constructs has resulted in some conceptions of personality being presented as more strongly genetically determined and less subject to modification than desirable. This section of the chapter will suggest, first, that transactions with the environment must take into account the temperamental givens. Second, the phenotypic aspects of personality have a past, present, and future history in the mutual processes whereby person and environment interact. I shall argue that a great deal of the quality of everyday life originates in the way the phenotypic, learned, and potentially changeable aspects of personality interact with environment. Both temperament and personality are characterized by major individual differences. A few of the major characterizations of such individual differences will be noted.

Temperament Types

Although the characterization of introvert and extrovert preceded Eysenck (1970), the best-known conception of temperament is his heavily biological personality theory. Eysenck presently conceives of personality as being describable in three dimensions, labeled introversion-extroversion (IE), emotionality or neuroticism (versus stability), and psychoticism (impulsiveness versus constraint). One cannot do justice here to the long stream of empirical research that has contributed to this formulation. Psychophysiological data and much basic genetic research support many of his hypotheses. The genetic component is clear in explaining the very early emergence of IE and neuroticism. One cannot miss the analogy between both neuroticism and introversion-extroversion and individual differences in the propensity toward negative affect and positive affect. This association has been best demonstrated by Costa and McCrae (1980a). Costa and his colleagues also documented the long-term continuity of such individual differences over the adult years (Costa et al., 1987).

A variation on Eysenck's types, more in accord with both neuropsychological and psychopathological data, is the dual-system array proposed by Gray (1981). On the neurobehavioral level, Gray reviews evidence for three systems involved in the integration of emotional behavior: the behavioral inhibition system, the behavioral activation system, and a "fight-flight" regulation system related to unconditioned punishment. Parallel to these neurophysiological systems are three personality types, which represent statistical rotations of Eysenck's types: anxiety, impulsivity, and constraint. Tellegen (1985), the proponent of another tripartite view of personality, notes the parallel between Gray's anxiety and his negative emotionality type, on the one hand, and Gray's impulsivity and his constraint type, on the other.

Neither Eysenck's personality measure (Eysenck Personality Questionnaire; Eysenck & Eysenck, 1975) nor most personality measures influenced by his original framework (e.g., the "Big Five"; see Costa & McCrae, 1992; Goldberg, 1990) have made an attempt to separate putative genotypic and phenotypic indicators from one another. In mixing many possibly learned behaviors (e.g., social behaviors, interests, or attitudes) that are statistically correlated with more genotypic indicators, factor-analytic approaches inevitably define personality types that have the appearance of genetic origin and higher persistence through the life span than may be warranted. Cloninger's (1986) research began with just such an attempt to specify, a priori, personality types that were consonant with genetically determined neuropsychological types and whose indicators were closely linked to the genotypes. (He has more recently developed another parallel set of "character" measures, which tap individual differences that are highly influenced by experience [Cloninger, Svrakic, & Przybeck, 1992].) Cloninger's three types are: novelty seeking, harm avoidance, and reward dependence. Each dimension is linked conceptually and empirically to neuropsychological research data. Gray (1987) concluded that Cloninger's novelty seeking shared conceptual and measurement space with his impulsive dimension, with a similar congruity between anxiety and harm avoidance, while Cloninger, Przybeck, and Svrakic (1991) note parallels between novelty seeking and harm avoidance, on the one hand, and Tellegen's (1985) positive and negative emotionality, respectively.

It should be evident that each of these conceptions' first two factors are relatively similar and that they may be interpreted in terms of their function in mediating personal needs and environmental resources. Extroversion draws on external stimuli and is in turn associated more strongly with positive affect. Neuroticism (stability) is associated with internal stimuli and learned schemata (as contrasted with the greater stimulus-boundedness of extroversion) and is related to negative affect.

It should be noted that these temperaments are also highly abstracted constructs. Statistically, they represent second-order factors composed of surface traits (Cattell, 1950) or facets (Costa & McCrae, 1989). Although the indicators that make up the subdimensions describe everyday cognitions, feelings, preferences, responses, attitudes, and behaviors, these specifics are lost as they become aggregated into scores measuring the Big Two or Big Three dimensions discussed above. Such aggregation contributes to the blending of genotypic and phenotypic attributes. Gray (1981), for example, criticizes Eysenck's revision of the original Eysenckian (1970) model for the emphasis put by the revised model on sociability, a phenotypic cluster, as the major marker of extroversion (impulsivity, originally a component of extroversion, was reconceived as a manifestation of psychoticism in Eysenck's second conception; Eysenck & Eysenck, 1975). Cloninger's dimensions are the only ones that were deliberately operationalized to emphasize the genotypic manifestations.

The research on the Big Five has converged better than has temperament research on the content of the factors, perhaps because subjective or peer ratings have been the major source of data, rather than leaning so heavily on characteristics tied to biological or neuropsychological processes. Introversion-extroversion and neuroticism emerge regularly in all Big Five models. Unlike the noncongruent and elusive third factors of the temperaments, the third Big Five factor—openness to experience (as named by Costa and McCrae, 1989, in the NEO Personality Inventory)—and factors they call agreeableness and conscientiousness show rough replicability across a number of the five-factor personality inventories (see review of the evidence for convergence and nonconvergence by Costa and McCrae, 1992).

One hypothesis worth considering is that the first three factors are the highest saturated with genetic variance because many of both the genotypic and phenotypic indicators were originally derived from research that included neurobiological thinking. By contrast, agreeableness and conscientiousness were defined by everyday behaviors with less-obvious neuropsychological and perhaps less genetic counterparts.

A basic point of the argument of this chapter is that by mixing temperament and personality measures, we quickly converge on a level of abstraction whose strongest markers are biogenetic. In doing so, we lose the ability to describe the individuality of the person and to define more specific personality traits that are formed through person-environment interaction and therefore more modifiable than those properly called temperament.

Preferences

Preferences constitute a familiar category in everyday language, but they have not been fully incorporated as an important personality process. A *preference* may be defined as a wish for an environmental object, primarily learned from past experiences of pleasure associated with attaining the object. A preference is thus distinguished from need by being learned, oriented toward external objects, and by usually being less intense and more elective than a need.

The research most relevant to preference is that of Reich and Zautra (1983, 1983). These investigators were concerned with the distinction between ''demands'' emanating either from within the person or from the environment, on the one hand, and ''desires,'' impulses to perform behaviors that are intrinsically motivated and freely chosen, on the other. Their research demonstrated that desire behaviors were likely to be associated with positive affect but not negative affect. They also found support for the two-factor conception whereby positive events and negative events selectively affected positive and negative affect, respectively.

The demands versus desires distinction has some similarity to Carp and Carp's (1984) complementarity versus congruence transaction and Lawton's docility versus proactivity. Each of these conceptions, as well as the research of Bradburn (1969), Lawton (1983, 1994b), and others, links preferences and their satisfaction to positive affect and to the external antecedents of positive affect. The research on positive and negative affect reviewed earlier, as well as a number of more recent attempts to analyze the structure of well-being (Andrews, 1984; Warr, Barter, & Brownbridge, 1983), establish definitively that favorable mental health must be conceived in terms of both the absence of negative states and the presence of positive states. Similarly, related research data help reinstate into our conceptions of healthy person-environment interactions those external stimulating conditions that elicit positive affect and whose motivational origins lie in learned preferences. So much classic writing in dynamic psychology conveys the idea that internalized sources of conflict (e.g., those stemming from conflictual family relationships) are the sole determinants of mental health. The lack of attention given by dynamic psychology to social diversion, leisure activity, novelty, learning, and other proactive behaviors conveys the idea that these are superficial aspects of the person that are largely irrelevant to mental health. This is true only if one defines mental health solely in terms of neuroticism or negative affect. The entire "other side" of mental health originates in these proactive behaviors, which are more related to positive affect than to negative affect.

General psychology has been less blind than clinical psychology to the proactive behaviors and their associated subjective states. White's (1959) conception of effectance suggested that behavior motivation was as likely to be directed toward the creation of tension (e.g., satisfying curiosity, need for change, for developing new skills for their own sake) as toward the reduction of tension. Berlyne's (1978) research examined the stimulus properties ("collative qualities") associated with proactive behaviors. Such properties as novelty, complexity, ambiguity, and incongruity, in moderate intensity, are motivating and associated with positive hedonic quality (see also Wohlwill, 1966).

Much contemporary leisure theory is based on the chain beginning with collative environmental properties as the generalized external motivators and learned preferences as the proximal internal motivators. The proactive person searches the external environment for objects (stimulants, activities, social opportunities) whose engagement is likely to arouse positive affect (Csikszentmihalyi, 1975; Iso-Ahola, 1980a, 1980b; Lawton, 1994b). Similarly, environmental psychology has demonstrated the positive affective experiences associated with aesthetic stimuli, novel environments (Berlyne, 1974), familiar environments (Zajonc, 1968), natural environments (Knopf, 1987), and so on.

TEMPERAMENT, PERSONALITY, PREFERENCES, AND THE ENVIRONMENT

The foregoing sections have discussed selectively some aspects of temperament and personality, these aspects having been chosen among all that could have been discussed because they have some particularly obvious connection with the environment. This distinction is artificial because all human action is transactional. Nonetheless, what has been referred to as "external stimulation" has a more direct and immediate association with the environment than do the "internal" aspects. Internal stimulation is more likely the result of temperament or of earlier person-environment transactions embedded in cognitive-affective schemata where memory and past learning of meaning, rather than current environmental input, are the major ingredients.

In this section, such intrapersonal processes that are selectively relevant to the environment will be discussed in greater depth. Specifically, temperament, personality, and preferences are seen as successively more concrete representations of motivational, cognitive, and affective processes. These three classes are also successively more subject to determination by experiential factors and therefore more subject to change. Finally, individual differences are major within each of the classes. It is such individual differences whose relationship to the environment requires the special attention of researchers. As Carp and Carp (1984) and others have argued, there is a great deal more to the P component of the ecological equation than competence, and there is a great deal more to the PXE interactional term than environmental cognition.

Temperament

The study of temperament has emphasized individual differences, including the neuropsychological aspects of autonomic reactivity and the base level of "arousal" (seen by Eysenck [1970], as a unidimensional continuum from high to low level of nervous system activity). In this view some individuals (introverts) are chronically overaroused and therefore seek environments that are low in stimulation or at least controllable in a way to achieve this level. Other people are chronically underaroused (extroverts) and therefore seek environments that provide high levels of stimulation (Geen, 1984). The later elaborations of temperament theory (Cloninger, 1986; Gray, 1981; Tellegen, 1985), although not easy to reconcile with one another, include similar broad propensities to admit or reject external stimulation or to increase or decrease the variety of such input.

The two major dimensions in temperament research concern, first, the regulation of input from the outside and the inside (extroversion-introversion) and, second, control of adaptive behavior through expectancies for security versus threat of loss of security (neuroticism/stability). By characterizing temperament as biogenetic in origin, a relatively fixed quality is thereby assigned to some aspects of the person. "Still Stable After All These Years" was the title of an article by Costa and McCrae (1980b), whose conclusion was that extroversion-introversion and neuroticism changed very little across a number of years of adulthood. The conclusion from temperament theory suggests that the importance of environmental input to a person's well-being is more a matter of genetics than of learning or circumstance.

We might conceive of these variations in temperament as setting broad (and individually/different) ranges wherein optimal functioning is set. The extrovert is predisposed to searching for external stimulation. If instead of *press* as the abscissa of Figure 1.1 in the Lawton-Nahemow ecological model, we substitute *strength of stimulus*, it is likely that for the extrovert the entire figure would be shifted to the right. Higher stimulus strength would still be within the tolerable level of the extrovert, and the stimulus deprivation level would be reached at a higher stimulus strength than is true for the introvert; adaptation level shifts in similar proportion to the right. Conversely, the introvert's adaptation level and other ecological model reference points would be displaced to the left.

Does neuroticism imply any analogous type of orientation to the environment? For an answer to this question, we need to consider the affective state outcomes associated with the two main temperaments. The extrovert searches for additional stimulation because the expected outcome is a positive affective state. More risks are taken in this search. Being open to the environment sometimes means experiencing extra punishment or frustration, even though the sheer amount of positive feeling is maximized. Thus, Gray (1981), Cloninger (1986), and others have described the "neurotic extrovert" as one of the blends that occur. For the person high in neuroticism, there may well be excessive alertness to danger, or fear of the unknown, because of the neurotic temperamental proclivity to react with pain to punishing aspects of the environment. Thus, we would have extroverts attempting to maximize positive states by proactive environmental activity and those high in neuroticism attempting to minimize negative states by caution and withdrawal. The extrovert risks punishment in the search for highs; the neurotic risks scarcity of positive states in the search for security.

Costa and McCrae's (1989) third major factor, openness to experience, is probably related to what others have called stimulus seeking (Zuckerman, 1979) or novelty seeking (Cloninger, 1986). Even more clearly than extroversion, openness to experience suggests a general willingness to experiment. In this case, however, the openness may be both to one's own feelings, impulses, associations, and private schemata and to novel external stimulation. The combination of extroversion and openness would be the most open to new environments; the combination of introversion and openness would be most likely to thrive on self-reflection and introspection.

In fact, the small number of studies that have addressed intraindividual change over time have usually identified changes with age that document a decrease (very small in magnitude) in extroversion (Costa et al., 1987), in novelty seeking

(Giambra, Camp, & Grodsky, 1992) and, to a lesser extent, in neuroticism. As noted earlier, one possibility is that the component that changes with age is concentrated in the experiential, phenotypic aspects of personality; in existing personality inventories they are typically measured along with the more stable genotypic aspects.

The most changeable aspects of the person are affective states and the motivators of the behaviors and internal events that lead to such states, preferences. There is a fine line between states and traits. As discussed at length by Epstein (1983), the repetition of states over time constitutes a trait, that is, the statistical probability that a state will recur in a given individual. Thus, negative affect may be a response to a stressful situation, but there are people who encounter more stressful situations than others or who find a given situation more stressful than does another person. Such a person is characterized by high neuroticism. On the other hand, states do change with circumstances, as in the case of bereavement (Thompson, Gallagher-Thompson, Futterman, Gilewski, & Peterson, 1991), natural disaster (Murrell & Norris, 1984; Norris & Murrell, 1988), or valence of daily events (DeLongis, Coyne, Dakof, Folkman, & Lazarus, 1982; Larsen, Diener, & Emmons, 1986; Lawton, DeVoe, & Parmelee, 1995).

The assertion here is that what we mean by the usual traits that describe personality represents the broad temperaments modified by the canalized dynamic experiences of a lifetime. The extent to which surface traits at a given age are correlated with measures at an earlier age varies with the time between the measurements. Sociability is an example of a behavioral trait composed of accumulated social experiences of reward and punishment superimposed on a temperamental proclivity toward introversion or extroversion. Social behavior at a given time is also highly conditioned by the contemporary context in which it occurs.

If we examine personality tests whose purpose is to assess such surface traits, rather than the second-order factors tapped by the Big Five, we find ample evidence for change, for development, or for elasticity superimposed on stability. For example, Haan, Millsap, and Hartka (1986) in a longitudinal study of the greatest part of the life span concluded that all traits showed evidence of experiential change; overall, 36% of the total pattern of change and lack of change could be ascribed to experience. Such a general pattern appears whether personality is construed in terms of Murray-type needs or in terms of behavioral traits such as affiliation, achievement, dominance, autonomy, and the like.

Compared to the relatively high consensus regarding the basic temperaments, there is considerably less consensus regarding which middle-level traits are basic. Therefore, it is more a matter of qualitative judgment as to whether a particular surface trait is especially relevant to the environment. Some possibilities for such environment-relevant traits follow. A person high in need for order might do well in an environment that was clearly legible and predictable. Such a trait might also describe a person who imposes her or his own order on any context and therefore would shape, rather than be shaped by, the given environment. An affiliative person would respond favorably to the easy availability of others but might, even in the absence of this condition, be adept at constructing a socially rich environment without the physical proximity of others. Locus of control (Rotter, 1966) and some of its derivatives such as desired control (Reid, Haas, & Hawkings, 1977) has an intimate relationship to the number, characteristics, and organization of others in one's environment and the social context of rules, laws, norms, and culture. Other traits such as hostility or emotional dependence appear less environmentally relevant.

One concludes that at the moderately stable but still modifiable level of surface personality traits, person characteristics may be matched to an environment capable of fulfilling this need. On the other hand, the very fact of trait and environment modifiability makes a range of person-environment incongruence possible. A favorable outcome would be contingent on change either in person (adaptation) or environment (environmental proactivity; Lawton, 1989). A second conclusion is that description of an individual personality demands use of the richness of vocabulary associated with surface traits and dominant needs. Attempting to describe personality only in terms of the Big Five intrinsically levels many individual differences.

Preferences

The boundary between surface personality trait and preference is as fuzzy as that between temperament and personality. If the conceptual domain of surface traits is redundant and unclearly organized, that of preferences is impossibly diverse. On the other hand, because of the great number and variety of preferences, it is theoretically possible to identify very concretely personal preferences, to diagnose an environment in terms of whether the preference can be met in that environment, and to supply the resource if the environment lacks the resource. Among the properties of the domain of preferences is their multiplicity, which operates in favor of satisfaction of the desire for an object. One preference may be substituted for another more easily satisfied. Although preferences vary in intensity within a person and across persons, preferences are inclined to be less intense and central to the self than are personality needs. Preferences may be described as needs of the moment, bearing the same relationship to personality needs that states have to traits. The quality of a day consists largely of the mix of positive preferences fulfilled and negative preferences avoided—the quality of the events (uplifts or hassles; Delongis et al., 1982) and the affective consequences (positive affective state or negative affect). I refer to this sequence as the *preference-event-affect state chain*. This chain is highly responsive to the environment. In other words, the environment represents an especially fertile entry point for influencing quality of daily life. The relative ease of building into an environment resources that can bring about recurrent events, which in turn can satisfy widely varying personal preferences, provides justification for the study of residential environments for elders in these terms.

Looking backward at the contributions of temperament, personality, and preferences to well-being, it seems clear that limits within which broad individual differences may be manifested are set by temperament. These influences are lifelong, and they affect personality in its more specific forms. Specific personality motives and traits vary more with accumulated experience and contemporary context than do the temperaments. Everyday life, and its accompanying affective states, is even more variable and less determined by biogenetic factors. In terms of psychological well-being, as Costa and McCrae (1980a) reported, there clearly are "happy people and unhappy people" as identified in long-term perspective; such dispositions are certainly partly determined by temperament. There are also happy periods and unhappy periods of life that are partially independent of temperament. Finally, there are good days and bad days. The presence of good days seems particularly controllable by external events and proactive choices, as seen in the recurrent correlations between external engagement and positive affect. Quality of life is partially defined by the mix of good days and bad days. The worth of life may be defined in terms of whether there still are some good days even if they are outnumbered by the bad ones (Lawton, 1991).

Leisure Activity and Positive Affect

A brief digression seems useful at this point to underline two previously asserted points. First, positive affective states have been the poor relation of mental health. Second, in most of the mental health literature, discretionary activities have been excluded from the list of lifestyle factors related to psychological well-being. Leisure science has thus developed somewhat in isolation from mainstream psychology, despite the occasional very successful effort to bridge this gap (Iso-Ahola, 1980a). One of the problems seems to be that a criterion of the psychological importance of an area of life has traditionally been whether it correlates with depression, anxiety, and other indicators of negative states. Although there have been exceptions, for the most part leisure activity participation has not been shown to exhibit such a relationship to negative mental health. When positive states are added as a criterion for mental health, however, leisure-time activity is clearly associated with positive mental health (Beck & Page, 1988; Lawton, 1983, 1994b).

A connection between leisure activity and the macro-aspects of the person as embodied in temperament and personality has been sought by many leisure researchers. The typical mode is to begin with macrolevels of leisure preference or leisure activity choices and search for structural organization of these characteristics that identifies personality needs or traits associated with these activities. Lawton (1993) organized many such empirical analyses into 12 rational categories, further grouped into larger categories referred to as experiential leisure and social leisure.

Environment and Positive Affect

Resources for leisure-time activity are an aspect of the environment toward which our attention should be directed. In analogous fashion, it would seem that uplift-producing aspects of the physical environment also require renewed attention, as Kaplan and Kaplan (1981) have done for the natural environment. It seems very likely that the ability of features of the natural environment to evoke positive affective states varies with temperament and personality. For example, extroverts or those more open to experience may be more immediately influenced by the visual aesthetic qualities of the environment.

Traitlike preferences for environmental features received the brief attention given by McKechnie (1970) and Windley (1973) in their explorations of environmental dispositions. This line of investigation has been relatively neglected since that time. What is needed to advance our knowledge is to look again through a chain going from temperament to personality to preferences to environmental resources and ending with the two major affective facets of mental health as outcomes.

HOUSING AND ENVIRONMENTAL THEORY

This brief final section of the chapter will sketch some implications of this conceptual orientation for the design and use of residential environments for the aged. Earlier writings have detailed the general relevance of person-environment models for housing (Lawton, 1985; Parmelee & Lawton, 1990; institutions—Kahana, 1982; and community—Golant, 1991). The thoughts to follow will use the added perspectives of individual differences in complementing our ability to foster high-quality environments and optimal matches of person and environment. An early finding that bears emphasis is Carp's (1966, 1974) study of Victoria Plaza showing that personality traits consistent with the social character of age-targeted housing, such as sociability (when measured before occupancy), predicted further engagement after becoming a tenant; by contrast, introverted people seemed to diminish their range of external engagement even further following occupancy.

Parmelee and Lawton (1990) identified a central dialectic of person-environment transactions in later life as the tension between the need for security and the need for autonomy. It is not a far step to link strong security needs to the neuroticism temperament, or autonomy to the extroverted, novelty-seeking temperament. It is important to note in this context both the universal and the individual-difference facet of the autonomy-security dialectic. Attainment of both autonomy and security is a universal need, whose mix and resolution vary at different times and in different contexts within the same individual. The mix characterizing the average range of the security-autonomy dialectic is in itself an individual difference.

For the present purpose, it is useful to the planner and the architect to have some idea of the average range on the continuum between autonomy and security into which prospective occupants of a housing environment may fall. This is exactly what is conveyed when planners decide that the target group should be vigorous, frail, ill, or cognitively impaired. Such broad designations are useful in guiding the general shape of a housing environment, but individual needs get lost among generalizations as abstract as those conveyed by autonomy or security.

The most in-depth consideration of how individual differences brought by tenants into a housing environment may affect quality of adaptation to the housing has been introduced by Golant (1991). He presents a ''whole-person perspective,'' which introduces a number of relevant person characteristics into our thinking about successful housing tenancy. Golant discusses 18 such bases on which people may differ, probing into both how each characteristic may affect housing adaptation and how interventions to adjust dysfunctional matches between person and housing might be introduced. Among these characteristics, Golant treats temperamental variations (preference for novelty, rigidity, ease of habituation), classic need-oriented personality traits (affiliation, control, order, dominance), social and self attitudes (social identity, age identification), and preferences (for homogeneity, privacy, leisure, urbanism/wilderness, environmental familiarity, and attachment to past). Also included are two basic structural personal characteristics (competence and consistency with expectations) and a psychological outcome (life satisfaction and happiness). Although the personal characteristics were not chosen to represent systematically or sample from all important levels of temperament, personality, and preferences, this very rich discussion illustrates the gain that may be expected from putting the person more firmly back into the ecological equation.

This section will end by noting several alternative approaches to enhancing the ability of housing to fulfill the needs of different individuals: initial selection, provision of maximum diversity, changing the person, and changing the environment.

Initial Selection

Where one lives is the result of an intricate, dynamic process of gathering information about the housing, considering alternatives, making a decision, and reaffirming that decision (Lawton, 1983). Thus, the person is a highly proactive participant in environmental choice. The environments so chosen are partially explainable by genetic factors; that is, genetic factors have been shown to lead to choices of environmental resources consistent with one's needs (Bergeman, Plomin, McClearn, Pedersen, & Friberg, 1988). Nonetheless, sponsors, planners, and administrators also have a say in decisions that determine who will enter.

Although it is unlikely that formal selection criteria would ever be based on temperament or traditional personality traits, level of competence is a familiar planning and selection basis. Lawton, Greenbaum, and Liebowitz (1980) characterized "constant" and "accommodating" environments in terms of whether initial selection criteria for competence were maintained as the environments aged. Other bases for selection may be correlated with personality. If the sponsor's preference for tenants from a specific social group operates strongly, the housing may attract people with a need for homogeneity, or familiarity, and therefore preference for "their own kind."

Even in unplanned housing, people's self-imposed selection criteria are likely to result in housing choices consistent with their own needs (Campbell, Converse, & Rodgers, 1976). It is possible that housing counseling embedded in a housing or multiservice agency could help make the elder aware of the possibility of matching such a choice to some basic personality needs.

Provision of Maximum Diversity

Another route toward better person-environment congruence is to deliberately encourage diversity among residents and their needs and match this diversity through environmental diversity. This situation of maximum congruence is, in fact, what healthy elders in comfortable economic circumstances find when they select or remain in homes in nonplanned age-mixed communities. Such unlimited choice of people, physical environment, and environmental resources helps explain some of the tenacity of elders in remaining in their homes. They have learned to get what they wish.

In planned housing, such high environmental diversity is expensive to provide. The housing environment must be relatively large to yield social choices for residents based on affinity of background and interests. In fact, such resource richness is characteristic of many continuing care retirement communities and is no doubt a factor related to their success. If the community is large enough, like-minded people are easier to find, and the variety of activities and personal styles that can be fruitfully pursued is increased. It is a continuing challenge to attempt to achieve this diversity of person and resource in smaller or less-expensive settings.

Changing the Person

Most people, regardless of age, do not require changing; they either adapt or impose choices and actions on the environment to reduce the extent of misfit. Planned housing constitutes a special situation, however, where group living is both more complex and likely to represent a major change in lifestyle. Further, some types of residences, in choosing occupants from the low-competent or security-oriented ends of the continuum, may be caring for people less able than the average elder to manage an incongruent situation. Both management and other personnel who interact with the tenant could benefit from an orientation to temperament, personality, and preferences and the limits of change possible in most people. The difference between lifelong isolation associated with high introversion and learned isolation associated with illness or an unfriendly social context is just one example of many principles that are useful in administration, programming, and counseling.

Preferences are the easiest to change. There is ample justification in theory for exposing tenants to new activities, training them to recognize and exert choices, and even for learning social skills that are pertinent to the planned housing environment. In-home services programs delivered to frail elders still living in their homes can attempt to change preferences by stimulating the elder to plan rearrangements of the home, decor, aesthetic aspects of the home, and so on. In any such application, the greater resistance to change of long-term personality and temperament needs to be considered by the professional.

Changing the Environment

Once more, the distinction between environments shaped by the person and those that shape the person is paramount. It is doubtful whether the potential of residents to create their own housing environments within a planned housing context has ever been achieved, despite the occasional efforts of a tenants' council or a therapeutic environment committee to facilitate such activity.

The main tool available for housing management is to keep an open mind and encourage adventurousness in making available both leisure activities and sometimes instrumental task opportunities. Sometimes the aging in place of a tenant population (Tillson, 1990) may stimulate a need to revise such a resource program. Cohort change will be just as important a consideration in modifying housing environments over time. The physical environment, the activity program, and psychosocial norms change with changing backgrounds of new arrivals. The changing mix of other tenants (the suprapersonal environment; Lawton, 1982), for example, the tendency of the mean age and health of tenants to change in an accommodating environment (Lawton et al., 1980), is a suprapersonal characteristic capable of being controlled by management admission and retention standards. If aging in place is accepted, the housing may require physical remodeling to increase accessibility or the addition of service spaces or social spaces consistent with increased frailty.

A suggestion that there may be reason to develop "place therapy" was elaborated on by Scheidt and Windley (1985) and Scheidt (1995). They note the many possibilities and dynamics involved in efforts to preserve or fortify desirable characteristics of neighborhoods and communities, citing the instance of small midwestern towns that have been the focus of much of their research. They include the notion of "behavior setting therapy," intervention measures applied to the system properties of individuals in the aggregate engaged in a standing pattern of behavior within a physically bounded physical environment

(Barker, 1968). Both planned and unplanned housing environments include such settings. Their standing patterns of behavior may or may not facilitate the most adaptive or satisfying behaviors for the majority of occupants, or the standing pattern may suit the majority but be maladaptive or aversive for some individuals. In planned housing, for example, the behavior settings around elevators are often the most conflict ridden. Interventions may include the purely environmental (building more elevators in the original design, lengthening the open-door cycle), personal (providing an operator at peak times), or system-level (establishing a timed order in which people finish meals and have access to the elevator). In another example, the enforced surveillance imposed on tenants by having a single entrance and exit pathway through a crowded lobby may be altered by searching for a second route that avoids having to run the gauntlet of scrutiny by one's fellow tenants. As aging in place occurs, the rules that govern the standing patterns of behavior may need to be modified deliberately—for example, persuading the tenant group to accept people in wheelchairs in the lobby or dining room.

All four ways of serving individual differences are considered to some extent in the present volume. In this chapter, these mechanisms are included simply to illustrate how awareness of such differences may be used in concert with environmental differences to enhance quality of daily life and generalized well-being.

REFERENCES

Altman, I., & Rogoff, B. (1987). World views in psychology: Trait, interactional, organismic, and transactional perspectives. In D. Stokols & I. Altman (Eds.), *Handbook of environmental psychology* (Vol. 1, pp. 7–40). New York: John Wiley.

Andrews, F. M. (1984). Construct validity and error components of survey measures: A structural modeling approach. *Public Opinion Quarterly, 48*, 409–442.

Barker, D. E. (Ed.). (1968). *Ecological psychology.* Stanford, CA: Stanford University Press.

Beck, S. H., & Page, J. W. (1988). Involvement in activities and the psychological well-being of retired men. *Activities, Adaptation, and Aging, 11*, 31–47.

Bergeman, C. S., Plomin, R., McClearn, G. E., Pedersen, N. L., & Friberg, L. T. (1988). Genotype-environment interaction in personality development: Identical twins reared apart. *Psychology and Aging, 3*, 399–406.

Berlyne, D. E. (Ed.). (1974). *Studies in the new experimental aesthetics.* New York: John Wiley.

Berlyne, D. E. (1978). Curiosity and learning. *Motivation and Emotion, 2*, 97–175.

Bradburn, N. M. (1969). *The structure of psychological well-being.* Chicago: Aldine.

Campbell, A., Converse, P., & Rodgers, W. (1976). *Quality of life in America.* New York: Russell Sage.

Carp, F. M. (1966). *A future for the aged.* Austin: University of Texas Press.

Carp, F. M. (1974). Short-term and long-term prediction of adjustment to a new environment. *Journal of Gerontology, 29*, 444–453.

Carp, F. M., & Carp, A. (1982a). Perceived environmental quality of neighborhoods. *Journal of Environmental Psychology, 2*, 4–22.

Carp, F. M., and Carp, A. (1982b). A role for technical assessment in perceptions of environmental quality and well-being. *Journal of Environmental Psychology, 2*, 171–191.

Carp, F. M., & Carp, A. (1984). A complementary/congruence model of well-being on mental health for the community elderly. In I. Altman, M. P. Lawton, & J. F. Wohlwill (Eds.), *Elderly people and their environment* (pp. 279–336). New York: Plenum Press.

Cattell, R. B. (1950). *Personality: A systematical, theoretical, and factual study*. New York: McGraw-Hill.

Cloninger, C. R. (1986). A unified biosocial theory of personality and its role in the development of anxiety states. *Psychiatric Development, 3*, 167–226.

Cloninger, C. R., Przybeck, T. R., & Svrakic, D. M. (1991). The Tridimensional Personality Questionnaire: U.S. normative data. *Psychological Reports, 69*, 1047–1057.

Cloninger, C. R., Svrakic, D. M., & Przybeck, T. R. (1992). *Mature character development as a process of identification: Relations of demographic and temperament to character*. St. Louis: Washington University Department of Psychiatry.

Costa, P. T., & McCrae, R. R. (1980a). Influence of extroversion and neuroticism on subjective well-being: Happy and unhappy people. *Journal of Personality and Social Psychology, 38*, 668–678.

Costa, P. T., & McCrae, R. R. (1980b). Still stable after all these years. In P. B. Baltes & O. G. Brim (Eds.), *Life span development and behavior* (Vol. 3, pp. 65–102). New York: Academic Press.

Costa, P. T., & McCrae, R. R. (1989). *The NEO/FFI Manual supplement*. Odessa, FL: Psychological Assessment Resources.

Costa, P. T., & McCrae, R. R. (1992). Four ways five factors are basic. *Personality and Individual Differences, 13*, 653–665.

Costa, P. T., Jr., Zonderman, A. B., McCrae, R. R., Cornoni-Huntley, J., Locke, B. Z., & Barbano, H. E. (1987). Longitudinal analyses of psychological well-being in a national sample: Stability of mean levels. *Journal of Gerontology, 42*, 50–55.

Csikszentmihalyi, M. (1975). *Beyond boredom and anxiety*. San Francisco: Jossey-Bass.

DeLongis, A., Coyne, C., Dakof, G., Folkman, S., & Lazarus, R. S. (1982). Relationship of daily hassles, uplifts, and major life events to health status. *Health Psychology, 1*, 119–136.

Diener, E., Larsen, R. J., Levine, S., & Emmons, R. A. (1985). Intensity and frequency: Dimensions underlying positive and negative affect. *Journal of Personality and Social Psychology, 48*, 1253–1265.

Epstein, S. (1983). Aggregation and beyond: Some basic issues on the prediction of behavior. *Journal of Personality, 51*, 360–392.

Eysenck, H. J. (1970). *The structure of human personality* (3rd ed.). London: Methuen.

Eysenck, H. J., & Eysenck, S. B. (1975). *Manual for the Eysenck Personality Questionnaire*. San Diego: Education and Industrial Testing Service.

Garling, T., & Evans, G. W. (Eds.). (1991). *Environment, cognition, and action*. New York: Oxford University Press.

Geen, R. G. (1984). Preferred stimulation levels in introverts and extroverts. *Journal of Personality and Social Psychology, 46*, 1303–1312.

Giambra, L. M., Camp, C. J., & Grodsky, A. (1992). Curiosity and stimulation seeking across the adult life span: Cross-sectional and 6- to 8-year longitudinal findings. *Psychology and Aging, 7*, 150–157.

Gibson, J. J. (1979). *The ecological approach to visual perception.* Boston: Houghton Mifflin.

Golant, S. M. (1991). Congregate housing for the elderly: Theoretical, policy, and programmatic perspectives. *Journal of Housing for the Elderly, 9*, 21–38.

Goldberg, L. R. (1990). An alternative description of personality: The Big Five factor structure. *Journal of Personality and Social Personality, 59*, 1216–1229.

Golledge, R. G. (1987). Environmental cognition. In D. Stokols & I. Altman (Eds.), *Handbook of environmental psychology* (Vol. 1, pp. 131–174). New York: John Wiley.

Gray, J. A. (1981). A critique of Eysenck's theory of personality. In H. J. Eysenck (Ed.), *A model of personality* (pp. 246–276). New York: Springer-Verlag.

Gray, J. A. (1987). Discussion of Cloninger's unified biosocial theory of personality. *Psychiatric Developments, 4*, 344–385.

Haan, N., Millsap, R., & Hartka, E. (1986). As time goes by: Change and stability in personality over fifty years. *Psychology and Aging, 1*, 220–232.

Helson, H. (1964). *Adaptation-level theory.* New York: Harper & Row.

Iso-Ahola, S. E. (1980a). *The social psychology of leisure and recreation.* Dubuque, IA: Wm. C. Brown.

Iso-Ahola, S. E. (1980b). Toward a dialectical social psychology of leisure and recreation. In S. E. Iso-Ahola (Ed.), *Social psychological perspectives on leisure and recreation* (pp. 19–37). Springfield, IL: Charles C. Thomas.

Kahana, E. A. (1982). A congruence model of person-environment interaction. In M. P. Lawton, P. G. Windley, & T. O. Byerts (Eds.), *Aging and the environment: Theoretical approaches* (pp. 97–121). New York: Springer.

Kaplan, S., & Kaplan, R. (1981). *Cognition and environment.* New York: Praeger.

Knopf, R. C. (1987). Human behavior, cognition, and affect in the natural environment. In D. Stokols & I. Altman (Eds.), *Handbook of environmental psychology* (Vol. 1, pp. 783–825). New York: John Wiley.

Larsen, R. J., Diener, E., & Emmons, R. A. (1986). Affect intensity and reactions to daily life events. *Journal of Personality and Social Psychology, 51*, 803–814.

Lawton, M. P. (1982). Competence, environmental press, and the adaptation of older people. In M. P. Lawton, P. G. Windley, & T. O. Byerts (Eds.), *Aging and the environment: Theoretical approaches* (pp. 33–59). New York: Springer.

Lawton, M. P. (1983). The dimensions of well-being. *Experimental Aging Research, 9*, 65–72.

Lawton, M. P. (1985). Housing and living environments of older people. In R. H. Binstock & E. Shanas (Eds.), *Handbook of aging and the social sciences* (pp. 450–478). New York: Van Nostrand Reinhold.

Lawton, M. P. (1989). Environmental proactivity and affect in older people. In S. Spacapan & S. Oskamp (Eds.), *Social psychology of aging* (pp. 135–164). Newbury Park, CA: Sage Publications.

Lawton, M. P. (1991). A multidimensional view of quality of life in frail elders. In J. E. Birren, J. E. Lubben, J. C. Rowe, & D. E. Deutchman (Eds.), *The concept and measurement of quality of life* (pp. 3–27). New York: Academic Press.

Lawton, M. P. (1993). The meaning of leisure. In J. R. Kelly (Ed.), *Activity and aging.* Newbury Park, CA: Sage Publications.

Lawton, M. P. (1994a). Aging and activity: A theoretical perspective. In D. C. Compton & S. Iso-Ahola (Eds.), *Leisure and mental health* (pp. 61–78). Parker City, UT: Family Development Resources.

Lawton, M. P. (1994b). Personality and affective correlates of leisure activity participation by older people. *Journal of Leisure Research, 26,* 138–157.

Lawton, M. P., DeVoe, M. R., & Parmelee, P. (1995). The relationship of events and affect in the daily lives of an elderly population. *Psychology and Aging, 19,* 469–477.

Lawton, M. P., Greenbaum, M., & Liebowitz, B. (1980). The lifespan of housing environments for the aging. *Gerontologist, 20,* 56–64.

Lawton, M. P., Kleban, M. H., Rajagopal, D., & Dean, J. (1992). The factorial generality of brief positive and negative affect measures. *Journal of Gerontology: Psychological Sciences, 47,* 228–237.

Lawton, M. P., & Nahemow, L. (1973). Ecology and the aging process. In C. Eisdorfer & M. P. Lawton (Eds.), *Psychology of adult development and aging* (pp. 619–674). Washington, DC: American Psychological Association.

Lawton, M. P., Windley, P. G., & Byerts, T. O. (Eds.). (1982). *Aging and the environment: Theoretical approaches.* New York: Springer.

Lazarus, R. S. (1966). *Psychological stress and the coping process.* New York: McGraw-Hill.

Lazarus, R. S. (1990). Theory-based stress measurement. *Psychological Inquiry, 1,* 3–13.

Lewin, K. (1951). *Field theory in social science.* New York: Harper & Row.

McDougall, W. (1926). *Outline of abnormal psychology.* London: Methuen.

McKechnie, E. (1970, October). *Measuring environmental dispositions with the environmental response inventory.* Proceedings of the conference paper presented at the meeting of the Environmental Design Research Association, Pittsburgh, PA.

Magnusson, D., & Endler, N. S. (Eds.). (1977). *Personality at the crossroads: Current issues in international psychology.* Hillsdale, NJ: Lawrence Erlbaum.

Mowrer, O. H. (1950). *Learning theory and personality dynamics.* New York: Ronald Press.

Murray, H. A. (1938). *Explorations in personality.* New York: Oxford.

Murrell, S. A., & Meeks, S. (1991). Depression symptoms in older adults: Predispositions, resources, and life experiences. In K. W. Schaie (Ed.), *Annual review of gerontology and geriatrics* (Vol. 11, pp. 261–286). New York: Springer.

Murrell, S. A., & Norris, F. H. (1984). Resources, life events, and changes in positive affect and depression in older adults. *Journal of Community Psychology, 12,* 445–464.

Norris, F., & Murrell, S. (1988). Prior experience as a moderator of disaster impact on anxiety symptoms in older adults. *American Journal of Community Psychology, 16,* 665–683.

Olds, J., & Milner, P. (1954). Positive reinforcement produced by electrical stimulation of the septal area and other regions of the rat brain. *Journal of Comparative and Physiological Psychology, 47,* 411–427.

Olds, J., & Olds, M. (1965). Drives, rewards, and the brain. In T. Newcomb (Ed.), *New directions in psychology* (Vol. 2, pp. 327–410). New York: Holt, Rinehart, & Winston.

Parmelee, P., & Lawton, M. P. (1990). The design of special environments for the aged.

In J. E. Birren & K. W. Schaie (Eds.), *Handbook of the psychology of aging* (3rd ed., pp. 464–487). New York: Academic Press.

Pribram, K. H., & McGuiness, D. (1975). Arousal, activation, and effort in the control of attention. *Psychological Review, 82*, 116–149.

Reich, J., & Zautra, A. (1983a). Demands and desires in daily life: Some influences on well-being. *American Journal of Community Psychology, 11*, 41–58.

Reid, D. W., Haas, G., & Hawkings, D. (1977). Locus of desired control and positive self-concept of the elderly. *Journal of Gerontology, 32*, 441–450.

Rotter, J. B. (1966). Generalized expectancies for internal versus external control of re-inforcement. *Psychological Monographs, 80* (1, Whole No. 609).

Rowles, G. D. (1978). *Prisoners of space?* Boulder, CO: Westview Press.

Rowles, G. D. (1980). Growing old "inside": Aging and attachment to place in an Appalachian community. In N. Datan & N. Lohmann (Eds.), *Transitions of aging* (pp. 153–170). New York: Academic Press.

Rowles, G. D. (1984). Aging in rural environments. In I. Altman, M. P. Lawton, & J. F. Wohlwill (Eds.), *Elderly people and the environment* (pp. 129–157). New York: Plenum Press.

Russell, J. A., & Snodgrass, J. (1987). Emotion and the environment. In I. Altman & D. Stokols (Eds.), *Handbook of environmental psychology* (Vol. 1, pp. 245–280). New York: John Wiley.

Russell, J. A., & Steiger, J. H. (1982). The structure in persons' implicit taxonomy of emotions. *Journal of Research in Personality, 16*, 447–469.

Scheidt, R. (1995, November). *Place transitions and the well-being of older persons: Interventive strategies.* Paper presented at the annual meeting of the Gerontological Society of America, Los Angeles.

Scheidt, R., & Windley, P. (1985). The ecology of aging. In J. E. Birren & K. W. Schaie (Eds.), *Handbook of the psychology of aging* (2nd ed., pp. 245–258). New York: Van Nostrand Reinhold.

Schooler, K. K. (1969). The relationship between social interaction and morale of the elderly as a function of environmental characteristics. *Gerontologist, 9*, 25–29.

Schooler, K. K. (1982). Response of the elderly to environment: A stress-theoretic perspective. In M. P. Lawton, P. G. Windley, & T. O. Byerts (Eds.), *Aging and environment: Theoretical approaches* (pp. 80–96). New York: Springer.

Tellegen, A. (1985). Structure of mood and personality and their relevance to assessing anxiety with an emphasis on self-report. In A. H. Tuma & J. Masser (Eds.), *Anxiety and the anxiety disorders* (pp. 681–706). Hillside, NJ: Lawrence Erlbaum.

Thompson, L. W., Gallagher-Thompson, D., Futterman, A., Gilewski, M. J., & Peterson, J. (1991). The effects of late-life spousal bereavement over a 30-month interval. *Psychology and Aging, 6*, 434–441.

Tillson, D. (Ed.). (1990). *Aging in place.* Glenview, IL: Scott, Foresman.

Tucker, D. M. (1981). Lateral brain function, emotion, and conceptualization. *Psychological Bulletin, 89*, 19–46.

Wapner, S. (1987). A holistic, developmental systems–oriented environmental psychology: Some beginnings. In D. Stokols & I. Altman (Eds.), *Handbook of environmental psychology* (Vol. 2, pp. 1433–1466). New York: John Wiley.

Warr, P., Barter, J., & Brownbridge, G. (1983). On the independence of positive and negative affect. *Journal of Personality and Social Psychology, 44*, 644–651.

Watson, D., & Tellegen, A. (1985). Toward a consensual structure of mood. *Psychological Bulletin, 98*, 219–235.

White, R. W. (1959). Motivation reconsidered: The concept of competence. *Psychological Review, 66*, 297–333.

Windley, P. G. (1973). Measuring environmental dispositions of elderly females. In W. F. Preiser (Eds.), *Environmental design research* (Vol. 1, pp. 217–228). Stroudsburg, PA: Dowden, Hutchinson, & Ross.

Windley, P. G. (1982). Environmental dispositions: A theoretical and methodological alternative. In M. P. Lawton, P. G. Windley, & T. O. Byerts (Eds.), *Aging and the environment: Theoretical approaches* (pp. 60–68). New York: Springer.

Wohlwill, J. F. (1966). The physical environment: A problem for the psychology of stimulation. *Journal of Social Issues, 22*, 29–38.

Zajonc, R. B. (1968). Attitudinal effects of mere exposure. *Journal of Personality and Social Psychology, 9* (2, Pt. 2), 1–28.

Zajonc, R. B. (1980). Feeling and thinking: Preferences need no inferences. *American Psychologist, 35*, 151–175.

Zuckerman, M. (1979). *Sensation seeking: Beyond the optimal level of arousal*. Hillsdale, NJ: Lawrence Erlbaum.

2

Changing an Older Person's Shelter and Care Setting: A Model to Explain Personal and Environmental Outcomes

STEPHEN M. GOLANT

Older persons must often modify their current housing arrangements or move to more supportive shelter and care settings because they feel uncomfortable living alone, are unable to maintain their households, have trouble carrying out everyday activities, or have unmet needs for therapeutic and nursing services. Housing and service providers have an obvious interest in knowing whether these residential adjustments are successful from the perspective of older persons themselves (Golant, 1986). Two issues are central: First, why do older persons view some aspects of their residential or environmental change more positively than others? Second, why do older persons dissimilarly evaluate their changed settings, even as they seemingly have similar personal qualities and the changes seem equally appropriate to them all (Golant, 1991; Moos & Lemke, 1994; Parmelee & Lawton, 1990)? This chapter outlines a conceptual model designed to answer these questions. It focuses on how changes in two broad categories of outcomes are experienced differently by older persons following their residential adjustments. These include personal state outcomes, such as morale, life satisfaction, and control; and environmental outcomes, such as project satisfaction, feelings of privacy, and compatibility of social relationships.

BACKGROUND

A Wealth of Empirical Studies

Many studies have investigated the consequences of older people moving from one residential setting to another and whether the resulting environment is more or less congruent with their needs or demands. Researchers have focused on a wide array of residential adjustments made by older Americans: moves from conventional dwellings and neighborhoods to other conventional residential sites in response to gentrification and urban renewal projects; moves from conventional market rate housing to public housing facilities; moves from conventional housing to group housing alternatives, such as congregate housing, continuing care retirement communities (CCRCs), assisted living, board and care, shared group living, and nursing homes; moves to the home of a child; and moves from one institutional setting to another.

A disproportionate number of these investigations have linked these residential shifts to negative outcomes, such as higher mortality and morbidity rates, poorer physical health, greater housing dissatisfaction, and declines in morale, happiness, and life satisfaction. Other investigations, however, have reported on the positive outcomes of these moves and the benefits older people experience as a result of living in more physically, socially, and organizationally supportive settings (Carp, 1987; Kasl & Rosenfield, 1980; Lawton, 1977, 1985b; Lieberman, 1991; Pastalan, 1983; Schulz & Brenner, 1977).

Given that most older persons do not cope with their new needs by moving but rather by changing some aspect of their current residential settings, an increasing number of studies have investigated the economic, social, and psychological consequences of aging in situ. These have particularly focused on how the introduction of professional services in the home and the assumption of new family caregiver roles have influenced the psychological well-being of these older residents, their ability to live independently, and the length of time that they are able to delay their move to a nursing home (Lawton, Brody, & Saperstein, 1989, Newman & Envall, 1995; Weissert, Cready, & Pawelak, 1988).

Past Theories and Models

Lieberman (1991) has offered two theoretical explanations for the negative psychological or physical outcomes that older persons may experience following their residential relocations. The first, the "symbolic meaning of relocation," focuses on the meanings older persons attribute to the moving event. When older persons do not fully anticipate the consequences of their move or when their experiences are not consistent with their expectations, they are more likely to interpret the move negatively and as a personal loss. Even the mere anticipation of a future move may be a source of stress and anxiety (Lieberman & Tobin, 1983). A second explanation, the "environmental discrepancy hypothesis," views relocation as a potential crisis or major stress demanding new adaptive efforts, because it "disrupts customary modes of behavior and imposes a need for strenuous psychological work" (Lieberman, 1991, p. 127). While shedding light on environmental change as a source of stress and the psychological adjustment problems experienced by elderly movers, these interpretations fall short in three ways: (1) by overemphasizing the negative consequences—especially morbidity and mortality outcomes—of these relocations; (2) by failing to consider adequately how changes in the physical characteristics of the new shelter environments influence the adjustment process; and (3) by failing to consider fully why individuals differently interpret and cope with unfavorable changes.

Several "ecology of aging" models developed by gerontologists have addressed these weaknesses. These models have examined the theoretical basis for the congruence of the "objectively and subjectively defined features of the physical and psychosocial environment" with the needs and capabilities of their older occupants (Scheidt & Windley, 1985, p. 245). Their central concern is how well older persons have adapted to their new surroundings, that is, "the processes governing the efforts of the aging individual to respond successfully to both endogenous and exogenous changes (needs and demands) occurring *over time*" (p. 246; emphasis added).

While these models have helped clarify the person and environmental characteristics that underlie older people's optimal living arrangements, they have all suffered from a major shortcoming. Despite their purported rationale of studying change—of environments and people—they have only incompletely or vaguely conceptualized either the characteristics of the individual or the environment in temporal terms. These theoretical perspectives have in Magnusson's terms (1981, p. 17) assumed a "momentary situation." The most prominent of these, the person-environment model developed by Lawton (1982), included personal and environmental characteristics that had the potential of being measured over time, but these were not formally assigned temporal attributes. This is exemplified by the central propositions of the model, the "environmental docility hypothesis" and later the "environmental proactivity hypothesis," that relate the level of competence of older persons to their ability to experience favorable adaptive outcomes (Lawton, 1983, 1989). When the model speaks of lower and higher competence, however, it is unclear whether reference is being made to a cross-sectional comparison of the competence levels of older persons at a point in time or to a longitudinal description of the competence levels of these persons over some period.

Another model developed by Schooler (1976) had considerable potential as a framework to predict the impact of environmental change, because it was closely derived from the psychological stress and coping theory of Lazarus (1966). Unfortunately, its author never formally specified the model's components and relationships, thereby reducing its value as a theoretical contribution.

Among the other notable person-environment models, change is also largely absent as a measurable construct. Other than positing that incongruence will result from a change in one's life situation or environment, Kahana's (1982) congruence model and its earlier formulation by French, Rodgers, and Cobb (1974) do not include a temporal dimension. This is largely true of Nehrke's et al. (1984) congruence model except in their identification of "discontinuity" as one of the environmental dimensions along which to assess person-environment congruence. Golant's (1984b) "environmental experience" model is also a static conceptualization of the determinants of environmental outcomes with the exception of its "duration in residence" construct. This is also an appropriate criticism of the complementary/congruence model of Carp (1987) with the exception of its "recent life events" construct.

Although these more formal models have largely failed to conceptualize individual or environmental change as constructs, several researchers have pointed to the importance of the past environmental views and attachments of older persons as predictors of how successfully they will adjust to new or different environments. These include Rowles's (1983) "autobiographical insideness," Howell's (1983) "individual psychoenvironmental histories," and O'Bryant and Wolf's (1983) "attachment to home."

RATIONALE AND OVERVIEW OF PROPOSED MODEL

An Interactional Worldview

In its construction, operation, and assumptions, this conceptual model adopts an interactional worldview as this philosophical position is understood in contemporary psychology (Altman & Rogoff, 1987). A set of distinct antecedents, which include personal qualities and behaviors, subjectively interpreted environmental attributes, and psychological processes, both independently and in interaction with each other, are construed as causal influences of a set of individually experienced outcomes. These relationships occur in an objectively defined environment or context, designated as including a set of content components and the behaviors of occupants transacting with this content.

The Temporal Context

The model's goal of explaining why older persons differently experience changes in their personal and environmental outcomes as a result of their residential adjustments sharply distinguishes it from most environmental optimality or person-environment congruence models that have focused on only a single slice of individual and environmental time. Its temporal emphasis is consistent with a major thrust of gerontological and human development research that seeks to understand the patterns, antecedents, and consequences of the aging process and how persons differently evaluate and adapt to both the forces of change and the resulting outcomes (Stokols, 1987). Adopting this temporal perspective is a recognition that older persons observed in new or changed settings have experienced different trajectories of individual and environmental change. Observed over some defined interval of time, their past experienced outcomes thus serve as individually defined subjective reference points by which to judge the impact of their currently occupied setting. This warns against declaring a group of individuals as homogeneous simply because they *currently* are attributed with having identical characteristics or experiences. The erroneousness of this assumption derives from their having reached their sameness from very different starting points.

Table 2.1

Temporal Context of Older Person's Current Environmental Outcomes: Change in Appraised Environmental Outcomes as a Result of Relocation

Worse*	Same*	Better*
NA	(1) Excellent	(2) Excellent
(3) Good	(4) Good	(5) Good
(6) Fair	(7) Fair	(8) Fair
(9) Poor	(10) Poor	NA

*Assumed current outcomes measured on a 4-point scale: Excellent, Good, Fair, and Poor.
NA = Not applicable.

Most important, it is unlikely that older people observed in a new shelter and care setting will all have previously occupied residential settings that were congruent with their needs and capabilities. Thus, programmatic goals designed to achieve individual-environment congruence in a new setting are unrealistically ambitious given that many of its occupants will not have achieved such optimality in their previous settings—indeed, perhaps in any of the settings that they have occupied in their adult lives. It is similarly presumptuous to believe that we can explain with a cross-sectional analysis the poor individual-environment fits of persons in a new setting who have for a long time assessed aspects of their previous housing arrangements as inappropriate and who have always had imperfect or ineffectual coping skills. The past psychological processes, individual qualities, and environmental transactions underlying such incongruence, and that still persist and influence how they evaluate their present situations, would not easily reveal themselves in any contemporary analysis. One is in effect trying to psychoanalyze an older person in a single session.

The potential pitfalls of interpreting the outcomes reported by older persons at a point in time can be illustrated with a simple example. Table 2.1 describes the current environmental outcomes reported by ten hypothetical residents and how each of these outcomes has recently changed. Compare the outcomes of residents 5 and 8 with that of resident 3. The former two residents experienced better environmental outcomes than in their prior residential setting, yet they are currently experiencing the same or fewer positive outcomes as resident 3. This is true even as resident 3 has judged the current setting as being worse than the previous setting. In effect, the researcher employing a cross-sectional research design would be misleadingly seeking an environmental explanation for why the outcomes of residents 5 or 8 are similar to or worse than resident 3, when in fact there would be reason to believe that the current environment has had an ameliorative effect on their experiences.

The above discussion suggests the need for more realistic analytical goals and applications. First, our conceptualization of the reasons for optimal environments or environmental congruence must be redefined using more meaningful temporal guideposts. Most persons have never lived in perfect settings, and thus our models should explain and predict how recently changed environments have *improved* or *worsened* their elderly occupants' quality of life. Second, consistent with the contention of Scheidt and Windley (1985, p. 246) that "research in the field is largely mission-oriented . . . and is directed toward interventive ends," our models should help us find solutions that minimize the negative changes and maximize the positive changes experienced by older persons in their new or different settings.

A "Whole Person" Perspective

Studies have consistently found that professionals judge what is harmful and what is beneficial about the qualities of a residential setting differently than the elderly occupants themselves (Golant, 1986; Lawton, 1983). Older persons simply do not assess their living conditions as negatively as would be expected given the inadequacies professionals attribute to their accommodations. This oft-observed discrepancy between objectively and subjectively evaluated environments reflects the complex array of perceptual, cognitive, and behavioral factors that influence how occupants of a setting interpret, evaluate, use, and respond to its objective properties. Thus, the outcomes experienced by older persons in their new setting are as much a product of their perceived life situation as they are of their setting's objective conditions (Golant, 1982, 1986). When older people evaluate changes in their shelter and care setting, they are telling us a great deal about themselves: what's important about their lifestyles, how happy they are, how mentally and physically vulnerable they are, how well they deal with change, what they expect from their environment, what activities are central in their lives, and how they cope with adversity.

This model attempts to portray the complex array of individual qualities that influence how older persons evaluate their shelter and care setting. In this respect, it is similar to treatments of the individual in selected relocation studies (Lieberman & Tobin, 1983) but contrasts with the earlier reviewed environment-behavior models that have only focused on the influences of one or two constructs, such as behavioral competence or personality styles. While such expedience may be demanded by the constraints of empirical research, it is an unsatisfactory basis to conceptualize fully the antecedents of an older person's changed individual and environmental experiences.

MODEL COMPONENTS AND RELATIONSHIPS

The following sections describe the model's constructs and relationships, and these are schematically portrayed in Figure 2.1.

Figure 2.1
Antecedents of the Changed Outcomes of Older Persons in Their New Shelter and Care Setting

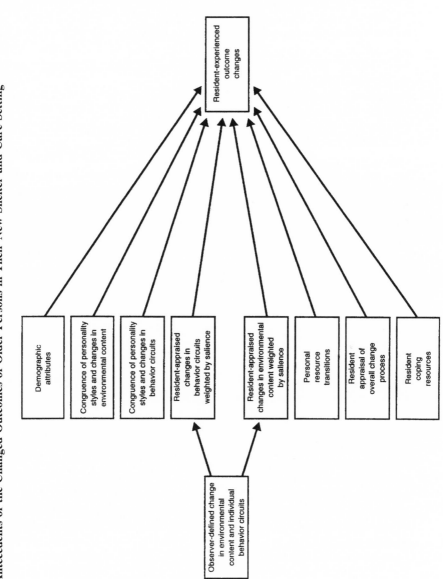

Observer-Based Conceptualization of Shelter and Care Settings

Changing Shelter and Care Settings

Shelter and care settings are here conceptualized as ranging from private or conventional homes and apartments to all categories of group residences designed for older persons (including congregate housing, assisted living, board and care, shared group housing, CCRCs, and nursing homes). A changed or a "new" shelter and care setting may encompass the following possibilities:

- A relocation to an entirely new shelter and care setting with very different physical characteristics and a different level of care or services.
- A relocation to another part (wing, floor, room) of a currently occupied shelter and care setting.
- Staying put in a currently occupied shelter and care setting in which the social situation or living arrangement has significantly changed such as, for example, when a spouse dies or moves to a nursing home, or a child, a live-in, or a grandchild moves in.
- Staying put in a currently occupied shelter and care setting in which the service supports have significantly changed such as, as for example, when the services of a home-care agency are hired.
- Staying put in a currently occupied shelter and care setting in which the physical setting has significantly changed such as, for example, when the dwelling has been significantly remodeled (e.g., a bathroom added) or the neighborhood is socially and physically declining.
- Staying put in a currently occupied shelter and care setting in which the organizational attributes have significantly changed such as when professionals assume the care responsibilities from family members, when there is a change in staff attitudes toward residents in a group housing facility, when the rules in a facility are significantly changed, or when staff morale declines.

Spatiotemporal Analytical Unit

The model distinguishes between a currently occupied (time 2) and previously occupied (time 1) shelter and care setting, and the model's focus is on older persons in their currently occupied setting. The amount of time that has passed since the individual departed from the old setting (or the unmodified setting) and occupied the new setting (or the newly modified setting) is left unspecified. Operationally, it will be necessary to specify an interval of time to measure change that is appropriate, given the research question. This interval must be sufficiently long to reasonably expect the occurrence of change without creating serious problems of sample attrition but sufficiently short to allow the valid reporting of change by both detached observers and older people.

Resident-Experienced Outcome Changes

Residents of the presently occupied setting are conceptualized as experiencing two categories of outcome changes: personal state outcomes and environmental outcomes. Personal state outcomes refer to attitudes (cognitive and affective evaluations) of individuals toward their self or life's (physiological, psychological, behavioral) circumstances and experiences. Environmental outcomes refer to attitudes of individuals toward their objective and external environmental referents. These attitudes may have become more positive or more negative over time or remained the same. Both personal state and environmental outcomes may distinguish qualities that are equivalent to the personality traits of an individual. Thus, individuals who evaluate their physical setting as depressing and controlling (environmental outcomes) and are depressed or unhappy about their lives (personal state outcomes) may have controlling or neurotic personalities. Operationally, these outcomes may be based on resident assessments (e.g., self-ratings, self-reports) or on observer-based appraisals (e.g., clinical assessments or observations).

Personal State Outcome Changes

The following are illustrative (Birren, Lubben, Rowe, & Deutchman, 1991; Lawton, 1983; Nydegger, 1977):

- Decline or increase in intrapsychic well-being (life satisfaction, self-esteem, morale, positive or negative affect).
- Increase or decrease in physical and psychophysiological symptoms (self-reports of fatigue, poor health).
- Increased or decreased control or dominance over life and environment.

Environmental Outcome Changes

The following are illustrative (Pynoos & Regnier, 1991):

- Loss of setting privacy.
- Loss of setting autonomy—fewer opportunities to make personal choices or control events.
- Increased or decreased satisfaction with one or more aspects of residential setting.
- Greater loneliness in setting.
- Loss of pride in surroundings.
- Surroundings feel less homelike.
- Increased sense of being secure and safe in setting.
- Feeling like a stranger in new surroundings.
- Greater sense of belonging in setting.
- Stronger involvement in setting activities.
- More emotionally rewarding or satisfying social relationships or exchanges (more compatible persons to talk over problems).
- More instrumentally rewarding or satisfying social relationships or exchanges (e.g., more helpful persons to rely on to help with chores).

• More aesthetically attractive and provoking (visually, auditorily, and olfactory) surroundings.
• Sense of increased accessibility in setting.
• Everyday activities becoming more restricted.
• Decline in compatibility of social situation.
• Greater confidence in way finding.
• Weaker sense of connection with "outside world."
• Fewer setting opportunities for spontaneity, deviancy.
• Boredom, insufficient stimulation in setting.

Observer-Defined Changes in Environmental Context of Shelter and Care Settings

The Functionally Relevant Environment

The functionally relevant environment includes those objects and activities in a setting that have the potential of evoking, reinforcing, or modifying an individual's or population's behaviors and experiences and that present both opportunities and constraints to residents seeking to satisfy their needs, goals, and preferences (Golant, 1984b). The model thus assumes the existence of an objective environment or situation having an empirical reality, independent of thinking and perceiving human beings, that is capable of being described in rational and detached terms. The portrayal and measurement of the functionally relevant environment rest with the researcher or "observer" who is responsible for selecting the relevant parts, properties, and behaviors of the setting. Multiple influences may drive this "selection" process. Definitional decisions may be linked to the verification of a particular theoretical proposition, the testing of a specific methodology, or the assessment of a specific public policy intervention. For some investigations the selected environmental categories and attributes will be constrained by research precedents; in other instances, the researcher may turn to preliminary qualitative research methodologies to identify the relevant personal constructs. Whatever the basis for the conceptual language, the researcher should be able to articulate its analytical basis, and it should be generalizable to other like settings.

Based on prior environmental taxonomies (Golant, 1984a), the shelter and care setting is categorized into three components: the social environment, the physical environment, and the organizational environment. Each of these components is further divided into several subcategories distinguished by attributes that describe their form (e.g., density, visual properties, age of residents, presence of close friends, architectural attributes, homogeneity), functioning (e.g., performance attributes such as the comfortableness of the furniture; the friendliness of the staff, convenience of the service, the ease of use of door-to-door van transportation), and structure (resident-staff relationships, resident interrelationships, staff cohesiveness or conflicts, facility rules and regulations).

Given that what constitutes an appropriate taxonomy of components is likely to depend on the specific goals motivating the investigation of the changed shelter and care setting, the classification below is suggestive rather than definitive. One could feasibly adopt other taxonomic dimensions and attributes having a like potential of eliciting relevant attitudinal responses from their older occupants.

Environmental Content Taxonomy

Social environment. Two subcategories of components and their attributes are distinguished. The first, the *social situation* (Sherif, 1967) of the setting, describes its overall social climate or ambiance. The second, the *personal situation* of the older person, differentiates the individuals found in a setting according to the social and psychological significance of their personal relationships.

- Social situation: people as objects, distinguished by such characteristics as age, sex, education, race, competence, activity levels, and cultural, ethnic, or religious background; the composition of a population group distinguished by their similarities and differences in these characteristics such as its age or ethnic homogeneity.

- Personal situation: people distinguished by their potential for satisfying human relationships in their instrumental and expressive roles as friends, acquaintances, family, caregivers, and professionals.

Physical environment. Four subcategories of largely self-explanatory components and their attributes are distinguished.

- Natural environment: landscape forms, temperature, humidity, precipitation, insects, and rodents.

- Built environment: physical and architectural aspects of spaces, rooms, common areas, dwellings, neighborhoods, or communities developed or adapted for human occupancy and use.

- Personal belonging environment: physical possessions that have emotional, practical, symbolic meanings, attachments, or sentiments for an individual (e.g., books, art, dishes, pets, furniture, photos, hobby collections) (Csikszentmihalyi & Rochberg-Halton, 1981).

- Urbanized environment: crime, noise, pollution, traffic congestion.

Organizational environment. This category is very similar to the "policy and program features" category in the Multiphasic Environmental Assessment Procedure (MEAP) of Moos and Lemke (1994):

- Staff/resident ratios
- Staff attitudes and behaviors toward residents
- Caregiver characteristics, attitudes, and behaviors
- Service availability
- Variety of sociorecreational activities
- Helping strategies
- Tolerated resident input

- Tolerated resident deviance
- Fairness of regulatory policies
- Clarity and unambiguity of rules and regulations
- Policy and program features
- Monitoring and oversight characteristics

Conceptualizing Changes in the Environmental Content

The components and attributes making up the environmental content of the functionally relevant environment must be capable of being conceptualized along a dimension of change denoting their increased or decreased availability, incidence, strength, intensity, distance, or other appropriate metric denoting the change in their presence. Operationally, these formulations must allow for the eliciting of responses by residents about how the content in their currently occupied and previously occupied setting differs. As an example, the change in presence of any component attribute in the *currently occupied setting* could be measured along a five-point scale ranging from LESS PRESENT to MORE PRESENT. Thus, a currently occupied setting could be evaluated by the residents as having "more (or less) present" storage space, rules and regulations, emergency devices, personal belongings, special design features, and confidants. To assure that the components and attributes of the currently or previously occupied environment can be expressed as a function of the other, the researcher must make as many as three sets of observations: (1) components and attributes found in both the previously occupied and the presently occupied setting; (2) components and attributes found in the presently occupied setting but not in the previously occupied setting (e.g., emergency call button, grab-bars, rules, formal staff roles); and (3) components and attributes found in the previously occupied setting but not in the presently occupied setting (e.g., grocery stores nearby, young neighbors).

Observer-Defined Changes in the Behavior Circuits of Residents in Shelter and Care Settings

Behavior Circuits

Older persons who occupy a new shelter and care setting will inevitably change (add, drop, modify) their everyday routines or activities. The model calls for the researcher to distinguish a set of *behavior circuits* conducted by residents in either or both of their currently or previously occupied settings. The researcher will select those behaviors that are likely to have strong instrumental, affective, or symbolic significance to the residents. Changes in these behavior circuits are expected to influence changes in the outcomes experienced by older persons.

"Behavior circuits" refer to "the round of behaviors people engage in order to accomplish each of their purposes, from start to finish. . . . [T]hey denote both the movement and the completion integral to tasks, errands, recreation, work, visiting, and so on" (Perin, 1970, pp. 77–78). These may involve the individual alone or as a participant in a group in a well-defined physical milieu as in Barker's (1968) behavior setting. Examples of behavior circuits include the daily walking of a pet in the neighborhood, the weekly card game at a friend's house, the watching of the Monday night football game either alone or with a friend, the Sunday morning restaurant brunch with friends, the twice-weekly shopping trip, the daily walk in the mall, the regular viewing of a favorite soap opera in one's favorite chair, the habitual drink before dinner, the scheduled meals of a group housing project, the weekly visit to the doctor, the regular gathering of a hobby group, the attendance of Sunday religious services, the regular conversations with staff, the regular arguments between residents, and the weekly visits with children.

The conceptualization of behavior circuits recognizes that the potential impact of a shelter and care setting cannot be understood only as a function of its content qualities. Additionally, it is necessary to understand the nature and significance of the transactions that individuals conduct with their environment's objects and attributes. Residents living in the same environment will not similarly occupy or utilize its contents and will engage in transactions having different potential consequences (Golant, 1984a). As examples, it is not just the neighborhood that is valued but the regular morning walk in the neighborhood. Similarly, it is not just the friend that is important but the regular weekly visit with that friend.

Behavior Circuit Taxonomy

The following classification distinguishes behavior circuits by their purpose.

- Barber/hairdresser
- Eating
- Financial (banking, broker)
- Leisure/recreational (reading, bingo, sports, radio, TV, entertaining, theater)
- Medical
- Political
- Religious
- Shopping
- Social (friends, neighbors, family)
- Spontaneous, unplanned
- Volunteer/advocacy
- Work

Conceptualizing Changes in Behavior Circuits

The behavior circuits conducted by residents in their functionally relevant environment must be capable of being conceptualized along a dimension of change denoting their increased or decreased frequency or presence. As in the case of environmental content changes, these formulations must operationally allow for the eliciting of responses by residents about how their behavior circuits in currently occupied and previously occupied settings differ. As a result of a shelter and care setting change, it is expected that some behavior circuits will continue unchanged (e.g., telephoning one's daughter twice a week), some will be lost (e.g., regularly scheduled neighborhood walks, playing with one's pet, eating alone with a spouse), some will be gained (e.g., new group-oriented leisure activities, talks with staff), and some will be modified. The researcher must make as many as three sets of observations to ensure that the behavior circuits of the currently or previously occupied environment are capable of being expressed as a function of the other: (1) behavior circuits present in both the previously or presently occupied settings (e.g., watching TV alone in one's room); (2) behavior circuits conducted in the presently occupied setting but not in the previously occupied setting (e.g., eating dinner every night in a congregate dining room; having to sign out every time one leaves the building); and (3) behavior circuits found in the previously occupied setting but not in the presently occupied setting (e.g., regularly watching Monday night football with a grandson; walking every morning with a close friend).

Resident-Appraised Changes in Environmental Content Weighted by Salience

Salience to Resident of Appraised Changes in Environmental Content

Judgments by older residents about how the contents of their currently occupied and previously occupied residential settings differ are unlikely to have the same salience or significance to them. Residents are expected to assign different "subjective values" (Golant, 1984b) or weights to these appraised changes. That is, older persons are expected to report that some environmental content changes more than others deter or facilitate desired actions, meet or block needs or goals, offer or prevent a solution to a problem, reduce or increase gratification in certain areas of life, and constrain or open up options for control and adaptation (Kahana et al., 1995, p. 464). Stokol's (1981) concept of "functional, motivational, and evaluative salience" and Lieberman's (1965) "symbolic salience" appropriately convey these distinctions. Operationally, it will be necessary for the researcher to elicit responses from residents allowing assessments of the unequal relevance of their environmental content changes.

Proposed Model Relationships

Environmental content changes that residents view consciously or unconsciously as representing greater gains or benefits or as being more supportive and enhancing of their goals are expected to lead to more positive outcome changes. On the other hand, those changes that residents view consciously or unconsciously as representing greater losses or as being more harmful, more unsupportive, or more inhibiting of their goals will lead to more negative outcome changes. It is also expected that the very same changes may yield at the same time both more positive and more negative outcomes. A change in environment may lead to the individual feeling more secure but at the same time feeling more dependent and restricted (Moos & Lemke, 1994; Parmelee & Lawton, 1990). What can be reasonably proposed is the following:

• The greater and the more salient the changes in environmental content attributes, the more likely they will contribute to changes in the outcomes experienced by residents in the presently occupied setting.

Resident-Appraised Changes in Behavior Circuits Weighted by Salience

Salience to Resident of Appraised Changes in Behavior Circuits

Judgments by older persons about how their behavior circuits have changed are also unlikely to have the same salience or significance to them. Residents are expected to assign different subjective values or weights to these appraised changes. Operationally, it will be necessary for the researcher to elicit responses from residents allowing assessments of the unequal relevance of their behavior circuit changes.

Proposed Model Relationships

Behavior circuit changes that residents view consciously or unconsciously as representing greater gains or benefits or as being more supportive and enhancing of their goals are expected to lead to more positive outcome changes. On the other hand, those changes that residents view consciously or unconsciously as representing greater losses or as being more harmful, more unsupportive, or more inhibiting of their goals will lead to more negative outcome changes. Again, the direction of these relationships cannot be theorized in advance, and what can be reasonably proposed is the following:

• The greater and the more salient the changes in behavior circuits, the more likely they will contribute to changes in the outcomes experienced by residents in the presently occupied setting.

Personal Resource Transitions

The model differentiates individuals in their presently occupied setting according to how their capacity to function normatively without assistance in the areas of "biological health, sensation and perception, motor behavior, and cognition" (Lawton, 1983, p. 350) has changed since they occupied their previously occupied setting. These personal resource transitions are expected to influence the outcomes older people experience in three linked ways: (1) by making it more or less difficult for them to use, manipulate, modify, or explore the environmental content of their settings and to engage in necessary, rewarding, and satisfying behavior circuits; (2) by influencing how they assess the appropriateness of the changed content and behavior circuit opportunities and constraints found in their new setting; and (3) by influencing how they assess their own well-being.

Typology of Personal Resources

The following personal capability or resource constructs are representative:

Behavioral Competence
- Ability to perform activities of daily living
- Ability to perform instrumental activities of daily living
- Ability to prepare and take prescribed oral medications

Cognitive Competence
- Problem-solving abilities
- Amount of memory loss
- Response to cues
- Way-finding abilities

Prognosis of Physical Health Conditions, Rehabilitation Potential, and Required Medical/Nursing/Prescription Regimens
- Arthritis
- Osteoporosis
- Hip fracture complications
- Vision impairment
- Urinary incontinence
- Cardiovascular disease
- Stroke
- Osteoarthritis
- Diabetes
- Parkinson's disease
- Deafness and hearing loss
- Dyspnea

Temporal Properties of Personal Resources

The change in the personal resources of an older person is specified by three temporal properties:

- Direction of change (e.g., improving, stable, declining).
- Amount or intensity of change (e.g., the amount of improvement or decline).
- Pace of change (e.g., tempo, quickness, suddenness, or speed).

Proposed Model Relationships

Unequivocal propositions are not possible as to how the personal resource transitions of older residents influence changes in their personal state or environmental outcomes. These relationships will foremost depend on what types of changed outcomes are of interest. It can be easily demonstrated, for example, that residents experiencing decrements in their personal resources can at the same time feel more physically secure but less independent than in their previous residence (Parmelee & Lawton, 1990).

The model proposes that the outcomes experienced by residents will depend on whether they believe the changes in their environmental content and behavior circuits are appropriate, given their personal resource shifts. For example, residents who have experienced substantial decrements in their resources, and who now receive more extensive care or monitoring than they had in their previous setting, may welcome these changes, view them as necessary, and feel less anxious and more secure. On the other hand, residents with the same decrements may believe that the setting has not been sufficiently responsive to their increased vulnerability (i.e., has provided inadequate services, staff, or design modifications). This may reflect the management's well-intentioned effort to create a more independent living environment or simply its failure to diagnose or serve their residents' needs correctly. Whatever the reasons, these residents could predictably feel more physically and psychologically insecure. Other residents may believe that the "protective" changes in their new setting are excessive given their personal resource shifts. They may feel that their privacy or independence has been unnecessarily eroded and that too many restrictions are placed on their activities (Krause, 1987). Thus, they view the introduction of "supportive" modifications as a blow to their self-esteem (Moos & Lemke, 1994; Parmelee & Lawton, 1990). Langer (1983), for example, argues that too supportive a setting reinforces a resident's sense of incompetence, leading to feelings of depression.

These alternative response repertoires result in the following sets of equally plausible propositions regarding the relationship between the changing personal resources of residents and their changing personal state and environmental outcomes. It remains for empirical research to confirm or disconfirm the validity of these alternative interpretations, which may well be setting-specific.

Decline in Personal Resources. When changes in the shelter and care environment are viewed as inappropriate (i.e., an insufficient or excessive increase in "supportive" environmental content), the following relationships can be proposed:

- The greater and the faster the decline in the personal resources of residents, the more likely they will experience a decline in their intrapsychic well-being, an increase in their negative physical and psychophysiological symptoms, and a decrease in their sense of control over their life and environment.

- The greater and the faster the decline in the personal resources of residents, the more negative will be their appraised environmental outcome changes.

When changes in the shelter and care environment are viewed as appropriate (i.e., a sufficient increase in "supportive" environmental content), the following relationships can be proposed:

- The greater and the faster the decline in the personal resources of residents, the more likely they will experience an increase (or less of a decrease) in their intrapsychic well-being, a decrease (or less of an increase) in their negative physical and psychophysiological symptoms, and an increase (or less of a decrease) in their sense of control over their life and environment.
- The greater and the faster the decline in the personal resources of residents, the more positive will be their appraised environmental outcome changes.

Increase in Personal Resources. When the personal resources of residents have increased over time, the possible personal state and environmental outcomes are no less equivocal. The following relationships can be proposed when changes in the shelter and care environment are viewed as inappropriate (i.e., an insufficient decrease or an excessive increase in "supportive" environmental content):

- The greater and the faster the increase in the personal resources of residents, the more likely they will experience a decline (or less of an increase) in their intrapsychic well-being, an increase (or less of a decrease) in their negative physical and psychophysiological symptoms, and a decrease (or less of an increase) in their sense of control over their life and environment.
- The greater and the faster the increase in the personal resources of residents, the more negative will be their appraised environmental outcome changes.

When changes in the shelter and care environment are viewed as appropriate (i.e., a sufficient decrease in "supportive" environmental content), the following relationships can be proposed:

- The greater and the faster the increase in the personal resources of residents, the more likely they will experience an increase in their intrapsychic well-being, a decrease in their negative physical and psychophysiological symptoms, and an increase in their sense of control over their life and environment.
- The greater and the faster the increase in the personal resources of residents, the more positive will be their appraised environmental outcome changes.

Stable Personal Resources. When changes in the shelter and care environment are viewed as inappropriate (i.e., an excessive increase or decrease in "supportive" environmental content), the following relationships can be proposed:

- The more likely they will experience a decline in their intrapsychic well-being, an increase in their negative physical and psychophysiological symptoms, and a decrease in their sense of control over their life and environment.
- The more negative will be their appraised environmental outcome changes.

When the changes in the shelter and care environment are viewed as appropriate, the following relationships can be proposed:

- The more likely they will experience an increase in their intrapsychic well-being, a decrease in their negative physical and psychophysiological symptoms, and an increase in their sense of control over their life and environment.
- The more positive will be their appraised environmental outcome changes.

Stable Individual Attributes

Observer-Evaluated Personality Styles

Other personal qualities of the older person are likely to be invariant over time (Kogan, 1990). These more stable, long-held values, preferences, and dispositions are also likely to influence what older persons judge as desirable or undesirable about their new or modified home. Kahana, Liang, and Felton (1980), for example, speak of internalized human needs and expressed preferences as determinants of the congruence of a setting with its occupants, while French, Rodgers, and Cobb (1974) similarly speak of individual demands. In its original formulation, Lawton's ''person'' component (now often identified only as a behavioral competence construct—implying individual capacities and capabilities) encompassed a person's ''personality style.'' This referred to the individual's ''enduring ways of perceiving, cognizing, and responding to the world outside oneself, ways that are relatively independent of specific needs'' (Lawton, 1982, p. 36).

Drawing on the models of Kahana, Liang, and Felton (1980) and Nehrke et al. (1984), our model distinguishes the following alternative personality dimensions by which to distinguish the ''needs'' or ''demands'' of older residents:

- Need for dominance
- Need for autonomy
- Need for affiliation
- Need for control
- Need for immediate rewards or gratification
- Need for predictability, order, or regularity
- Need for privacy
- Disposition toward risk-taking or adventure
- Need for variation or change
- Orientation to future as opposed to past
- Need for active versus sedentary (passive) activities
- Need for solitary versus group activities
- Need for individualized treatment
- Need to interact with old as opposed to young people (Rosow, 1967)

The Congruence of Personality Style with Changes in Environmental Content and Behavior Circuits

Both the person-environment congruence models of Kahana and Kahana (1983) and Nehrke et al. (1984) demonstrate how the personality styles of older individuals can be conceptualized as influences of their personal state and environmental outcomes. They assume that environmental optimality exists when individuals are occupying a setting that is consistent with their stable or enduring demands and needs. This requires the conceptualization of both the personality styles of the person and the attributes of the setting along commensurate dimensions to allow an assessment of the similarity or closeness of the two constructs. An example from the model of Nehrke et al. (1984) is illustrative. One indicator of individual need (personality style) was *"I prefer to live where residents do things alone,"* and the commensurately defined environmental indicator was *"Around here residents do things alone."*

The model here similarly assesses personality style–environment congruence but with two notable differences. First, both a setting's environmental content and a person's behavior circuits must be matched with the older individual's personality style. Second, congruence depends on the equivalence between personality style and the *changes* in the individual's environmental content and behavior circuits. Thus, a comparable behavior circuit attribute would be expressed as: Compared with where I lived before, I am less likely to eat alone. A comparable environmental content attribute would be expressed as: Compared with where I lived before, there are more likely to be older people around me. Similarly, the operationalized "resident-experienced outcome change" would be: Compared to where I lived before, I feel I have less privacy. This results in an interpretation of "incongruence" that differs somewhat from prior models that emphasized how both the oversupply or undersupply of environmental features may be inconsistent with an individual's needs or demands. Rather, the focus of this model is on whether the changes in environmental content attributes or in an individual's behavior circuits have resulted in the qualities of the setting becoming *closer to* or *further away* from an individual's personality style. For example, the increased presence of frail older residents in a new setting would result in it becoming less consistent with an individual exhibiting a need to associate with younger persons. Similarly, having meals more frequently in a centralized dining room would result in a less congruent shelter and care setting for persons exhibiting a need for solitary activities.

Proposed Model Relationships

- Residents will experience more negative changes in their individual state and environmental outcomes when their environmental content attributes are evaluated as changing in a direction that make them less consistent with their personality styles.

- Residents will experience more negative changes in their individual state and environmental outcomes when their behavior circuit attributes are evaluated as changing in a direction that make them less consistent with their personality styles.

Other Stable Individual Attributes

Demographic Attributes

Residents can also be differentiated by the following representative set of individual attributes that over a relatively short observation period are also likely to be unchanging or stable.

- Age
- Sex
- Education
- Race
- Ethnicity
- Religious preference
- Economic status (cash income, asset wealth, in-kind benefits such as subsidized services or products)

Proposed Model Relationships

The rationale for specifying these individual constructs as antecedents is three-fold. First, individuals who have demographic characteristics that are more consistent with their changed social situation are likely to experience more positive outcomes. Second, it can be theorized that certain individual state outcomes (e.g., life satisfaction or depression) and environmental outcome changes are more likely to be experienced by individuals with certain demographic characteristics than others. And third, the possibility exists that older persons with certain demographic characteristics are more likely than others to display environmental content and behavior circuit changes, to experience declining personal resource transitions, or to have distinctive personality styles. Controlling for the demographic diversity of the residents thus avoids spurious conceptual interpretations.

Resident Appraisals of the Overall Change Process

The psychological adjustment problems experienced by older persons as a result of their changing settings have been linked to several factors (Cumming & Cumming, 1963; Golant, 1984a; Lieberman, 1991; Mirotyznik & Ruskin, 1985; Pastalan, 1983; Schulz & Brenner, 1977). Older persons often find themselves occupying an unfamiliar setting where they must learn anew about a place's opportunities and risks and adopt new routines and activities (Golant, 1984a). They have often left a long-occupied and familiar setting, requiring them to loosen or sever strong and valued attachments with possessions, people, and activities (Kalish & Knudtson, 1976). These losses may be especially traumatic when the move was unexpected or the rationale of the move was not well understood (Lieberman & Tobin, 1983). A major environmental change also may temporarily or permanently disrupt the organization of the individual's ego. The individual often enters a new setting as an unknown entity—a stranger with no history. Because the person's "concept of himself no longer receives automatic reinforcement" (Cumming & Cumming, 1963, p. 48), it becomes necessary for new residents to reestablish their personal identities to gain people's recognition and acceptance. In so doing, individuals are forced to reexamine critically their realized goals and accomplishments and the value of their lives. This self-scrutiny may be a painful or unpleasant experience. For all these reasons, a residential change may result in older people feeling that they have lost control over their lives or environment and in their experiencing stress and anxiety (Rodin, 1986).

Other theoretical interpretations of the relocation experience are more positive. Kahana and Kahana (1983, p. 206) argue, for example, that a relocation is a pathway toward "personal control and hope for improving one's future in later life" that "allows older persons to plan for a more satisfying future, improve their living situation, and increase person-environment (P-E) fit." Moves may also be interpreted more positively when they are believed to involve only a short-term stay. Such a "temporary" move might be in response to disabilities or medical episodes that require short-term nursing care and rehabilitation, following which residents are expected to attain their prior level of behavioral functioning and return to their previously occupied setting. A move may also be viewed more positively by residents who consider that their new situation is better than that experienced by most of their age peers (Festinger, 1954).

Proposed Model Relationships

The above arguments suggest that residents will experience more positive changes in their personal state and environmental outcomes in the following instances:

- They have viewed their move or environmental change as a necessary adjustment to their living conditions.
- They have prepared (physically and psychologically) for the changes.
- They have viewed their move or environmental change as consistent with those experienced by the majority of older persons they identify as their age peers.
- They have viewed their move or environmental change as voluntary, a product of their own choices, and under their own control.
- They have viewed their move or environmental change as temporary.
- The changes they have experienced in their new setting are consistent with their anticipations, expectations, or predictions.

Coping Resources of Residents to Deal with Unfavorable Changes in Environmental Content and Behavior Circuits

The extent to which individuals will experience negative outcomes from their setting change will not only reflect the "demand characteristics of a potential stressor'' (Kahana et al., 1995, p. 464) or negative "environmental press" (Lawton, 1982); it will also depend on their ability to cope with the changes appraised as offensive. This implies that a simple causal relationship cannot be proposed between environmental press and an individual's level of behavioral competence (Lawton, 1982). Individuals are not passive human organisms "acted upon by an overwhelming environmental context" (Holahan, 1978, p. 11). Rather, "they utilize a variety of coping strategies, anticipating and evaluating what might happen and what has to be done, planning and preparing, changing the environment, retreating when necessary, postponing action for maximum effect, tolerating frustration and pain, and even deceiving themselves in order to feel better and to maintain hope and a sense of self-worth" (Lazarus & Cohen, 1977, pp. 111–112). Individuals thus engage in a "secondary appraisal" process (Lazarus, 1966) in which they assess what options they have available to eliminate, avoid, weaken, counteract, or ignore worsened environmental conditions.

Two categories of coping strategies can be distinguished (Lazarus, 1966). By *direct actions* individuals attack or avoid the source of the more negative outcomes. They may, for example, manipulate their environmental content to mitigate the impact of negative outcomes, such as by their establishing a "control center" to boost their sense of autonomy and better access information (Lawton, 1985a), or they may complain vigorously to staff members about a problem. Residents may also selectively attend less to offending aspects of setting, such as by avoiding contact with certain other residents. Alternatively, they may change or modify their behavior circuits, such as by reducing their participation in certain of a setting's activities or by establishing territorial barriers or buffers to reduce contact with offending content (Baron & Rodin, 1978). Second, through *defensive reappraisals*, residents can employ cognitive strategies whereby they deceive themselves about the seriousness of unfavorable aspects of their setting. This may involve such cognitive strategies as resignation, denial, and withdrawal.

The initiation of these coping strategies will depend in part on the extent that residents can draw on two types of coping resources: ego resources and situational resources (Lazarus, 1966).

Ego Resources

Individuals will differ as to how strongly they hold beliefs (whether realistic or not) regarding their capacity to weaken or eliminate more negatively appraised outcomes. A weak belief strength (e.g., I am broken; I cannot resist change; I'm too weak to deal with it) has been associated with persons having lower self-esteem and stronger feelings of inadequacy.

Situational Resources

The types, quantity, and reliability of the social or organizational resources that residents can draw on to change their environment or avoid its appraised noxious qualities will differ. Such tangible assistance, emotional help, and informational support (Krause, 1987) may be available from the following sources:

- Counseling and other sources of information to increase individual resources or coping skills
- Significant others (family, friends) to confide in or rely on
- Staff members willing to listen to complaints
- Management alert to resident problems
- Management willing to change policies in response to resident dissatisfaction
- Flexible or mutable rules and regulations

Proposed Model Relationships

- The greater and more reliable the coping resources available to residents, the more likely their coping strategies will involve direct actions and the less likely they will experience personal state and environmental outcomes appraised as more negative than in their previously occupied setting.
- The fewer and less reliable the coping resources available to residents, the more likely their coping strategies will involve defensive reappraisals and the more likely they will experience declines in their personal state and environmental outcomes.

CONCLUSION

The proposed model is intended to have both heuristic and practical applications. On the one hand, it demonstrates the pitfalls inherent in point-in-time or cross-sectional models and the complexities of theoretically explaining personal state and environmental outcome changes. It thus offers a set of conceptual guidelines by which to assess the strengths and weaknesses of investigations designed to measure the effects of environmental change. On the other hand, the model itself is designed to be operationalized, recognizing that the researcher seeking to measure its constructs and establish causal relationships for its antecedents faces some formidable challenges.

Even as the model is already operationally demanding, a theoretical justification can be made for three additional refinements that add further complexities. First, the personal state and environmental outcomes experienced by older persons in their *previously occupied* settings are themselves likely to influence how subsequent residential changes are interpreted (Golant, 1984b, pp. 125–127). In the words of Fromm (1947, p. 182), ''[T]he functioning of our mental and emotional capacities is influenced by our happiness or unhappiness.'' That is, the outcomes experienced by older persons in their new setting are unlikely to be independent of the outcomes they have experienced in their past. This implies, for example, that individuals who enter a residential situation with low morale or with a history of maladaptive environmental experiences will be more likely to display negative affective and evaluative responses to objects and events in their new setting. To assess these effects empirically, the researcher must control statistically for the (baseline) individual state and environmental outcomes that characterize older persons prior to their residential changes.

Figure 2.2
Influence of Environmental Outcome Changes on the Personal State Outcome Changes of Older Persons in New Shelter and Care Setting

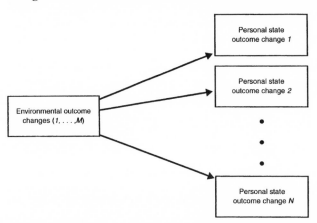

A second set of refinements is demanded by the strong likelihood of inter-action effects among the proposed determinants of outcome change. How in-dividuals appraise the changes in their environmental content or behavior circuits, for example, will be mediated by their personal resource transitions, their appraisal of overall change, and their coping resources. While the testing for interaction effects can be readily handled empirically, the interaction effects that are theoretically possible in this proposed model are both many and com-plex, and space constraints preclude their full specification and rationale.

A third model refinement is the need to specify a causal relationship between an individual's personal state and environmental outcomes. It is theoretically likely that the changed personal state outcomes of older residents will be influ-enced by their environmental outcome changes. Changes in the morale levels of older persons, for example, are likely to be a function of appraised changes in their residential satisfaction. An obvious extension to this model is to propose a causal ordering of *N* personal outcome state changes and *M* environmental outcome changes, as illustrated in Figure 2.2. This would allow for two types of analytical insights: first, an assessment of the extent that the variability of any given personal state outcome change can be explained by different envi-ronmental outcome changes; and second, an assessment of the extent that the variability of different personal state changes can be explained by the variable importance of any given environmental change.

REFERENCES

Altman, I., & Rogoff, B. (1987). World views in psychology: Trait, interactional, organ-ismic, and transactional perspectives. In D. Stokols & I. Altman (Eds.), *Handbook of environmental psychology* (Vol. 1, pp. 7–40). New York: John Wiley.

Barker, R. (1968). *Ecological psychology.* Stanford, CA: Stanford University Press.

Baron, R. M., & Rodin, J. (1978). Personal control as a mediator of crowding. In A. Baum, J. E. Singer, & S. Valins (Eds.), *Advances in environmental psychology: The urban environment* (Vol. 1, pp. 145–190). Hillsdale, NJ: Lawrence Erlbaum.

Birren, J. E., Lubben, J. E., Rowe, J. C., & Deutchman, D. E. (Eds.). (1991). *The concept and measurement of quality of life in the frail elderly.* New York: Academic Press.

Carp, F. M. (1987). Environment and aging. In D. Stokols & I. Altman (Eds.), *Handbook of environmental psychology* (Vol. 1, pp. 329–360). New York: John Wiley.

Csikszentmihalyi, M., & Rochberg-Halton, E. (1981). *The meaning of things: Domestic symbols and the self.* Cambridge, MA: Cambridge University Press.

Cumming, J., & Cumming, E. (1963). *Ego and milieu.* New York: Atherton Press.

Festinger, L. (1954). A theory of social comparison processes. *Human Relations, 7,* 117–140.

French, J. R. P., Rodgers, W., & Cobb, S. (1974). Adjustment as person-environment fit. In G. V. Coelho, D. A. Hamburg, & J. E. Adams (Eds.), *Coping and adaptation* (pp. 316–333). New York: Basic Books.

Fromm, E. (1947). *Man for himself: An inquiry into the psychology of ethics.* New York: Rinehart.

Golant, S. M. (1982). Individual differences underlying the dwelling satisfaction of the elderly. *Journal of Social Issues, 39,* 11–133.

Golant, S. M. (1984a). The effects of residential and activity behaviors on old people's environmental experiences. In I. Altman, J. Wohlwill, & M. P. Lawton (Eds.), *Human behavior and the environment* (pp. 239–279). New York: Plenum Press.

Golant, S. M. (1984b). *A place to grow old: The meaning of environment in old age.* New York: Columbia University Press.

Golant, S. M. (1986). Subjective housing assessments by the elderly: A critical information source for planning and program evaluation. *Gerontologist, 26,* 122–127.

Golant, S. M. (1991). Matching congregate housing settings with a diverse elderly population: Research and theoretical considerations. In L. W. Kaye & A. Monk (Eds.), *Congregate housing for the elderly: Theoretical, policy, and programmatic perspectives* (pp. 21–38). New York: Haworth Press.

Holahan, C. J. (1978). *Environment and behavior: A dynamic perspective.* New York: Plenum.

Howell, S. (1983). The meaning of place in old age. In G. D. Rowles & R. J. Ohta (Eds.), *Aging and milieu* (pp. 97–107). New York: Academic Press.

Kahana, E. (1982). A congruence model of person-environment interaction. In M. P. Lawton, P. G. Windley, & T. O. Byerts (Eds.), *Aging and the environment: Theoretical approaches* (pp. 97–121). New York: Springer.

Kahana, E., & Kahana, B. (1983). Environmental continuity, futurity, and adaptation of the aged. In G. D. Rowles & R. J. Ohta (Eds.), *Aging and milieu* (pp. 205–228). New York: Academic Press.

Kahana, E., Liang, J., & Felton, B. J. (1980). Alternative models of person-environment fit: Prediction of morale in three homes for the aged. *Journal of Gerontology, 35,* 584–595.

Kahana, E., Redmond, C., Hill, G. J., Kercher, K., Kahana, B., Johnson, J. R., & Young, R. F. (1995). The effects of stress, vulnerability, and appraisals on the psychological well-being of the elderly. *Research on Aging, 17,* 459–489.

Kalish, R. A., & Knudtson, F. W. (1976). Attachment versus disengagement: A life-span conceptualization. *Human Development, 19,* 171–181.

Kasl, S. V., & Rosenfield, S. (1980). The residential environment and its impact on the mental health of the aged. In J. E. Birren & R. B. Sloane (Eds.), *Handbook of mental health and aging* (pp. 468–498). New York: Prentice-Hall.

Kogan, N. (1990). Personality and aging. In J. E. Birren & K. W. Schaie (Eds.), *Handbook of the psychology of aging* (3rd ed., pp. 330–346). New York: Academic Press.

Krause, N. (1987). Understanding the stress process: Linking social support with locus of control beliefs. *Journal of Gerontology, 42,* 589–593.

Langer, E. J. (1983). *The psychology of control.* Beverly Hills, CA: Sage Publications.

Lawton, M. P. (1977). The impact of the environment on aging and behavior. In J. E. Birren & K. W. Schaie (Eds.), *Handbook of the psychology of aging* (pp. 276–301). New York: Van Nostrand Reinhold.

Lawton, M. P. (1982). Competence, environmental press, and the adaptation of older people. In M. P. Lawton, P. G. Windley, & T. O. Byerts (Eds.), *Aging and the environment: Theoretical approaches* (pp. 33–59). New York: Springer.

Lawton, M. P. (1983). Environment and other determinants of well-being in older people. *Gerontologist, 23,* 349–357.

Lawton, M. P. (1985a). The elderly in context: Perspectives from environmental psychology and gerontology. *Environment and Behavior, 17,* 501–519.

Lawton, M. P. (1985b). Housing and living environments of older people. In R. Binstock & E. Shanas (Eds.), *Handbook of aging and the social sciences* (2nd ed., pp. 450–478). New York: Van Nostrand Reinhold.

Lawton, M. P. (1989). Environmental proactivity and affect in older people. In S. Spacapan & S. Oskamp (Eds.), *The social psychology of aging* (pp. 135–163). Newbury Park, CA: Sage.

Lawton, M. P., Brody, E. M., & Saperstein, A. R. (1989). A controlled study of respite service for caregivers of Alzheimer's patients. *Gerontologist, 29,* 8–16.

Lazarus, R. S. (1966). *Psychological stress and the coping process.* New York: McGraw-Hill.

Lazarus, R. S., & Cohen, J. B. (1977). Environmental stress. In I. Altman & J. Wohlwill (Eds.), *Human behavior and environment* (Vol. 2, pp. 89–127). New York: Plenum Press.

Lieberman, M. A. (1965). Psychological correlates of impending death: Some preliminary observations. *Journal of Gerontology, 20,* 181–190.

Lieberman, M. A. (1991). Relocation of the frail elderly. In J. E. Birren, J. E. Lubben, J. C. Rowe, & D. E. Deutchman (Eds.), *The concept and measurement of quality of life in the frail elderly* (pp. 120–141). New York: Academic Press.

Lieberman, M. A., & Tobin, S. S. (1983). *The experience of old age: Stress, coping and survival.* New York: Basic Books.

Magnusson, D. (1981). Wanted: A psychology of situations. In D. Magnusson (Ed.), *Toward a psychology of situations: An interactional perspective* (pp. 3–32). Hillsdale, NJ: Lawrence Erlbaum Associates.

Mirotyznik, J., & Ruskin, A. P. (1985). Inter-institutional relocation and its effects on health. *Gerontologist, 25,* 265–270.

Moos, R. H., & Lemke, S. (1994). *Group residences for older adults: Physical features, policies, and social climate.* New York: Oxford University Press.

Nehrke, M. F., Morganti, J. B., Cohen, S. H., Hulicka, I. M., Whitbourne, S. K., Turner, R. R., & Cataldo, J. F. (1984). Differences in person-environment congruence between microenvironments. *Canadian Journal on Aging, 3,* 117–132.

Newman, S. J., & Envall, K. (1995). *The effects of supports on sustaining older disabled persons in the community.* Washington, DC: Public Policy Institute, American Association of Retired Persons.

Nydegger, C. N. (Ed.). (1977). *Measuring morale: A guide to effective assessment.* Special Publication No. 3. Washington, DC: Gerontological Society.

O'Bryant, S. L., & Wolf, S. M. (1983). Explanations of housing satisfaction of older homeowners and renters. *Research on Aging, 5,* 217–233.

Parmelee, P. A., & Lawton, M. P. (1990). The design of special environments for the aged. In J. E. Birren & K. W. Schaie (Eds.), *Handbook of the psychology of aging* (3rd ed., pp. 465–488). New York: Academic Press.

Pastalan, L. A. (1983). Environmental displacement: A literature reflecting old-person-environment transactions. In G. D. Rowles & R. J. Ohta (Eds.), *Aging and milieu* (pp. 189–203). New York: Academic Press.

Perin, C. (1970). *With man in mind: An interdisciplinary prospectus for environmental design.* Cambridge, MA: MIT Press.

Pynoos, J., & Regnier, V. (1991). Improving residential environments for frail elderly: Bridging the gap between theory and application. In J. E. Birren, J. E. Lubben, J. C. Rowe, & D. E. Deutchman (Eds.), *The concept and measurement of quality of life in the frail elderly* (pp. 91–119). New York: Academic Press.

Rodin, J. (1986). Aging and health: Effects of sense of control. *Science, 223,* 1271–1276.

Rosow, I. (1967). *Social integration of the aged.* New York: Free Press.

Rowles, G. D. (1983). Place and personal identity in old age: Observations from Appalachia. *Journal of Environmental Psychology, 3,* 299–313.

Scheidt, R. J., & Windley, P. G. (1985). The ecology of aging. In J. E. Birren & K. W. Schaie (Eds.), *Handbook of the psychology of aging* (2nd ed., pp. 245–258). New York: Van Nostrand Reinhold.

Schooler, K. K. (1976). Environmental change and the elderly. In I. Altman & J. F. Wohlwill (Eds.), *Human behavior and environment* (Vol. 1, pp. 265–298). New York: Plenum Press.

Schulz, R., & Brenner, G. (1977). Relocation of the aged: A review and theoretical analysis. *Journal of Gerontology, 32,* 323–333.

Sherif, M. (1967). *Social interaction: Process and products.* Chicago: Aldine.

Stokols, D. (1981). Group x place transactions: Some neglected issues in psychological research on settings. In D. Magnusson (Ed.), *Toward a psychology of situations: An interactional perspective* (pp. 393–415). Hillsdale, NJ: Lawrence Erlbaum Associates.

Stokols, D. (1987). Conceptual strategies of environmental psychology. In D. Stokols & I. Altman (Eds.), *Handbook of environmental psychology* (Vol. 1, pp. 41–70). New York: John Wiley.

Weissert, W. G., Cready, C. M., & Pawelak, J. E. (1988). The past and future of home- and community-based long-term care. *Milbank Quarterly, 66,* 309–388.

3

Gender and Housing for the Elderly: Sorting Through the Accumulations of a Lifetime

SUSAN SAEGERT AND DOLORES E. McCARTHY

Women in later life provide a particularly vivid illustration of the paradox of feminist thought in at once identifying the oppression of women and challenging social conceptions of the category "woman" (Benhabib, Butler, Cornell, & Fraser, 1995; Young, 1990). Older women are especially likely to suffer from a paucity of material and social resources that are the cumulative product of social inequality, as illustrated in many statistical portraits of older women (Hardy & Hazelrigg, 1995). Yet more qualitative studies of older women often reveal the ingenuity and strength with which they remake themselves and their circumstances in unpredictable ways (Laferriere & Hamel-Bissell, 1994; Saegert, 1989). In our everyday lives, most of us experience both aspects as our mothers, grandmothers, aunts, spouses, or ourselves age. Through our own experiences, we know that many of our ideas about how to live come from the positive and negative lessons we learn from the elderly—and if we are women, especially from older women. This chapter applies a feminist perspective to the issue of gender, housing, and the elderly. The viewpoint of the authors is also situated in the framework of environmental psychology, where issues are seen as multidetermined and contextualized. Environmental psychological theory supports the consideration of gender, age, and housing as interactions of political, social, economic, psychological, geographic, and cultural factors; further, it critiques some assumptions made by rigidly defining "age" and "gender" in a linear or monolithic theoretical position.

Women's homes and neighborhoods are deeply woven into the nature and outcome of what Erikson has categorized as the developmental challenge of later life—despair versus integrity. Yet beyond a certain level of habitability, the material quality of the home may not be the most significant issue. Constraint on housing choice, the ways that a particular home sets limits on other choices, and how the home gets made within these limits may be more important. The saga of the first author's mother-in-law from retirement until her present age of 81 has been a source of lessons about successful development in later life and the role homes play in this development:[1]

> When I first met Cathy, she had been widowed for four years and had just retired at 61, taking this option when the company she had worked for for many years went bankrupt. Having married young, she and her husband had moved to California during the depression, leaving behind East Coast families to make a fresh start for themselves. She had worked all her adult life while raising two children with her husband. Like most women of her era (and ours), her earnings were modest and so was her pension. Her husband, who worked at a better-paying job as a steelworker but who was forced into early retirement during a period of economic decline for the industry, left her with a small sum of money and a comfortable but rented apartment in a large, safe, and attractive housing complex convenient to transportation, shopping, and entertainment in Los Angeles.
>
> Despite the fact that she worked, her marriage had been fairly traditional. In all her years in California, she did not learn to drive. In the drama of family life, the males had had the starring roles and the women the supporting parts. The children bore the expectations for improving the lot of the family in traditional ways, the boy through education and achievement in work, the girl through a good marriage. Cathy's dual contribution as breadwinner and wife were respected by her family, as was the fine figure she cut in her trademark spike heels. How she would live after retirement, for the first time alone and without daily demands on her time, was an open question.

At this point in her life, Cathy faced the economic and social transition from being part of a couple to being a woman alone, which is the statistical norm for older women and the beginning of many gender differences in the experience of aging. The constantly changing contingencies that she then experienced also characterize the unpredictability of the later years for many women as they move back into and sometimes in and out of old family roles.

> Life quickly supplied an answer when her son-in-law suffered an untimely death, leaving her daughter with three very young children in the San Fernando Valley, an hour's drive away. The daughter had not worked nor completed college after an early marriage. The brother from New York (my husband) stepped in to try to help get her financial affairs in shape. Yet it soon became apparent that eventually she had to take over the daily running of her husband's business. After a period of commuting, Cathy moved into the daughter's home to help raise the children.
>
> As the children grew into teenagers, Los Angeles was changing. The mostly working-class customers of the family furniture store lost buying power. Crime and declining quality in the public schools were worrisome. At the same time, the house was seeming very small with two growing girls, one boy, and the two adult women. Yet house prices had skyrocketed.
>
> Looking for a positive solution to a rather negative situation, Cathy and her

daughter went scouting for a new home in a new community. They found a large five-bedroom home overlooking Monterey Bay at a price far below the selling price of their San Fernando Valley home (with a pool). Exercising the financial acumen she developed while running the business, and with the help of a trusted accountant, the daughter sold the business at a good price, despite the somewhat deteriorating neighborhood in which it was located. The family moved to Monterey. By pooling the financial resources of mother and daughter, the daughter could afford to stay home with the children and enroll them in private schools. An inheritance from the paternal grandmother could be put away for their college educations.

Intergenerational households may offer financial advantages and social support, but the different developmental trajectories of various household members are often hard to balance and weigh heavily on the women who try to juggle them.

For several years, life seemed nearly idyllic. However, the pressures of necessity that had brought this particular household together were no longer there. Family dynamics were complicated by the usual challenges teenagers bring to the adults who raise them and most likely by the double sets of mother-daughter struggles over independence.

In retrospect, Cathy remembers feeling overburdened, stressed, and anxious. She was also discontented and unchallenged by the way she was living. She felt that moving to a new place had left her without points of reference for organizing a meaningful future.

The tensions in the household became more apparent when Cathy was hospitalized briefly for an unspecific illness. Cathy's daughter was very supportive of her during this period, helping her identify various treatments for the anxiety-related aspects of her condition. After some experiences with tranquilizers and group therapy sessions with mostly much younger people, she settled on biofeedback, which proved quite successful. During this period she and the family decided to look for supported housing for the elderly. She found and moved into a HUD [Housing and Urban Development]-sponsored senior citizen building that offered meals, some activities and outings, some health monitoring, and beautifully formally landscaped grounds. For a while she also had a home attendant who came in to keep her company and do chores. For some time she continued to struggle with depression, although she made efforts to conceal it from the family, especially those of us back East.

The housing Cathy moved to provides a typical example of good, enriched subsidized housing for the elderly, and her experience of it also illustrates some of its limitations.

Gradually she began to feel, as she explains it, "the beauty and tranquility of being on my own once again." She began volunteer work in the development's service offices and started to widen her circle of friends. HUD sold the building to a private sponsor, and rents rose to $1,000 a month. As Cathy became more comfortable with her life, the support services seemed unnecessary. And while she enjoyed the friends she made in the building, the concentration of only elderly people seemed a bit confining and somewhat depressing, particularly when friends began to decline in health.

Her next experiences need to be understood against the context of the housing and employment markets in Monterey. The area has little industry or private sector employment opportunities outside of tourism but has been the site of a large military base and training institute. As a result, it has many small apartment complexes catering to transient military personnel and students. However, rents are not cheap. (The rental market today has become less predictable because of a military base closing there, coupled with increased popularity as a resort and retirement area and the opening of a new university.)

Soon she moved into a beautifully sited, but somewhat remote, larger apartment with a view of the bay and swimming pool, which she didn't use. At this point, my husband, I, and our baby daughter began visiting for a month in the summer. Usually, we stayed in her apartment while she stayed with her daughter.

Then in her early seventies, Cathy began to volunteer at the local hospital and continued an active social life. With friends she would take excursions to San Francisco, go shopping, to the library, and to restaurants. The big problem was that she lived far away from almost everyplace she wanted to go. She also worried about the high cost of her rent. She addressed the first problem by writing letters to the local newspaper and becoming active in local politics around the issue of improving mass transit.

The issue of finances was not so easily addressed. Her pension value declined with inflation, and she attempted to protect the principal of the money her husband left her. She became quite knowledgeable about global markets and different investment choices. Her daughter began to find that her nest egg was dwindling and would soon be inadequate. Once again, housing played a role in the solution. As children left home, the daughter began taking in boarders from a local postgraduate school. Cathy continued to make some financial contribution to cover property taxes. Once again, she began to look for somewhere else to live.

She found a larger but less expensive apartment near the ocean walk between Monterey and Pacific Grove. It, too, had a view of the bay and was within walking distance from stores, church, and an entertainment/tourist/aquarium complex and right on the major bus line. She took five-mile walks along the ocean and walked regularly to shopping and church. She started container gardening on her two balconies. Her choices for using her time greatly expanded as she made new friends and kept up with old ones.

While her grandchildren and daughter had always stayed in close touch with her, the new location was more convenient for dropping by whenever someone had time. My own family continue to visit her for a month in the summer, enjoying the new location even more than the woodsy beauty, but isolation, of the old one. As our daughter got out of infancy and after Cathy had a health scare that reminded us all of how much we enjoyed being together, she began to remain in the apartment when we visited, sleeping in the living room with our daughter. These times have been extremely special to each of us. For me, the fact that we four could get along for such long stretches of time and actually increase our appreciation of each other has been remarkable. We have had time for talks, for sharing shopping at the green market, cooking, barbecuing, and playing games after dinner, as well as for excursions to the new discoveries she makes each year.

The positive opportunities the loose housing market offered Cathy arose in part from the limited employment options in the area that had a more adverse effect on the younger generations of her family. Gender roles had much to do with how these overall economic constraints were handled by various family members.

> My sister-in-law has followed in her mother's footsteps as children have periodically moved back in between times in college or when they were strapped financially. One granddaughter and the grandson married, and now Cathy has great-grandchildren. The grandson lives in the area, and his wife and children drop by frequently to let Cathy get to know her great-granddaughter, to take her to church, or to do errands.
>
> The effects of economic restructuring on both men and women and the economics of female-headed households continue to challenge the different family members. The daughter works long hours as a day-care teacher and holds two jobs. The grandson works two jobs. His family has moved back in with his mother. The unmarried daughter's college work has been disrupted by shrinkage of the University of California (UC) system that discontinued courses she needed for her major. She also moved back home, working at the day-care center with her mother and trying to forge a new educational path at the local UC campus.
>
> Cathy seems to be able to maintain her financial independence, but it must take a great deal of ingenuity. At 82, she still dresses well and just gave away *some* of her spiked heels this year. Over the years she has given most of the fine china and crystal, pots and pans, and other household possessions of her married life to her daughter. Her own apartment is tastefully but sparely furnished, reminding me of the apartment of a young single working woman. Despite occasional thoughts of moving due to declining maintenance and a fire downstairs from her apartment, signs of improving conditions and the many benefits of her location have kept her there. She credits the sea view, wonderful climate, and the aesthetically appealing, unthreatening small-town environment with prolonging and improving her life. The high-quality public amenities and medical care have been important. For example, after sustaining a back injury, she was able to get low-cost physical therapy at a public sports facility. Her grown grandchildren call up and drop by to seek advice about jobs and life in general. Our daughter considers being with her one of the treats in life and wrote an essay about the most perfect place in the world to live, in grandma's apartment.

FEMINIST THEORIES AND ELDERLY HOUSING

Cathy's story illustrates several feminist themes concerning housing for the elderly: one that highlights the political, social, and economic context in which gender and age are intertwined with the economics of housing; a second that emphasizes the embeddedness of both male and female lives in a web of relationships involving both power differentials and mutual assistance; a third that stresses the complexity and diversity of women's experiences and conditions; and a fourth that emphasizes the deconstruction and reconstruction of what it means to be a particular woman. Her story also shows that these different aspects converge in the actual living of life. Feminist theory or, more correctly, feminist theories are understood in this chapter as a kind of critical social theory that examines the way in which the framing of social facts hides their limitations and participates in the perpetuation of socially structured inequalities (c.f. Fraser, 1989; Rose, 1993). Although feminist theory does not speak with one voice (Benhabib et al., 1995), the root critique of feminism centers on the aspect of social inequality that is structured by the idea of men as the privileged center of knowledge and rights and women as dependent on or defined by men. Thus, feminist theory leads us to ask: How has aging been socially constructed so that housing for the elderly is a topic? How does this construction mask the gendered nature of aging? Likewise, we may ask, How does a focus on gender help or hinder our understanding the aging nature of gender? A critical approach to social scientific research on housing and aging also directs our attention to other forms of structured social inequality (Young, 1990), especially race and economic stratification.

Using this framework of questioning, the following topics require further examination: (1) the gendered nature of poverty, ill health, longevity, and living conditions, looked at in the context of race and economic stratification; (2) the assumptions involved in a discourse about the housing needs of the elderly and how gender is related to this discourse; (3) how assumptions about gender affect conceptions of aging and the life course, especially as they relate to appropriate housing; and (4) the kind of housing for the elderly that would emerge from a social and political discourse unburdened by gender inequality.

The Disadvantages of Being an Older Woman: Implications for Housing

To some extent, the disadvantages of being both aged and female tend to converge since women greatly outnumber men in the oldest age groups. Poverty, poor health, living alone, and widowhood all endanger the quality of life for older people. The prevalence of these conditions tends to increase with very advanced age and especially among women (Barer, 1994; Hardy & Hazelrigg, 1993). Even studies that use gender as a predictive variable often underestimate the cumulative risk women experience because of their likelihood of also experiencing these other conditions. While poverty among the elderly in the United States has been eclipsed by the rise in poverty among households with children, it has been increasingly feminized at all ages (Dressel, 1991; Goldberg & Kremen, 1990; Pearce, 1979). It can be argued that females were historically more likely to be affected by poverty than males but that in previous eras this was hidden in household statistics (Abramovitz, 1988); however, in the last several decades, the "femininity of poverty" has become statistically apparent. Hardy and Hazelrigg (1993) used data from the U.S. Census data, the Luxembourg Income Study of seven countries, and their own survey of 2,103 Florida residents over age 55 to document the greater incidence of poverty among older women than among their male age cohort. Among the elderly, the feminization of poverty was largely confined to unmarried women living alone. One fifth of unmarried women living alone had incomes of under $5,000—twice as many as unmarried men living alone and unmarried women living with others, and four to five times as many as married women and men. Regression analyses indicating the significant independent contributions made by race, gender, age, education, marital status, employment, and accumulated capital confirm the overdetermination of poverty by the factors that stratify American society. The data suggest that the greater lifetime wages and asset accumulation of men as compared to women, whites as compared to African Americans and Hispanics, and those who are more educated explain much of the variance of who ends up in poverty. With advancing age, declining probability of employment and depletion of assets occur. The higher survival rates for women in later years further increases the likelihood of poverty. Social Security income in this study was inadequate. For unmarried women living alone, both income from employment and from investments was required to improve chances of avoiding severe poverty.

The feminization of poverty among the elderly puts women at greater risk for living in substandard housing and for problems with affordability. Even among homeowners, women and especially African-American women pay substantially more in housing costs than men (Leavitt, 1995). Elderly and single-person households make up over a sixth of all households who are caught between paying their housing costs and even minimally meeting other needs (Stone, 1993). These elderly are mostly older women, living alone, and subsisting on Social Security or supplemental security income (SSI).

Stone also notes a mismatch between the availability of housing subsidies for the elderly and need. For the lowest income elderly, who are mostly women, the subsidized housing costs are still too high to permit them to cover other needs. However, income ceilings of $17,000 for singles and $19,000 for couples mean that some subsidized elderly would not be shelter poor even without subsidies. Subsidized housing for the elderly may not reach those most in need for other reasons as well. Frequently, communities will dedicate public housing to the elderly as a means of targeting it to a white population (Citizens' Commission on Civil Rights, 1986; Kravitz & Collings, 1986). Seventy percent of the mostly female-headed elderly households in public housing are white (Bratt, 1986).

In the United States and most other developed nations, women stand a much greater chance of being without a spouse and are more likely to live alone

(Altergott, 1988). Within the United States, studies find that African-American and Hispanic elderly women and men are more likely to live with others (Leavitt & Welch, 1989). African-American women are more likely to be unmarried and to head their own households, but their household composition is often fluid (Hatch, 1991). The presence of grandchildren and extended kin, either full- or part-time, in the households of elderly minority women makes it difficult for them to take advantage of housing designed especially for the elderly (Seamon, 1992).

While living with others may often be an economic survival strategy, it can have other benefits. Living alone can be a risk factor for depression and ill health (Dean, Kology, Wood, & Matt, 1992; Fuhrer, Antonucci, & Dartriques, 1992; Seamon, Berkman, Blazer, & Rowe, 1994). Impaired older women who live alone were less likely to use services (Webber, Arnsberger, Fox, & Burnette, 1994) and more likely to wind up in a group home or an institution (Foley, Ostfeld, Branch, & Wallace, 1992; Woroby & Angel, 1990). Gender itself strongly relates to health outcomes (Barer, 1994; Horton, 1995). Men have shorter but less impaired lives (Horton, 1995). Older African-American women are more likely to be health pessimistic than African-American men and than white men and women; this pessimism is associated with engaging in fewer health-promoting activities (Ferraro, 1993; Penning & Strain, 1994).

Time-use studies from various countries indicate that men in most cultures remain more physically active into later life (Altergott, 1988). The health problems that plague older women (arthritis/rheumatism, depression, hypertension, high cholesterol levels, obesity, osteoporosis) could be particularly susceptible to improvement through exercise (Horton, 1995; O'Brien & Vertinsky, 1991; Simonsick, 1991). Since both the habits of elderly women (Altergott, 1988) and continuing responsibilities for housekeeping and caring for others result in women being less active than men (Altergott, 1988; Danigelis & McIntosh, 1993), providing attractive, accessible opportunities for physical exercise could be one of the ways in which housing for the elderly would especially benefit women (Regnier & Pynoos, 1992).

Living alone or in enriched housing for the elderly may be more attractive to women because it affords them an autonomy they may have lacked for much of their lives (McCartney, 1988). Many studies show that over their lifetimes elderly women receive and give more assistance than men (Chappell, Segall, & Lewis, 1990; Gottlieb, 1989; Guberman, Maheau, & Mille, 1992; Kaye & Monk, 1991; Moen, Robison, & Fields, 1994; Penning & Strain, 1994). Their caregiving activities are deeply intertwined with the internalization of social norms and with assumptions made in public policy that they will provide this care. The imbalance between their caregiving activities and those of men, and the difficulties inherent in the role, make women especially sensitive to the imbalance in help-giving relationships and especially limits the emotional benefits of assistance from children (Henwood, 1993). The positive effects of enriched age-segregated housing, which is mostly occupied by women, appear to stem more from the programmed opportunities and safe, supportive environment for engaging in activities and social contact with others than from age concentration itself (Kaye & Monk, 1991; Ward, LaGory, & Sherman, 1988). Ward and his colleagues document that women living in communities are more likely to have varied social networks, to depend less on spouses for support, to know more about community services, and to be more central in the networks of their elderly neighbors. However, they also are more often poor and experience impediments to mobility. In the oldest age groups, women were more likely to think of themselves as old, an identity also associated with poorer health. Despite the strengths women showed socially, community environments studied did not provide either the support needed to overcome resource limitations or access to opportunities to use their abilities in a satisfying way.

The problems experienced more by elderly women than elderly men stem largely from their accumulated economic disadvantages, from their longevity, and from their pervasive roles as caretakers and unpaid household workers. The caretaking and domestic activities of older women lead them to spend more hours even into very old age in ''productive activity,''—but not of a sort that either strongly benefits them or improves the physical and psychological quality of their lives (Danigelis & McIntosh, 1993). The social skills and connections women hone in these caring relationships appear often to be latent resources needing an appropriate context for realization.

While enriched housing schemes for the elderly are one potential way to provide this context, the availability of this option is constrained by the social priorities that limit women's claims on resources and the web of relationships in which women are embedded. The extent to which elderly women remain caretakers also reminds us that housing schemes that segregate the elderly from others in their community need to take into account the way the housing affects these relationships. The social context that tends to sort women into lower-paying jobs and to assign them to unpaid caretaking roles and low-paid caretaking occupations affects the political viability of projects for the elderly.

Gender and the Social Context of Aging and Housing

Housing for the elderly is provided primarily through the market, secondarily through government subsidies, and in a very small part through private charitable institutions (Howe, Clark, & Butler, 1993). Most housing that has been designed specifically for the elderly has been developed with the use of substantial governmental subsidies. Similarly, programs to allow the elderly to remain in their homes as they age, such as homemaker services and home health care, have also depended on governmental support. The current political climate calls into question the future of such support. Even regulatory statutes like the Disabilities Act of 1990, which makes housing more supportive for impaired elderly, may not have continuing political support.

At this time, the claims the elderly have felt they could securely make on the government in the United States have been thrown into doubt. The market, rather than the government, is being looked to increasingly to provide for the needs of all citizens, even those too old to be employed. However, threats to the Social Security system and Medicare arouse particular anxiety for the elderly. Thus far, the extensive popular support for such programs has protected them to a large degree. However, the fate of housing programs for the elderly is more in question.

The popularity of Social Security and Medicare contrasts markedly with the absence of public support for Aid to Families with Dependent Children (AFDC), which goes mostly to female-headed families. In addition, cuts to programs that disproportionately benefit women may add to the cumulative disadvantage they face in later life in many ways. Fraser (1989) compares the underlying assumptions of Social Security and AFDC programs to explore what she calls the gendered subtext of the politics of fiscal austerity. Fraser states:

> In each of the major ''means-tested'' programs in the U.S., women and the children for whom they are responsible now comprise the overwhelming majority of clients. For example, more than 81 percent of households receiving . . . (AFDC) are headed by women, more than 60 percent of families receiving food stamps or Medicaid are headed by women, and 70 percent of all households in publicly owned or subsidized housing are headed by women. High as they are, these figures actually underestimate the representation of women. . . .
>
> Women also predominate in the major U.S. ''age-tested'' program. For example, 61.6 percent of all adult beneficiaries of Social Security are women, and 64% of those covered by Medicare are women. In sum, because women as a group are significantly poorer than men—indeed, women now compose nearly two-thirds of all U.S. adults below the official poverty line—and because women tend to live longer than men, women depend more on the social-welfare system as clients and beneficiaries. (pp. 147–148)

She goes on to summarize the variety of studies that show that women do more of the work of administering and providing the social services being threatened by budget cuts and few of the jobs promoted by shifting resources to the military budget (Ehrenreich & Piven, 1984). Women are also affected by cutbacks in these services because they provide almost all of the unpaid caring in households, extended families, and communities. Thus, the decline of government services has a triple impact on women, reducing direct support and services and replacing paid caring jobs with greater demands for unpaid care.

The gendered differences among welfare programs noted by Fraser come not just in terms of recipients but in terms of how eligibility is defined. Unemployment insurance and Social Security entitles individuals to benefits based on their participation in the paid labor force. She notes that recipients of these programs, to which men have the greatest access because of their more continuous and better-paid labor force participation, are not construed as being ''on the dole.'' (Women's high rate of Social Security receipt occurs because about half receive benefits based on their husband's employment.) These benefits are claimed as a right by virtue of participation in the labor force. "Welfare" in the pejorative sense is usually applied to AFDC, food stamps, and Medicaid, which go to households and are means tested. Benefits are not understood as the "right" of the woman, or even the household, but rather as providing for the needs of households who cannot provide for themselves. When benefits are dependent on need rather than right, Fraser argues, the claimant has less ability to define what the need is and to choose how to meet it.

These different constructions of government assistance programs, and the more general threat to all such programs, have implications for the very concept of housing for the elderly. Most elderly people live in communities, not in specially designed or funded housing for the elderly. Thus, in its statistically most general form, housing for the elderly is just housing occupied by older people. The most important housing programs for the elderly, then, are the largest housing subsidy program, tax deductions for homeowners; second, the programs that increase the adequacy of incomes of the elderly for covering their shelter and nonshelter expenses, Social Security and Medicare; and third, the largest federally subsidized housing programs, public housing, Section 8 rental subsidies and HUD's Section 202 housing for the elderly. The first benefits higher-income people more than those of modest means, and thereby more men than women, especially among household heads. The second appears inadequate to prevent severe poverty among the elderly, especially women living alone and racial minorities (Hardy & Hazelrigg, 1993). The latter, directly subsidized housing, benefits women disproportionately.

Elderly women make up the majority of residents of housing "for the elderly" and are substantially represented among the majority of female-headed households in subsidized housing, most of which is means tested and defined as meeting needs rather than fulfilling rights. The kinds of questions that social science research often tries to answer have usually been framed within the discourse of needs, such as: What kind of housing is good for the elderly? Who benefits in what ways from different kinds of programs, designs, services? Perhaps it is this discourse that social scientists must challenge if the interests of elderly women are to be served. The following section explores the ways in which women's constructions of their own lives differ from the social construction of the life cycle that provides the rationale for "housing for the elderly."

Gendered Life Cycles

Traditional life cycle theory, such as that of Erikson (1959, 1985), has viewed human development as a trajectory of "ages and stages," with later life being the "completion." Erikson, especially in his later work (1985), also focused on the concepts of cohort and, in his theorizing, linked developmental challenges to culture. However, his overarching theory still presumed a specific ordering of tasks, with later life being seen as a period of philosophical and existential concern for achieving a final integrity and wisdom in the face of the disintegration of the physical self.

Feminist theorists have challenged the usefulness of the fixed stage model for women (Allatt, Keil, Bryman, & Bytheway, 1987; Franks, 1992; Franz & Stewart, 1994; Helson, 1992; Katz & Monk, 1993; Rice, 1994) and of the requirement or possibility of individual resolution (Hare-Mussen & Maracek, 1990). They see a woman's life as consisting of "chapters," with later life being yet another chapter.

Feminist psychologists also challenge the "deficit model," which stresses the limitations of aging; they prefer a "coping model," describing how people cope with life challenges (Banyard & Graham-Bermann, 1993; Garner & Young, 1994). According to this position, there is little that is "inevitable" about aging. Coping theory combines individual characteristics with sociopolitical realities of particular situations. Anthropologists Kerns and Brown (1992) assembled studies of midlife women in 13 societies and their indigenous perspectives on aging. Diverse cultural norms and practices were found; biological changes associated with menopause do not produce uniform physiological or psychological reactions, nor did they dictate future transformations in later life.

Certainly the challenges of aging, including physical changes, losses, and need for a philosophical attitude, require the ability for coping. Coping is not a trait but a process, and that, with its social components, varies from situation to situation. Women seem to employ other strategies than men, such as negotiation and forbearance, partially as a result of limited amounts of social, political, and economic power, but traditional research may place such coping mechanisms in a negative light. Further, in many situations, institutionalized ageism and sexism may induce feelings and behaviors of powerlessness and passivity in older women, rather than actually being a trait of older women (Sharpe, 1995). For example, health-care settings that impose childlike qualities on older women are not only demoralizing but may also create dependency. Housing arrangements, when designed by others "for" the elderly, may also engender such reactions; the disempowering aspects of housing for the elderly may be most likely when the advantages of enriched programming are greatest.

The social and emotional resources women develop throughout their lifetimes can stand them in good stead in later life, despite the disadvantages accruing to older women. Studies indicate that women have a wider variety of social contacts and social skills (Hansson & Carpenter, 1994). However, community contexts and cultural norms can be a major barrier to the use of these resources (Ward, et al., 1988). One study showed that U.S. women demonstrate significantly less anxiety about aging and seem more prepared to cope with loss and change (Barer, 1994; Lasher & Faulkender, 1993). This advantage appears particular to cultures and groups within a culture. A study comparing Turks and Swedes found that women had less positive attitudes toward aging and higher feelings of loneliness in both cultures, although gender differences were more pronounced among Turks (Imamoglu, Kuller, Imamoglu, & Kuller, 1993). Many studies indicate that women are more likely to assume new leadership roles in later life when circumstances either require or facilitate leadership (Saegert, 1989; Schultz & Galbraith, 1993).

Banyard and Graham-Bermann (1993), in suggesting an alternative model to understanding coping, challenge the interpretations of what is "healthy" and propose an acceptance of diversity. Pratt and Hansen (1993), studying women and work across the life cycle, highlight the sense of women's "multiple stories"; many successful women do not start careers until midlife; others recycle careers, part- and full-time, while juggling family responsibilities, rather than necessarily leaving employment entirely. They remind us that gender is socially constructed, that the category of "woman" is created and recreated differently even through individual women's lives and within cultures. All people, male or female, may change in values and aspirations, in opportunities available, and in constraints placed before them by the historical time and geographic space that frame their life course. Katz and Monk (1993) propose certain concepts for understanding the life course of women, including the importance of prior experience; the potential for continuing changes in motivation and behavior; the diversity of roles that women fulfill in the home, workplace, and community both simultaneously and over the years; and the ways in which ideologies about gender and age affect individual opportunities and structure collective experiences. They stress that women live "at the nexus of production and reproduction," but the spaces and temporal/spatial scales that organize these two spheres are vastly different.

Rubinstein and Parmelee (1992) develop a model of place attachment, constructed specifically to frame the elderly, that centers on life course and life experience. They focus on factors of cultural space and individual place and of cultural roles and personal relationships. Because numerous aspects of the identities of many elderly people have been lived out in distant times and places, the arrangements, contents, and other physical qualities of their homes carry important confirmations of their unique identities. This confirmation of identity appears to support a sense of psychological integrity in later life.

Ecological psychology provides some important concepts for contextualizing the discontinuity in women's lives within the continuities provided by culture and society. Elder (1995) views the life course paradigm as a blend of social change and individual development, combining two analytic frameworks. He offers four concepts of analysis: lives in time and place, human agency, the timing of lives, and linked lives. He sees a "life course paradigm" as more than just a single career but a dynamic of multiple, interlocking pathways. Thus, the life course approach studies the developmental tasks in a situational context and in a historical cohort.

Feminists also accept such a frame of analysis in understanding women's development. Bateson (1989) refers to the "multiple lives" of women, which are extensions of her multiple roles. Helson (1992) stresses acts of "rewriting life stories" that women may undertake during difficult life experiences. Katz and Monk (1993) use the concepts of "juggling" and "recycling," while Franz and Stewart (1994) highlight the relative "discontinuities" in women's life course as they balance various roles. Tomlinson-Keasey (1994) proposes five factors that are crucial to an appreciation of women's development: the importance of relationships; the force of serendipity; the impact of discontinuity; personal attributes that alter one's life; and social barriers that minimize women's intellectual skills. Rice (1994) critiques the "epigenetic" view of both family life cycle and women's life cycle, challenging the systematic, stepwise paradigm of stage theory and normative role expectations. Much of traditional life course theory with such a normative approach can be challenged on racial, ethnic, class, and gender lines.

Like ecological psychology, feminist theory also stresses the necessity for seeing phenomena in context. In fact, there is no one "elderly person" nor one true "elderly woman"; individuals exist in relational/social contexts. An elderly woman, for example, is defined by various social contexts and roles. In a familial context, she may be a mother, a grandmother, a spouse, a widow, a divorcee, or an elderly lesbian, even as a never-married person, most likely embedded in relationships such as peers, friends, community members, and so on. Another context is socioeconomic status. While many elderly, especially women, are in lower-income categories, they are nevertheless defined by personal and social history.

Katz and Monk (1993) also note the importance of cohorts to understand shared cultural beliefs and experiences of women within a certain age group. For example, behaviors associated with certain life stages may be related to the conditions through which certain groups have collectively lived, such as access to education, career expectations, or common ages for giving birth to a first child. Cohort issues also influence the elderly because they have mutually lived through a specific period of history. Current, elderly women may have lived through the end of World War I, the Great Depression, and World War II. They grew up in an atmosphere of relatively well-defined gender roles, with fairly clear expectations of women as primary caretakers. The cohort of women who will soon emerge as elderly lived through at least some challenge to tradition. There is more independence, higher economic expectation, and less family stability. She is more likely to have been separated or divorced, sometimes more than once, from a partner. She is more likely to have worked outside the home for a more significant period and may have identified with a "career" rather than a "job." She may live longer, be in better health, and have had children at various ages in her life. Some women, in fact, have borne children in their twenties, divorced, remarried, and borne children again later in life. Blended families, extended families of "stepchildren," exist who may or may not feel an obligation to care for stepparents in later life.

While later life is often considered "retirement" age, for women it is hard to know what they "retire" from. Many caregiving activities continue throughout all life phases. Women often begin caretaking activities early in life, by babysitting, caring for younger siblings, then caring for a mate, children of her own, her own aging parents, her grandchildren, and so on. Further, some may earn a living as a professional caretaker such as nurse or nanny.

For the elderly woman, housing issues often involve an intergenerational context. Housing concerns include whether the elderly person will live with her children and, if so, if she is really "wanted" by all family members, if she moves to a retirement community and is or is not visited frequently by family, if she will "be put" (not her choice) in a nursing home, and so on. For elderly women in a couple, there is mutual concern about each other and who may outlive the other. For those in relative poverty, financial questions concerning housing and medical care may become extended family issues.

Many of these issues may also apply to elderly men, but they are less transparent. Since traditionally women are caretakers, even in their housing decisions, they are likely to contextualize decisions: How will where I live affect others? Will I be a burden? What can I contribute? Am I "entitled" to care because I have provided care? From this, what are the woman's expectations of housing in her elderly years? Have the realistic parameters of her choices matched her expectations? Thus, there are social components to the formation of expectations, and disappointments in such expectations as one ages, which are also related to cohort differences between generations.

Changes in economic trends may also create conflicts for future cohorts. When life had been seen in a stepwise way, a predictable retirement age was set for early "later life." However, many elderly of current and future cohorts, both men and women, may not be able to retire. They may need to continue part-time employment, which will have housing implications. This will affect where they live geographically as well as the specifics of neighborhood location and house size. "Retirement" may be gradual rather than a specific cutoff event.

Women's increased labor market participation may have effects lasting well beyond the period of actual employment. Bernard (1995) examines the erosion of male identity based on the "good provider" role as women assume (or taking a longer historical time frame, reassume) the role of coprovider. The increase in married women's labor force participation has not been accompanied by equivalent increases in male domestic activities (Hochschild & Machung, 1989). Differences in caretaking activities and different employment histories position men and women differently as they approach and experience retirement (Hatch, 1992; Szinovacz, 1982). Women more often face retirement from a poor financial situation that limits their ability to use their free time in desirable ways. Studies indicate that married, mostly white, women often have positive expectations about sharing time and household tasks with their husbands that are unrealized, leading to disappointment and sometimes resentment (Altergott, 1988; Szinovac, 1982). While African Americans are less likely to be married in later life, they show more egalitarian patterns in carrying out household responsibilities and caregiving, and African-American men seem often to view retirement more positively, perhaps having experienced less rewarding work histories than white men (Danigelis & McIntosh, 1993).

These changes in labor force participation and retirement raise questions about the future and generality of the idea of elderly housing. The concept has been predicated on the idea that residents would mostly be no longer working. In the private market "retirement housing" and "adult only" communities have catered to couples. Evaluations of these "prepackaged" communities have suggested that residents are often very happy with them (Rappaport, 1985). However, how husbands and wives may differ in their use and evaluation of these residences has not been explored.

EXPANDING THE BOUNDS OF GENDER IN ELDERLY HOUSING

The literature on gender and housing (Peterson, 1987; Saegert, 1980, 1985; Tognoli, 1987), while not always specifying age, emphasizes the conflicts inherent in the joint roles of wage earner and mother for women and the less personal identification of men with the home (Tognoli, 1980). Studies of housing options for the elderly rarely treat gender in a formal way and are often based on high proportions of female respondents. Gender differences in the symbolic meaning and forms of place attachment to housing in later life have been largely unexplored. However, the gender identity in younger age groups has been strongly associated with the meaning of home (Rose, 1993; Saegert, 1980; Tognoli, 1987). It is not just an expanded time frame that is needed in the literature on gender and housing. Our understanding of this topic also encompasses the dual aspect of a gender critique: (1) how gender, along with race and position in the economy, structures advantage and disadvantage in society and (2) how particular women and men attempt to realize different human potentials, including new spatialized forms of dwelling, and through doing so to remake the social relationships that constrain them. As we suggest, gender and housing continue to be intertwined throughout life. Male- and female-headed elderly households have very different access to housing. Domestic work remains largely the business of women throughout their lives and expands with the presence of a man in the household, even if he is retired. Mobility limitations appear to make the home a greater focal point of women's activity. For example, elderly women, more than men, restrict their geographic sphere (Rosenbloom, 1993). Women either may not have had driver's licenses or were more likely to stop driving at an earlier age than men. Some studies show that elderly women are less willing to move (Ward et al., 1988) or/and less able physically and financially to travel (Altergott, 1988; Szinovacz, 1982). Research measuring functional health finds them to be physically less mobile (O'Brien & Vertinsky, 1991).

There may be a special urgency to the remaking of these relationships for older people. Erikson has spoken of the challenges of old age, highlighting conflicts of integrity versus despair. For many older people, especially women, the conflict appears to be not just a psychic struggle. In a concrete way, housing accommodations should support this need for integration and opportunity to transmit wisdom to others. Yet the choices facing many elderly women are living alone in housing that may be hard to keep up, unaffordable, or dilapidated; being dependent on inadequate transportation; or living in institutions that separate them from society. From a feminist perspective, the quest for integrity in later years is but a continuation of the struggle women have throughout their lives to achieve a vision that takes into account their ''objective'' limitations but is self-reflective and leaves room for transformation in a context of ''fractured identity'' (Morawski, 1990, p. 177).

Losses, Relocation, and Change

For the elderly, changes in residence and social role, such as from wife to widow or from worker to retiree, may in many instances constitute a deprivation; yet these changes also provide an occasion for the reworking of the self and the social and physical world in which that self is embedded (Hormuth, 1990). While bereavement is in most instances a major life stress, it can also be the start of a new social identity. For men, the aftermath of the loss of a spouse through divorce or death is most often remarriage. For women, social identity changes may be more fundamental, and perhaps more contingent. For example, one study that followed adults from age 30 to age 70 found that, generally, men's well-being in later life was more related to their personalities and that women's well-being was more responsive to environmental options (Maas & Kuyper, 1974). A subset of widows, mostly living in more urban areas, did very well, taking up life paths that had been foreclosed at marriage.

Loss of the spouse in widowhood frequently means heightened awareness of housing issues while also requiring the survivors to reinterpret their social and personal identity. For almost all, the home itself contains objects and memories linking the survivor to the past shared domestic life. The companionship and assistance lost may precipitate further readjustment through relocation and can include moving into a three-generation household, a smaller apartment, or a retirement community. Such relocations require shifts in role to accommodate to the new environment and new people in the environment. In many cases, relocation is ambivalent. The extent to which the positive ''pulls'' outweigh the negative ''pushes'' can be critical; however, even when relocation constitutes a net loss, elderly women's interpretation of their circumstances can lead to personal growth and self-acceptance (Ryff & Essex, 1992).

The material process of moving and resettling involves many decisions and choices, as well as facing up to loss and limits. In situations of residential relocation, many decisions are made, including choices of what possessions to keep and what to discard. Often these decisions entail a ''life review.'' Feminist psychologists stress connectedness and attachment to place and to person as the basis for psychological growth. They recognize that conflicts arise from the tensions between needs for intimacy and needs for autonomy and independence. This life review may provide the occasion for a creative reworking of these tensions. For example, in McCarthy's clinical practice, a retired professional woman suffering from depression was asked to make a "collage" of her life; she reported the most influential part of the process was deciding which photos of whom to include and which to leave out. In her psychotherapy, this led to a moving review of "who" was really significant in her life in the long view.

Leadership for Change

Social scientists are coming to recognize the leadership role of women of many different ages, races, and walks of life around issues related to their homes (Edelstein & Wandersman, 1987; Feldman & Stall, 1994; Lawson, Barton, & Joselit, 1980; Saegert, 1989). Although elderly women are frequently among these leaders, the potential for their leadership in developing their own housing and living options has not been fully recognized.

Leavitt and Saegert (1990), in their study of low-income housing in abandoned buildings in African-American and Latino communities, unexpectedly found many older people, primarily women, in leadership roles. These women developed tenant cooperatives not only to preserve their own homes but also "to make a more homelike world" for all tenants. Older male leaders usually described their leadership as an extension of work roles, whereas older women from a wide range of backgrounds, from professionals to domestic workers to welfare recipients, talked about saving and improving their buildings as an extension of their lifelong activities in finding and maintaining decent housing for themselves and their families, as well as their efforts to create and maintain a viable community. Through group action and self-help, residents secured their buildings against vandals and drug dealers, repaired roofs open to the rain, restored light, heat, and hot water to apartments, and generally brought buildings almost beyond saving back to habitability. Elderly leaders brought to their neighbors remembrances of their buildings and communities when they were newer and stronger, when lobbies had mirrors and doormen, and famous singers lived next door. In doing so, they aided not only the restortion of their homes but also a positive collective identity. In this study, the buildings themselves, old and in disrepair, literally mirror the Eriksonian tasks of despair versus integrity and wisdom. These older buildings themselves went from abandonment to hope and grew into viable, strong entities, as did their tenants.

Feldman and Stall (1994) have documented elderly African-American women in similar roles as they struggle to restore and improve their public housing development in Chicago. The work of the women leaders is seen as a continuation of African-American women's efforts to appropriate a homeplace. What began as the reopening and refurbishing of a field house for youth programs went on to establishing a tenant-owned laundromat and small store and to leading a community-wide fight against construction of a stadium.

In a New York City Housing Authority development, women leaders of all ages worked together to physically improve their own developments, provide youth programs, and initiate economic development projects. These leaders started a coalition of 8,000 households, attempting to remake the physical and social landscape of East Harlem into a community that works for its residents. Some of the projects the leaders have organized have specifically addressed the needs of the elderly through food programs, senior activities, and programs bringing together youth and seniors to plan activities they could both enjoy. In one effort, a gardening project, active residents were surprised and pleased to see older men, who usually did not take part in tenant association activities, adopt the gardens and ensure their productivity. Vegetables were given away, and a final harvest feast was held, serving freshly cooked produce and other dishes.[2]

Women's leadership is proving especially crucial in programs aimed not at just serving but personally and politically empowering the elderly in many countries. In Mexico, an 88-year-old Belgian woman emigrant forced into retirement began a project to raise consciousness about the problems of aging. Discussion groups of older women were organized because they seldom spoke in mixed-sex settings. Out of these discussions, they developed a day center, started a garden, fired the cook so they could prepare their own meals, and found many ways to help each other cope with poverty, isolation, and cultural barriers faced by the aged. Groups to discuss aging and compare experiences were later opened to women of all ages (Ruiz, 1995). In Britain, the National Council for Single Women and Her Dependents formed an organization to improve the financial and social circumstances of the mostly never-married single women who were responsible for 95 percent of the home care of elderly (McKenzie, 1995). Middle-aged Japanese professional women concerned about losing their jobs when faced with the demands of elder care brought together a conference on the issue and became the basis for the Women's Group for Improvement of Aging Society. The group holds seminars on topics such as long-term care, women and financial stability, housing for the elderly, and medical services; they conduct research, publish books, organize visits to nursing homes and hospices, and encourage older women to run for political office (Sodei, 1995). Linking up such empowerment-oriented organizations with the large female populations in housing for the elderly and public housing in the United States might prove synergistic. The practical experience and leadership of older women could also be brought to bear in the development and design of housing options for older people.

All of these projects reveal not just the practical gains that older women leaders bring about but also the cultural significance of their leadership for empowering marginal people within their own societies. Dolores Hayden and her colleagues (Hayden, 1995) have touched a similar wellspring in their "Power of Place" project in Los Angeles. Sidewalks, plazas, and parts of building facades have been used to tell the stories of extraordinary but unknown women and men, African Americans, Chinese, and other groups who have made the city. In the New York City co-ops described above, tenants have often carefully restored the woodwork, tiles, and stained-glass windows, gathered scrapbooks and picture albums, and passed down the meaning of the places they live in to other generations. Such projects bring out the talents of older residents and also greatly enrich the younger ones. The physical design of housing and community space gains in meaning from the visible reminders of previous generations.

Equalizing and Improving Housing Access for the Elderly

Housing cost and availability constitute a major barrier to the largely female poor elderly. In the late twentieth-century political climate, the subsidies that have disproportionately served women in the United States and other developed countries are being cut back. How far this trend will go, and the extent that housing designed especially for the elderly will be affected, is unclear. However, research has found that elderly leaders play a significant role in low-income tenant co-ops and public housing developments. These roles might be extended into formal management arrangements as privatization progresses. Elderly women appear to benefit from the home-based nature of the activity and bring substantial skills from their life histories of managing homes and working co-operatively with others to provide goods and services they cannot afford in the market (Leavitt & Saegert, 1990). Resident control enhances the informal supports and services available to the elderly and provides a fertile setting for intergenerational initiatives. However, none of these options could operate without substantial public subsidy, even if ownership or management is privatized. The more pessimistic view is that, at least in the short term, such changes are likely to force older people, especially unmarried women, into poorly funded institutions. Women of all ages can also be expected to have increased workloads of unpaid care placed upon them.

Within the ability of market provisions for housing, the trend toward allowing accessory apartments in previously single-family zoned areas can be beneficial for the elderly (Leavitt, 1996). Without adequate and appropriate public transportation, many of these elderly may become shut-ins (Brail, Hughes, & Arthur, 1976). For elderly people with resources, the market has become especially creative in producing "adult only" communities and, increasingly, continuing care residences. These residences are the most likely sites for innovative programs and attractive facilities to support women in becoming more physically active and to sustain men's predilections to stay active. For the wealthy elderly, the "smart house" and other technological developments in communications and prosthetics promise to make independent living more feasible and enjoyable (Leavitt, 1996) The combined loss of subsidies for housing, cost consciousness, and privatization in health care may make these options affordable to only the better-off elderly, thus excluding a large proportion of elderly women. In other developed countries, redesigned suburban blocks incorporate housing and services for the elderly, and continuing care facilities have been more often provided by the state. The future of these innovations remains unclear as these countries also try to trim their social welfare costs. The burden on private philanthropies and religious institutions to support enriched housing for the elderly will most likely increase if this is to remain an option. Churches may also be important sources for increasing the support systems of elderly people living at home, especially for African-American women (Hatch, 1991).

Reframing Gender in Design

The numerous design innovations and evaluations of elderly housing options provide a good guide to ways to improve the lives of men and women in housing built specifically for the elderly (Carp, 1987; Howe, Clark, & Butler, 1993; Lawton, 1977; Regnier & Pynoos, 1987). New approaches to shared housing that maximize privacy while increasing the opportunities for shared activities and hobbies and cutting costs may be particularly attractive to women (Clark et al., 1992). Generally, the designs that work well are presented as gender neutral. It would be useful to include gender as a differentiating factor. For example, in our experience, men's minority status in elderly housing may lead them to avoid community spaces and activity programming or to take over particular areas and activities as male preserves.

Three divergent approaches to understanding the link between design and gender may have particular importance for housing for the elderly. One emphasizes the different goals and design processes that derive from feminist architectural practice. For example, Franck (1989) argues that feminist design practice can be distinguished by the following values: (1) connectedness and inclusiveness; (2) an ethic of care and the valuing of everyday life; and (3) valuing of subjectivity and feeling. The kinds of design processes and decisions she identifies would bring the often well-developed housing design intelligence of older women into the design process and also address attention to the practical and emotionally supportive qualities of housing that may particularly impact the lives of the elderly. A second approach looks at changes people make in their own dwellings over time as a way of understanding how changes in family roles and dynamics get reflected in design, renovations, and less formal spatial changes (Howell, 1994). Such observations will help us better understand what relational and identity goals household members are trying to achieve. A third approach draws attention to another potentially significant kind of architectural artifact revealing and challenging patriarchal conventions in design (Friedman, 1995). Her fascinating research program studies architect-designed houses commissioned by women clients. In a recent presentation, one convention she identified as typically reinterpreted by women clients was the master bedroom and the separation of activities into sleeping versus working versus food preparation and serving versus socializing.[3] The sort of design revisions that evolved in the client-architect dialogue might be particularly appealing to elderly women who live alone in that they make the most of small spaces in flexible and innovative ways. The particular buildings for women clients tend also to reflect their own struggles to achieve full personhood in settings designed by men and communities dominated by male-headed household conventions.

In conclusion, a feminist critique of housing for the elderly within the field of environmental psychology calls our attention to the ways in which gender shapes access to housing, public support for housing for the elderly, and the physical form and functions of that housing. Our hope is that by recognizing that decisions and constraints affecting elderly housing are intertwined with options and limits for personal growth in older age, new options and approaches can be opened up through dialogue with the women and men who are to use them. Further, we believe it is important to recognize that decisions about elderly housing affect the relationships, values for living, and visions of society that we all experience.

NOTES

1. The indented sections denote that they were written by the first author, Susan Saegert, in collaboration with Catherine Winkel, for this book chapter.

2. This project is being documented by the Housing Environments Research Group (HERG) of the Center for Human Environments at the City University of New York Graduate School. Technical assistance is provided by HERG as part of a HUD-sponsored Community Outreach Partnership Center grant. Documentation is supported by a grant from the Edna McConnell Clark Foundation.

3. Presented at "Re-Visioning Design and Technology: Feminist Perspectives," organized by Joan Rothschild and sponsored by the Center for Human Environments, City University of New York Graduate School and University Center, November 1995.

REFERENCES

Abramovitz, M. (1988). *Regulating the lives of women: Social welfare policy from colonial times to the present*. Boston: South End Press.

Allatt, P., Keil, Y., Bryman, A., & Bytheway, B. (1987). *Women and the life cycle*. New York: St. Martin's Press.

Altergott, K. (Ed.). (1988). *Daily life in later life: Comparative perspectives*. Newbury Park, CA: Sage Publications.

Banyard, V. L., & Graham-Bermann, S. A. (1993). Can women cope? A gender analysis of theories of coping with stress. *Psychology of Women Quarterly, 17*, 303–318.

Barer, Barbara. (1994). Men and women aging differently. *International Journal of Aging and Human Development, 38* (1), 29–40.

Bateson, M. C. (1989). *Composing a life*. New York: Plume.

Benhabib, S., Butler, J., Cornell, D., & Fraser, N. (1995). *Feminist contentions: A philosophical exchange*. New York: Routledge.

Bernard, J. (1995). The good-provider role: Its rise and fall. In M. S. Kimmel & M. A. Messner (Eds.), *Men's lives* (pp. 149–164). Boston: Allyn & Bacon.

Brail, R. K., Hughes, J. W., & Arthur, C. A. (1976). *Transportation services for the disabled and elderly*. New Brunswick, NJ: Center for Urban Policy Research.

Bratt, R. G. (1986). Public housing: The controversy and the contribution. In R. G. Bratt, C. Hartman, & A. Meyerson (Eds.), *Critical perspectives on housing* (pp. 335–361). Philadelphia: Temple University Press.

Carp, F. (1987). Environment and aging. In D. Stokols & I. Altman (Eds.), *Handbook of environmental psychology* (pp. 329–360). New York: Wiley.

Chappell, N. L., Segall, A., & Lewis, D. G. (1990). Gender and helping networks among day hospital and senior center participants. *Canadian Journal on Aging, 9*, 220–233.

Citizens' Commission on Civil Rights. (1986). The federal government and equal housing opportunity: A continuing failure. In R. G. Bratt, C. Hartman, & A. Meyerson (Eds.), *Critical perspectives on housing* (pp. 296–324). Philadelphia: Temple University Press.

Clark, H., Saegert, S., Chapin, D., Silverblatt, R., Iltus, S., & Hoffman, J. (1992). *A shared housing model for the elderly*. New York: Center for Human Environments.

Danigelis, N. L., & McIntosh, B. R. (1993). Resources and the productive activity of elders: Race and gender as context. *Journal of Gerontology: Social Sciences, 48*, S192–S203.

Dean, A., Kology, B., Wood, P., & Matt, G. E. (1992). The influence of living alone on depression in elderly persons. *Journal of Aging and Health, 4*, 3–18.

Dressel, Paula L. (1991). Gender, race, and class: Beyond the feminization of poverty in later life. In M. Minkler & C. L. Estes (Eds.), *Critical perspectives on aging* (pp. 245–252). Amityville, NY: Baywood.

Edelstein, M. R., & Wandersman, A. (1987). Community dynamics in coping with toxic contaminants. In I. Altman & A. Wandersman (Eds.), *Neighborhood and community environments* (pp. 69–112). New York: Plenum.

Ehrenreich, B., & Piven, F. F. (1984). The feminization of poverty. *Dissent, 31*, 162–170.

Elder, G. H. (1995). The life course paradigm: Social change and individual development. In P. Moen, G. H. Elder, & K. Luscher (Eds.), *Examining lives in context: Perspectives on the ecology of human development* (pp. 101–140). Washington, DC: American Psychological Association.

Erikson, E. (1959). *Identity and the life cycle*. New York: International Universities Press.

Erikson, E. (1985). *Childhood and society* (35th anniversary ed.). New York: Norton.

Feldman, R. M., & Stall, S. (1994). The politics of space appropriation: A case study of women's struggles for homeplace in Chicago public housing. In I. Altman & R. Churchman (Eds.), *Women and the environment*. New York: Plenum Press.

Ferraro, K. F. (1993). Are black older adults health-pessimistic? *Journal of Health and Social Behavior, 34*, 201–214.

Foley, D. J., Ostfeld, A. A., Branch, L. G., & Wallace, R. B. (1992). The risk of nursing home admission in three communities. *Journal of Aging and Health, 4*, 155–173.

Franck, K. (1989). A feminist approach to architecture. In E. P. Berkeley & M. McQuaid (Eds.), *Architecture: A place for women* (pp. 201–218). Washington, DC: Smithsonian Institution Press.

Franks, B. A. (1992). Developmental psychology and feminism: Points of communication. *Women's Studies Quarterly, 1–2*, 28–39.

Franz, C. E., & Stewart, A. J. (Eds.). (1994). *Women creating lives: Identities, resilience and resistance*. Boulder, CO: Westview Press.

Fraser, N. (1989). *Unruly practices: Power, discourse, and gender in contemporary social theory*. Minneapolis: University of Minnesota Press.

Friedman, A. (1995). The best laid plans: Housing built for women. Paper presented at the conference *Re-visioning design and technology: Feminist perspectives*, City University of New York Graduate School and University Center, New York City.

Fuhrer, R., Antonucci, T. C., & Dartriques, M. (1992). Depressive symptomology and cognitive functioning: An epidemiological survey in an elderly community sample in France. *Psychological Medicine, 22*, 159–172.

Garner, J. D., & Young, A. A. (1994). *Women and healthy aging: Living productively in spite of it all*. Binghamton, NY: Haworth Press.

Goldberg, G. S., & Kremen, E. (1990). *The feminization of poverty: Only in America?* Westport, CT: Greenwood Press.

Gottlieb, B. H. (1989). A contextual perspective on stress in family care of the elderly. *Canadian Psychology, 30*, 596–607.

Guberman, N., Maheau, P., & Mille, C. (1992). Women as family caregivers: Why do they care? *Gerontologist, 32*, 607–617.

Hansson, R. O., & Carpenter, B. N. (1994). *Relationships in old age*. New York: Guilford Press.

Hardy, M. A., & Hazelrigg, L. E. (1993). The gender of poverty in an aging population. *Research on Aging, 15*, 243–278.

Hardy, M. A., & Hazelrigg, L. E. (1995). Gender, race/ethnicity, and poverty in later life. *Journal of Aging Studies, 9*, 43–63.

Hare-Mussen, R. T., & Marecek, J. (Eds.). (1990). *Making a difference: Psychology and the construction of gender*. New Haven, CT: Yale University Press.

Hatch, L. R. (1991). Informal support patterns of older African-American and white women: Examining effects of family, paid work, and religious participation. *Research on Aging, 13*, 144–170.

Hatch, L. R. (1992). Gender differences in orientation toward retirement from paid labor. *Gender and Society, 6*, 66–85.

Hayden, D. (1995). *The power of place: Urban landscapes as public history*. Cambridge, MA: MIT Press.

Helson, R. (1992). Women's difficult times and the rewriting of the life story. *Psychology of Women Quarterly, 16*, 331–347.

Henwood, K. L. (1993). Women and later life: The discursive construction of identities within family relationships. *Journal of Aging Studies, 7*, 303–319.

Hochschild, A. R., & Machung, A. (1989). *The second shift: Working parents and the revolution at home*. New York: Avon.

Hormuth, S. E. (1990). *The ecology of the self: Relocation and self-concept change*. Cambridge: Cambridge University Press.

Horton, J. A. (1995). *The women's health data book: Profile of women's health in the United States*. New York: Elsevier.

Howe, J. L., Clark, H., & Butler, R. N. (1993). *The optimal environment for the elderly*. New York: Sasakawa Health Science Foundation.

Howell, S. (1994). Environment and the aging woman: Domains of choice. In I. Altman & A. Churchman (Eds.), *Women and the environment* (pp. 105–131). New York: Plenum Press.

Howell, S. (1995, August). *Rethinking stereotypes of family housing in Japan and USA*. Paper presented at the fourth Japan-U.S. Seminar on Environment-Behavior Research, Clark University, Worcester, MA.

Imamoglu, E. O., Kuller, R., Imamoglu, V., & Kuller, M. (1993). The social psychological worlds of Swedes and Turks in and around retirement. *Journal of Cross Cultural Psychology, 24*, 26–41.

Katz, C., & Monk, J. (Eds.). (1993). *Full circles: Geographies of women over the life course*. New York: Routledge.

Kaye, L. W., & Monk, A. (1991). Social relations in enriched housing for the aged: A case study. *Journal of Housing for the Elderly, 9*, 111–126.

Kerns, V., & Brown, J. K. (Eds.). (1992). *In her prime: New views of middle-aged women*. Urbana: University of Illinois Press.

Kravitz, L., & Collings, A. (1986). Rural housing policy in America: Problems and solutions. In R. G. Bratt, C. Hartman, & A. Meyerson (Eds.), *Critical perspectives on housing* (pp. 325–334). Philadelphia: Temple University Press.

Laferriere, R. H., & Hamel-Bissell, B. P. (1994). Successful aging of oldest old women in the Northeast Kingdom of Vermont. *Journal of Nursing Scholarship, 26*, 319–323.

Lasher, K. P., & Faulkender, P. J. (1993). Measurement of aging anxiety: Development of the Anxiety about Aging Scale. *International Journal of Aging and Human Development, 37*, 247–259.

Lawson, R., Barton, S., & Joselit, J. W. (1980). From kitchen to storefront: Women in the tenant movement. In G. R. Wekerle, R. Peterson, & D. Morley (Eds.), *New space for women* (pp. 26–41). Boulder, CO: Westview.

Lawton, M. P. (1977). The impact of the environment on aging and behavior. In J. E. Birren & K. W. Schaie (Eds.), *Handbook of the psychology of aging* (pp. 276–301). New York: Van Nostrand Reinhold.

Leavitt, J. W. (1995). Gender expectations: Women and early 20th-century public health. In L. K. Kerber, A. Kessler-Harris, & K. K. Sklar (Eds.), *U.S. history as women's history: New feminist essays*. Chapel Hill: University of North Carolina Press.

Leavitt, J. (1996). Modernization and aging. In *Encyclopedia of gerontology* (pp. 9-1–9-5). New York: Academic Press.

Leavitt, J., & Saegert, S. (1990). *From abandonment to hope: Community households in Harlem*. New York: Columbia University Press.

Leavitt, J., & Welch, M. B. (1989). Older women and the suburbs: A literature review. *Women's Studies Quarterly, 17*, 35–47.

Maas, H. S., & Kuyper, J. M. (1974). *From thirty to seventy*. San Francisco: Jossey-Bass.

McCartney, J. R. (1988). Elderly women who want to live alone: Lessons learned. *Journal of Geriatic Psychiatry and Neurology, 1*, 172–175.

McKenzie, H. (1995). Empowering older persons through organizations. In D. Thursz, C. Nusberg, & J. Prather (Eds.), *Empowering older people: An international approach* (pp. 83–90). Westport, CT: Auburn House.

Moen, P., Robison, J., & Fields, V. (1994). Women's work and caregiving roles: A life course approach. *Journal of Gerontology, 49*, S176–S186.

Morawski, J. G. (1990). Toward the unimagined: Feminism and epistemology in psychology. In R. T. Hare-Mussen & J. Marecek (Eds.), *Making a difference: Psychology and the construction of gender* (pp. 150–183). New Haven, CT: Yale University Press.

O'Brien, S. J., & Vertinsky, P. A. (1991). Unfit survivors: Exercise as a resource for aging women. *Gerontologist, 31*, 347–357.

Pearce, D. (1979). Women, work, and welfare: The feminization of poverty. In K. W. Feinstein (Ed.), *Working women and families* (pp. 103–124). Beverly Hills, CA: Sage Publications.

Penning, M. J., & Strain, L. A. (1994). Gender differences in disability, assistance, and subjective well-being in later life. *Journals of Gerontology, 49*, 202–208.

Peterson, R. B. (1987). Gender issues in the home and urban environment. In E. H. Zube & G. T. Moore (Eds.), *Advances in environment, behavior, and design* (Vol. 1, pp. 187–220). New York: Plenum Press.

Pratt, G., & Hansen, S. (1993). Women and work across the life course: Moving beyond essentialism. In C. Katz & J. Monk (Eds.), *Full circles: Geographies of women over the life course* (pp. 27–54). New York: Routledge.

Rappaport, A. (1985). Thinking about home environments: A conceptual framework. In I. Altman & C. M. Werner (Eds.), *Human behavior and environment: Vol. 8, Home environments* (pp. 255–286). New York: Plenum Press.

Regnier, V., & Pynoos, J. (1987). *Housing the aged: Design directives and policy considerations.* New York: Elsevier.

Regnier, V., & Pynoos, J. (1992). Environmental interventions for cognitively impaired older persons. In J. Birren, R. B. Sloane, & G. D. Cohen (Eds.), *Handbook of mental health and aging* (pp. 764–793). San Diego: Academic Press.

Rice, J. K. (1994). Reconsidering research on divorce, family life cycle and the meaning of family. *Psychology of Women Quarterly, 18*, 559–584.

Rose, G. (1993). *Feminism & geography.* Minneapolis: University of Minnesota Press.

Rosenbloom, S. (1993). Women's travel patterns at various stages of their lives. In C. Katz & J. Monk (Eds.), *Full circles: Geographies of women over the life course* (pp. 208–242). New York: Routledge.

Rubinstein, R. L., & Parmelee, P. A. (1992). Attachment to place and the representation of the life course of the elderly. In I. Altman & S. M. Low (Eds.), *Place attachment* (pp. 139–163). New York: Plenum Press.

Ruiz, C. (1995). Empowering older Mexicans through study and action. In D. Thursz, C. Nusberg, & J. Prather (Eds.), *Empowering older people: An international approach* (pp. 121–128). Westport, CT: Auburn House.

Ryff, C. D., & Essex, M. J. (1992). The interpretation of life experience and well-being: The sample case of relocation. *Psychology and Aging, 7*, 507–517.

Saegert, S. (1980, Summer). Masculine cities and feminine suburbs: Polarized ideas, contradictory realities. *Signs: An Interdisciplinary Journal of Women and Culture*, Special Supplement. Reissued as K. Stimpson, M. Nelson, & K. Yaktrakas (Eds.), *Women and the American city* (pp. 93–108). Chicago: University of Chicago Press, 1981.

Saegert, S. (1985). The androgenous city: From critique to practice. *Sociological Focus, 18*, 161–176.

Saegert, S. (1986). The role of housing in the experience of dwelling. In I. Altman & C. Werner (Eds.), *Human behavior and environments: Vol. 8, Home environments.* New York: Plenum.

Saegert, S. (1989). Unlikely leaders, extreme circumstances: Older black women building community households. *American Journal of Community Psychology, 17*, 295–316.

Schultz, C. M., & Galbraith, M. W. (1993). Community leadership education of older adults: An exploratory study. *Educational Gerontology, 19,* 473–488.

Seamon, F. (1992). Intergenerational issues related to the crack cocaine problem. *Family and Community Health, 15,* 11–19

Seamon, T., Berkman, L. F., Blazer, D., & Rowe, J. W. (1994). Social ties and support for neuroendocrine function: The MacArthur studies of successful aging. *Annals of Behavioral Medicine, 16,* 95–106.

Sharpe, P. A. (1995). Older women and health services: Moving from ageism to empowerment. *Women and Health, 22,* 9–17.

Simonsick, E. M. (1991). Personal health habits and mental health in a national probability sample. *American Journal of Preventive Medicine, 7,* 425–437.

Sodei, T. (1995). Tradition impedes organizational empowerment in Japan. In D. Thursz, C. Nusberg, & J. Prather (Eds.), *Empowering older people: An international approach* (pp. 91–98). Westport, CT: Auburn House.

Stone, Michael. (1993). *Shelter poverty.* Philadelphia, PA: Temple University Press.

Szinovacz, M. (Ed.). (1982). *Women's retirement: Policy implications of recent research.* Beverly Hills, CA: Sage Publications.

Tognoli, J. (1980). Differences in women's and men's responses to domestic space. *Sex Roles, 6,* 838–842.

Tognoli, J. (1987). Residential environments. In D. Stokols & I. Altman (Eds.), *Handbook of environmental psychology.* New York: John Wiley.

Tomlinson-Keasey, C. (1994). My dirty little secret: Women as clandestine intellectuals. In C. E. Franz & A. J. Stewart (Eds.), *Women creating lives: Identities, resilience, and resistance* (pp. 227–241). Boulder, CO: Westview Press.

Ward, R. A., LaGory, M., & Sherman, S. R. (1988). *The environment for aging: Interpersonal, social and spatial contexts.* Tuscaloosa: University of Alabama Press.

Webber, P., Arnsberger, P., Fox, P., & Burnette, D. (1994). Living alone with Alzheimer's disease: Effects on health and social service utilization patterns. *Gerontologist, 34,* 8–14.

Woroby, J. L., & Angel, R. J. (1990). Functional capacity and living arrangements of unmarried elderly persons. *Journals of Gerontology, 45,* S95–S101.

Young, I. M. (1990). *Justice and the politics of difference.* Princeton, NJ: Princeton University Press.

4

The Phenomenology of Housing for Older People

ROBERT L. RUBINSTEIN

In this chapter, we explore the phenomenology of housing for older adults. In a first section, we will trace the origins and outline the theoretical underpinnings of this perspective. In particular, we will highlight aspects of the personal and cultural constitution of the self and the environmental zone represented by housing. These constructs will then be illustrated with reference to one case example. In a final section, we will discuss the interrelationship of person and home with a concern for the discrete experiential elements of self and society.

By *phenomenology*, we mean simply the nature and content of experience. Thus, this chapter is about how older persons, in general, experience the environment and, more specifically, housing. We will be concerned not only with housing built specifically for the aged but also with all housing inhabited by elders. Issues of meaning for housing for the elderly have been addressed by Steinfeld (1981) in an important paper.

In this chapter, we will use the terms *phenomenology* and *experience* interchangeably. Implicated in a phenomenological approach are subjectivism, reflexivity, and concern with the individual's experiences. To summarize, this perspective may be seen as containing a bundle of related subjective views described by the terms *emic perspective, subjectivity, experience near, life world, insideness, lived experience*, and *personal meaning*. However, as we will describe in this chapter, we are also concerned with those constructs or elements that may crosscut individual experience. To be sure, while individual subjectivity may vary greatly and is in some sense ultimately irreducible, such experience is largely shaped in conventional or cultural ways. This is certainly as true for how one experiences the environment as it is for the experience of other important entities. Further, as we will point out, it is always important to remember that the object of the phenomenological approach, subjective experience of the individual, concerns an entity, the individual, that is itself a cultural construct; person and personhood vary from culture to culture (Heelas & Locke, 1981; Marsella, DeVos, & Hsu, 1985; Shweder & LeVine, 1984).

While the concerns here draw from a variety of scholarly disciplines, as a single approach this chapter may be seen as contrasting with or complementing the approach of mainstream environment and aging methods and assumptions.

First and foremost, the term *phenomenology* is most familiar from philosophy, where it is primarily used to describe a concern with the appearance of reality in consciousness or an understanding that sees intuitive experience and the perception of irreducible essences of phenomena as central to human life; there it is formatively associated with the work of Husserl and Merleau-Ponty among others (Bauman, 1978; Gurwitsch, 1970; Husserl, 1931, 1970; Korosec-Serfaty, 1985; Lauer, 1965; Merleau-Ponty, 1962, 1970). For example, the notion of the "life world" or experiential or phenomenological space of the person is found in Husserl's work. It is through the work of Merleau-Ponty (Spurling, 1977) and, especially, Alfred Schutz (1967, 1970) that there has been a greater concern with combining phenomenological philosophy or psychology with the social sciences. Schutz's work can be interpreted as supporting the priority of the subjective and of the primacy of distinctive worldviews. Besides Schutz's interest in the work of Weber (Wagner, 1970), as Frank (1979, 1980) has noted, Schutz's influence can be clearly found in modern ethnomethodology, such as the work of Goffman (1961, 1963) that has included classic studies of institutional environments and social identities.

In a related but distinctive vein, a focus on the constitution of experience has been the object of scrutiny from cultural anthropology and may be referred to as "the anthropology of experience" (Turner & Bruner, 1986). While here we may trace several discrete contributing bodies of work, we should mention the subfields of psychological and symbolic anthropology as especially germane. In particular, the work of Hallowell (1955b) on "culture and experience" and on "the culturally constituted behavioral environment" helped outline and highlight the distinctive nature of time, space, and person axiomatically characterizing different cultures (Hallowell, 1955a, 1955c, 1955). In a sense, the cultural notion of worldview—the distinctive perceptual and cognitive understandings associated with each cultural system of meaning—may be thought of as the cultural analog to the life world of the individual. From the perspective of cultural anthropology, four additional experiential and methodological perspectives are critical to understanding this perspective.

The first concerns the use of life histories in anthropological research. The life history, widely used in the social sciences, represents an important method and research product (Crapanzano, 1985; Langness & Frank, 1981; Shostak, 1981; Watson & Watson-Franke, 1985). To be sure, collection of life history materials is salient in the phenomenological study of later life and of person-environment interaction. As Frank has noted (1980; Frank & Vanderburgh, 1986), the life history phenomenologically represents a collaboration for meaning making between informant and researcher. One important aspect of life history work is its inherent subjectivity; life history work may be characterized as a form of person-centered ethnography or writing about cultural life from the perspective of subjectivities. Related to a general ethnographic concern with the life history is a complementary, yet more gerontological, interest in life review and the life span or life course perspective, a point of view obviously central to the study of later life (Fry, 1990; Fry & Keith, 1982; Kaufman, 1981, 1986). As we will discuss below, the subjective interpretation and construal of the life course is an important aspect of the phenomenological or experiential accounting of home environments in later life.

A second stream in the anthropology of experience concerns meaning and the acts of cultural and personal interpretation (Geertz, 1973, 1984). In a sense, this represents the analog in cultural studies of the philosophical phenomenological concern with intuition and the perception of essences. Many anthropologists would argue that intuitive essentialism, if it does exist, exists only with respect to the cultural or the behavioral environment as it is outlined culturally or in the context of a distinctive political economy. For example, cultural differences in notions of time, space, and person suggest that while there may be some identifiable domains of human nature shared by all of the species, in fact there is little in the way of personally experienced essentialism. Anthropologists would likely argue that "objects" in a phenomenological field do not have perceptible essences but rather are afforded meaning by the culture into which they are meaningfully embedded. Following the work of Geertz and others from the symbolic anthropology perspective, many anthropologists would argue that people live in worlds of meaning and that interpretation is the most human of acts. We would argue, too, and do below, that meaning must be construed along two domains, namely, what is shared (collective or cultural meaning) and what is personal (or meaning ascribed with reference to prior personal experience and acts of interpretation). It should be obvious that both of these domains are salient for senior adults and their environmental relations. The ways in which experience is *experienced*, as it were, makes continual reference to these two domains.

Third, and again related to the above concern, is an interest in the role of ritual and its spatial aspects in community life. From Durkheim on, a central problem in anthropology has been the relationship of ritual behavior to subjective experience. An obvious example is how ritual might lead to the internalization of values and behaviors of the group. A considerable body of work has explored the relationship of ritual, collective action, and subjectivity (Myerhoff, 1978; Turner, 1967, 1969). While American life contains much in the way of collective behavior, here problems of ritual and subjectivity face a strong emphasis on individualism and individual efficacy and mastery and the deemphasis of collective life (in the 1980s, at least). Thus, experientially, this perspective suggests, for the study of an understanding of the environment in later life, an interest in personal and home-based ritual.

Fourth and last is a continuing concern with social action, behavior, or practice. At first glance, this may seem at odds with the notion of experience, which is often perceived as a primary cognitive process (it is not). However, methodologically and phenomenologically, a concern with experience must be undertaken with an added concern for what people actually do: the constitution of their own categories, the meaningful interpretation of behaviors and actions, and the relation of these to aspects of social value and the merit ascribed generally to such behaviors and actions. For example, systems of significance built around the accomplishment of some daily routines or chores or the maintenance of an independent home, while perhaps developing in a larger social context that devalues elders, may, because of the concomitant experience of a failing body or decreased social value, be seen as especially valuable or satisfying by a senior adult. Thus, theoretical approaches subsuming issues of praxis are germane here (Bourdieu, 1978; Ortner, 1984).

POINTS RELATED TO THEORY

These two overarching perspectives, the philosophical phenomenological and the cultural experiential, are useful in studies of aging and the environment. One focus that might be seen as unifying these two general approaches is a concern with the experience of *home*. Indeed, the difference between the insider's (the phenomenological or experiential) perspective and that of the outsider is perhaps best illustrated by the meaning-content difference between the words *housing* and *home* (Saegert, 1985). *Housing* is general, generic, typological; *home* is intimate, meaningful, and personalized. The focus on home negotiates a concern both with housing and any number of objective features that may contribute to satisfaction and with home as an experienced place with subjective meaning. This interest in home as an experiential phenomenon has been taken up by many scholars (Bachelard, 1969; Bollnow, 1967; Boschetti, 1984; Buttimer, 1980; Dovey, 1978, 1985; Eliade, 1961; Hayward, 1975; Loyd, 1981; Porteous, 1976; Rakoff, 1977; Rapoport, 1985; Relph, 1976; Rowles, 1978, 1980, 1981, 1983a, 1983b, 1983c, 1984, 1987), as have the experiential aspects of territory (Tuan, 1974, 1977; cf. Taylor & Brower, 1985).

Second, this body of work and the general experiential approach it represents may be seen as existing either in opposition or as complementary to the majority of work undertaken in the subfield of environment and aging (e.g., see Altman, Rapoport, & Wohlwill, 1980; Carp & Carp, 1984; Lawton, Altman, & Wohlwill, 1984; Lawton & Nahemow, 1973; Lawton, Windley, & Byerts, 1982; Moos & Lemke, 1984). While it is easy to overgeneralize, by and large this mainstream subfield can be characterized in the following terms. It has been generally concerned with the nature and theoretical underpinnings for managed or supportive environments (although cf. Golant, 1984). In addition, it is largely concerned with measurable characteristics of person-environment (P-E) interaction and in particular with domains of *personal competence* and *environmental press*, taking a rather objective view of these. And finally, the object of study in this field is the human organism, and this subfield tends to view the relationship of organism and environment as unmediated by social or cultural constructs or meanings; it is not much interested in social or cultural embeddedness or context nor in personal experience or meaning (cf. Rapoport, 1982a).

To a great extent, this objectivist preoccupation can be explained and justified by the context in which most environmental and aging studies exist, namely, that of health, health-care issues, and the often diminishing physical health resources of elders.

Indeed, as Eckert and Murray (1984), Rowles (1987), and others have done, types of housing (''residential options'') for the elderly can be graphed on a continuum that represents a range of increasing levels of support for states of being from maximal physical dependence to maximal physical independence. Thus, representing maximal independence in such schemes is community-based housing such as single-family residents, apartment blocks, independent planned housing, and retirement communities with few supportive services. A midrange includes a variety of congregate supportive alternatives that are available, ranging from the relatively independent with few supports to more intensive personal care or assisted living homes. Finally, there are highly supportive medically oriented environments, including continuing care retirement communities, nursing homes, and other long-term care environments, for those exhibiting the greatest dependencies (Rowles, 1987). While these alternatives calibrate their distinctions on the basis of physical health and a bodily based definition of independence or dependency, there is little accounting with how independence or dependency might be defined socioculturally, psychologically, experientially, or in the context of the life course associations of person and place. To be sure, independence is a key cultural construct in American culture (Clark, 1972; Kaufman, 1986), but it is one that is only partially based on health status and also derives meaning from analogies to psychological control or mastery and cultural notions of social agency and autonomy.

While types of residences can be graded in terms of their environmental physical affordances, as in the above scheme, the lack of attention to the coordinate social, historical, and experiential aspects of dependence and independence is unfortunate. A listing of such ''residential options'' for the elderly is a false representation in that not all elderly have the same access to these forms of environment since many are too costly for all but the wealthiest elders.

Further, there is neglect of the ongoing and often supportive relationship that senior adults may have with their home environments. Here we may distinguish several components. Despite the image that most or many elders live in nursing homes or move to the Sunbelt upon retirement, neither impression is true, and in fact, most elders continue to live where they have always lived, both in the sense of community and neighborhood as well as dwelling. Known as *aging in place*, this phenomenon beckons an understanding of the evolving experience of home and the continuing relationship of person to place, which is only beginning (Guteman & Blackie, 1986; Myers, 1982; Pollak, 1985; Tilson, 1990).

Thus it is that the image or model of the person in phenomenologically based P-E relations is distinctive, axiomatically embodying a constructivist and socially embedded perspective. Increasingly, literature on aging and the environment has employed a proactive or transactional perspective and views the older person as both the environmental initiator and responder (Lawton, 1980a). Related traditions, for example, place attachment and habituation, serve as complements to experiential approaches to the environment.

Place attachment may be, and has been, used as a proxy for studies of the experiential perspective, in that attachment to place concerns the experienced emotional binding of person and place. However, in the view developed in this chapter, attachment to place per se may be seen as one relatively minor aspect of the totality of the phenomenology of housing. The phenomenology of housing and place is best understood, we feel, with reference to the symbolic and experiential perspectives described above. "Place attachment" is a part of the experience of place. Place attachment may be thought of as "a set of feelings about a geographic location that emotionally binds a person to place as a function of its role as a setting for experience" (Rubinstein & Parmelee, 1992); it does not subsume the totality of that relationship. Rather, as we will discuss below, attachment to place is a gloss on a more complex set of issues involving the life course, the body, and the cultural ordering of the home.

For senior adults and others, it is necessary to distinguish the realm of present-day places from the realm of past places in a way analogous to the experiential distinction between present-day life and past life "chapters." Several points are notable here. The remembered environment needs to be distinguished from the current environment, and both from significant present-day "away places" (Rowles, 1978) that themselves represent an active, current-day domain of "geographical fantasy." Second, while space is any territory, place has an assigned and personal meaning, through time spent in or with it, through the processes of association, appropriation, or personalization. Concerning past significant places, there may be a conflation of time and space so that attachment to a special place may also be attachment to a special time. However, again, it is incorrect to equate attachment to the *totality* of spatial or geographic experience. Defining a place does not automatically lead to attachment to it, nor does residing there automatically lead to having memories of it. Attachment may subsume a variety of discrete components. And finally, place attachment is not a fixed state but a process (Rubinstein & Parmelee, 1992).

Additionally, from the experiential or phenomenological perspective, the subject matter of habituation theory, the routinization of behaviors and the over-adaptation to routines—such as those that occur in the home—would not necessarily be regarded as mental stagnation or fatigue (Kastenbaum, 1981; Norris-Baker & Scheidt, 1989) from the perspective taken here. Suggestions that should we want to understand person-environment relations in later life, we must "try to budge the one and see what happens to the other" (Norris-Baker & Scheidt, 1989, p. 255; comma omitted) may be most appropriate for institutional and other possibly "fixed-stimulus" environments. But we know little about the stimulus affordances of community home environments, in which affordances may be emotional or cognitive rather than tangible, in part because for many so much past life experience has been put into the home environment by the resident and is periodically "reflected back" to her (Rubinstein, 1987). While habituation may be defined as the "decline of the organism's state of attention with prolonged exposure to the same stimulus" (Norris-Baker & Scheidt, 1989, p. 242), we know little about the phenomenology of home habituation (ritualization) or how routines or personal rituals are experienced. However, as has been suggested, there may be experiential manipulations of time and space, so that long-inhabited home environments are experienced as stimulus or symbol rich (Rowles, 1978; Rubinstein, Kilbride, & Nagy, 1992; Williams, 1988), rather than boring, understimulating, or impoverished.

A less problematic, but still cautionary, relationship is acknowledged with such mainstream, objectivist notions as environmental quality and environmental satisfaction, as objectively measured (Lawton, 1980b; Weideman & Anderson, 1985). Certainly, it is important for many purposes to have an objective environmental fix on such notions as quality and satisfactions; this is indisputable. We merely point out the irreducibly varied, rich, and multiple factors, particularly those derived from the idiosyncratic events of the life course as individually experienced, that may enter into objectivist categories underlying satisfaction (e.g., "personal factors," "long-term occupation," or "strong sense of attachment"). We must also acknowledge that too heavy a reliance on the subjectivist perspective can be used by some as an excuse for the continuation of objectively decrepit circumstances. As has often been noted, the housing stock inhabited by elders is often itself older and of objectively poorer quality than that of other age groups. Understanding the subjective evaluation or interpretation of housing can itself only be embedded in these larger social circumstances and the larger task of social knowing.

METHODOLOGICAL CONSIDERATIONS

Social science methods used to explore the notions described and outlined above are largely qualitative and are in most part dictated by the environmental level under investigation (objects in the home, home, around the home, institution, neighborhood, or community) and the overall topical focus (e.g., personal meaning, transactions, social support, the life course). There has been no explicit or comprehensive treatment of experiential or phenomenological research methods in environment and aging, but such a work would surely be timely (see Lawrence, 1985). Qualitative methods in old age research are increasingly utilized, and there is a body of descriptive literature on them (Fry & Keith, 1986; Reinharz & Rowles, 1988; Rubinstein, 1992; Thomas, 1989). Most experience-centered environment and aging literature includes careful descriptions of methods employed; most are either ethnographic or driven by analysis of a single or small set of semistructured or open-ended items but are interpretive in nature.

It is important to note that what is described from the experiential or phenomenological perspective is often not pure experience but rather immediately interpreted experience. That is, as people living in cultural and social context, we are provided with a system that *orients* the interpretation of experience. It is difficult for an experience to be independent of its meaning context, although people struggle with the process of interpretation, and meaning may often be ambiguous, contested, or personalized. Thus it is that pure experience is shaped by categorization and interpretation. Consider, for example, the request we might make of an older informant to describe the meaning of her home or of personal objects within her home. This cannot really be done without the larger context of the life course or a life story for explanatory grounding. The life story itself is an interpretation of experience: It is not the actual experience but the telling of experience through the processes of narration, editing, and condensing as well as the utilization of the appropriate cultural formats for the narration of such a life story (Luborsky, 1990).

A CASE EXAMPLE

The above theoretical and methodological discussion can be illustrated with reference to an example that will also be utilized for further analysis. The case is condensed from a much longer description (Rubinstein, Kilbride, & Nagy, 1992), which itself is condensed from a much longer set of interview transcripts.

Mrs. Cohen

Mrs. Cohen is an 83-year-old widow with several health problems who inhabits a small row house in a decaying Philadelphia neighborhood. She has no children. She came from a Protestant background and described a generally happy, but lonely, childhood. Mrs. Cohen's first marriage was subsumed by her narration of that early period of her life. She said of her first husband, "He was a friend from that time." The pace of her life slowed after her first marriage. Jobs and apartments began to last longer. Her home is her current residence, the place she shared with her second husband for nearly 50 years.

She noted that when she and her husband first moved to their home, some 40 years ago, she did not immediately feel comfortable, but gradually she began to feel more at home as the years went on. Mrs. Cohen worked for the first 6 years of this marriage until health problems forced her to stop. The first few years of their marriage Etta and Fred lived in two rooms of his family's home, but that arrangement became tense. "And then Fred saw this house up here, and he liked it. And, he decided that we should move.

"Fred started fixing the new home up. We changed [things], we took doors off there and put arches. And, we painted. We put tile floors. We made improvements. It was no drastic change in the house. Except that we made it more comfortable. . . . I didn't care for it here [at first], and then when I got to know the people . . . I talked to the different neighbors, then I started to like it.''

She now evaluated her present home in these terms: "This place is worth . . . just about everything I have. First of all, my husband's lifeblood was put into this house. He . . . painted walls, he tore out partitions, he put arches in. And he always kept everything nice. He would turn over in his grave, as dead as he is, he would turn over in his grave if he could see what is going on in the neighborhood.

"This house means an awful lot to me. It's the best place for my morale, but definitely not the best place for my whole body. The trouble I have physically is not going to improve with dampness, like [I have] in here. . . . That isn't helping my condition any, I know that.''

She added, "I'm very comfortable here. It has always, no matter when I have come back. Sometimes in the winter time I would be sitting out at the table, I sit there in the chair next to the refrigerator. And, I would look in here and the soft lights were on, in winter time you know, and I had my heavy drapes up. I have like gold color drapes that go up there in the winter time. And, the light there, and little sparkly things around that I had. I used to sit out in the kitchen and I'd look in, 'Oh, that room looks pretty.' The gold drapes did make a big difference. I always had my cover on the davenport. I used to say, 'Gee, I've got a pretty little home.' '' She had lived in this space for 40 years, 20 with Fred and then 20 alone after he died. Although she tried, she had a hard time imagining living anywhere else; this place, she said, was her life. When we listen to Mrs. Cohen discuss her past and her present-day life it is hard to tell where, or even if, she and her home were separated. So much of her life had occurred in that place.

"Fred was sick the last 3 or 4 years that he lived. He was sick without knowing why, he was a big man, and he kept getting thinner and thinner and thinner. And then his feet got to the point where he couldn't walk any more, then he went to the doctor. That's what they found diabetes, so from then on in he worked, but then he would fall asleep. . . . He was endangering himself. They told him they couldn't use him any more, and he came home a broken man.'' His health declined, and he was falling frequently and increasingly disoriented. Mrs. Cohen remembers this period with sadness.

By the time Fred died, the neighborhood had begun to change, but by then, her 20 years there had engendered a complex relationship with the neighborhood, the house, and the experiences she'd had. And she lacked the finances even if she had been willing to move. So Mrs. Cohen stayed.

She said:

"Being alone in this home has never bothered me that much. Now, there are two thoughts on that. One is loneliness, the missing of other people around you. And, being alone that's different, different altogether. Now, being alone has never bothered me because I have been alone all my life. Loneliness is another thing. But being alone, the fact that I had to live here alone did not bother me. But I did not know how long I would feel Fred's presence, you know what I mean. Some people can't live in a place after their loved ones are gone. If they are by themselves they can't live that way.

"I can keep myself. All my life I played alone. I was alone with everybody. . . . So I was inside of me. It's a heck of a way to explain something but. Often times people say, 'I don't see how you stay here by yourself.' I'll be more alone where I move to than I would ever be here. But as far as being lonely for people, I am not. I enjoy having someone come in, if someone would come in and sit down, we'd talk. I like to hear about what is going on in the outside world."

In recent years, she has faced the challenge of designing and managing, in her home space, a life that enables her to live with the limitations of health and age. Afflicted by arthritis, she has limited mobility, making walking, reaching, bending, sitting, and even sleeping uncomfortable, if not painful. She notes:

"My age is against me. You have got to realize that after a certain age, you are not as active and can't be as active, especially crippled with arthritis as I am. You see how I have to walk. Now, I can do without this cane in the house. I don't do it, but I can. I can't straighten up. When I'm sitting in a chair, no one would know there was anything wrong with me. Then I get up and start to walk all bent over, because right here at the base of my spine I have arthritis, then it runs into the hip, especially my right one. . . . I can move my legs while I am here . . . but, when I go to get up on my feet that's a different story. . . . There are days when I don't want to get out of bed. The mornings are not without tears.

"I don't know how I got to be 83 almost, but somewhere along the line I grew up. I had never thought of myself as an old person until [lately]. Then I had realized that age has an awful lot to do with your ailments and your attitude. I used to see elderly people; all I can remember about elderly people is that they complained that they were so nervous or they couldn't do this or they couldn't do that. And, I used to say, 'If they wanted to do it they could do it.' Well, I find *they* can't. No matter how much I want to do some things, I can't. I try to make it as convenient for myself as I can. So that the things that are the hardest for me to do, I leave until the very last minute. . . . And if I have any energy left, I dust. . . . The changes came gradually. It didn't happen over night. It took a long time for these legs to get to the point that I had to give things up."

She gradually changed her routine in order to accommodate changes in health. She said, "About a year and a half ago I could still walk down here to the Avenue and get on the bus and get off at Cole Street, that was where the doctor was and the grocery and all, and since they delivered the groceries, I didn't have to carry anything home. They would bring it. Then I'd get back on the bus, which was right outside of the store. But, after that, I began to get to the point where, by waiting the 20 or 25 minutes that I had to. . . . They did have at one time have a place where you could sit and wait, but the kids tore all the benches up. So there was no place to sit, and I had to stand.''

More and more simple home maintenance tasks took on the nature of a major performance. For example, she described in considerable detail an elaborate and rather consciously constructed procedure for doing her laundry. But while she has managed, even with impairments, in her home, the dramatic changes in her neighborhood have also affected her, most severely the general deterioration of the housing stock. Many homes in the area were built improperly, over inadequate landfill, and eventually they began to shift, sink, and collapse. In the late 1980s the city informed the residents that, due to such poor conditions, they would have to relocate. While some residents did so immediately, it took longer for others. The emigration from the neighborhood quickened the process of deterioration, as homes were left vacant and became subject to fire, vandalism, and occupation by squatters, homeless, and drug dealers. Mrs. Cohen was still in her home, one of the last residents on her block. The majority of the homes were vacant, boarded up, and vandalized, and some were set afire and remained only as shells. Others were vacated, occupied by drug users and the homeless, and stripped of fixtures, which were sold for cash.

While her reaction to these changes was complex, one perception she had is important to describe here. Noting that her friends wondered how she could stay in her neighborhood with abandoned and burned-out houses, she added, ''I have news for you. *I don't see those houses across the street.* In my mind's eye those are the houses that I've seen for 40 years, and that's the way I look at them. I remember the people that used to live there. I remember how it used to be in the summer time, and all like that. And, I'm sad about it because the death of a street is as serious as the death of a person. . . . There are . . . still people who are grieving inside for their homes the same as I grieved, and am still grieving for it. Because if they could pick this house up and move it somewhere and sit it on another lot, I would rather have that.''

Even in this relatively brief account summarizing what one articulate informant had to say about her relationship with her home and neighborhood, we are able to see the richness of a P-E relationship in the experiential field. Some factors that this informant mentioned and that appear to be meaningful to her in the way that she experiences and perceives her environment include the following. She listed life course dimensions, including her married life and her early life solitude, as grounding her experience and sense of home. She evaluated her home in terms of the needs and states of her body and her health: She espoused a rather elaborate, praxis-based theory of home task management. She discussed personal objects and arrays of objects—the effects made by her draperies, for example, in terms of sensuousness. The nature of her attachment to place was multilayered, recognizing both her love of home, the reality of neighborhood change, and the attitudes of her friends to her attachment. Finally, she recognized and acknowledged the subjective nature of her perceptions; remarkably, she noted, while acknowledging the profound changes that had occurred, she still saw the neighborhood as it had been as well. In sum, experientially, her relationship with her neighborhood was complex and rich.

SELF AND SOCIETY IN ENVIRONMENTAL PHENOMENOLOGY

We can discuss such relationships in the context of a complementary set of theoretical notions. Culture and experience-based investigations of the relationship between person and the environment must consider two sorts of linkages—those between person and place and those between self and society.

There is wide evidence that house form, structure, or organization obeys or is responsive to culturally distinctive principles of spatial organization (Altman & Chemers, 1980; Bourdieu, 1990; J. Duncan, 1981; Hardie, 1985; Loyd, 1981; Pratt, 1981; Rapoport, 1969, 1981, 1982b). Similarly, in American society at least, it is also clear that the home is the symbol of the self (Cooper, 1976; Kron, 1983). In some sense, as has often been noted, the home negotiates the relationship between self and society, between individuality and communality (Agnew, 1981; N. Duncan, 1981; Rakoff, 1977). The home has both an inward and an outward face. Rubinstein and Parmelee (1992) have suggested that the dichotomy between self and society is central to understanding person-environment relations in later life. They have elaborated a theoretical model that incorporates a distinction between personal (individual) environmental meaning and collective (cultural) environmental meaning, over domains of geographic behavior (space versus place), identity (life course versus life experiences), and interdependence (roles versus relationships).

Experiential aspects of relocation are underexamined but clearly fall under the effects of an overall concern with culture and social structure, since, at the very least, any relocation involves both cultural and personal meaning as well as a number of ritual events, such as integration into a new community. Again, Steinfeld (1981) has reviewed many issues here, and others are discussed by Hartwigsen (1987), Rowles (1983a), and others.

In addition, there is a concomitant relationship between the person and the home itself, albeit one that is embedded in this greater dichotomy between self and society. Yet this relationship is distinctive in that it can be a relationship that is largely reflective only of the self, for example, in emphasizing the role of home for elders as an environment that contrasts the self-as-is with the self-as-was, among other possibilities. Further, the relationship of person to home may, in part, be emotional or sensual, in the sense of love or sadness or loyalty or beauty, as described by Mrs. Cohen. And, in part, this relationship can also be distinctive from that between person and society per se, encompassing the relationship between person and the home as an object in relationship. But this is only part of the story; in fact, the relationship can be negotiated on other terms, some of which we will describe below.

Viewing Society

Phenomenologically, from the perspective of a house or home, society can be conceived in several ways, most significantly as an undifferentiated "the world out there" and in a related fashion as experientially segmented (cf. J. Duncan, 1985). Thus, there have been studies of the relationship of the elderly person to such environmental zones as objects or possessions within the home (Kalymun, 1983; Redfoot & Back, 1988; Rubinstein, 1987; Sherman & Newman, 1977); the surveillance zone—the world under convenient view of the home (Rowles, 1981); the street or block (Rose, 1987 Williams, 1988); the neighborhood or community; and faraway places experienced vicariously (Rowles, 1978). Similarly, in a cross-cultural context, there has been an examination of the conceptual relationship between house form and organization and societal or cosmic organization. The narrative of Mrs. Cohen, a frail and impaired older person living alone in a decrepit neighborhood, strongly suggests the experiential domains of "at home" and "away from home." For her, the realm of home is a safe haven, desirable, suffused with feeling, and segmentally manageable; the world outside is troubled and increasingly difficult to manage.

Viewing the Self

Culture- and experience-based studies of the person-environment nexus have relied on or emphasized a variety of conceptualizations of the self, most often those that emphasize organismic development issues or those that emphasize individual biography or personal interpretation of the life course (Starr, 1983).

Developmentally, Rochberg-Halton (1984) has examined the relationship of the person to significant personal possessions, these usually a part of the home environmental field. Largely critical of subjectivism, but reliant on individual testimony and interpretation, he views the environment as a "socializing sign-complex" and the relationship of the person with personal possessions or objects in and around the home as a form of developmental cultivation of the self (Csikszentmihalyi & Rochberg-Halton, 1981); material possessions are signs of the self, in his view. His work also demonstrates a shift in significant objects over the life course from those of action to those of contemplation or reflection.

In a related way, Proshansky, Fabian, and Kaminoff (1983) suggest that "the development of self-identity is not restricted to making distinctions between oneself and significant others, but extends with no less importance to objects and things" (p. 57) and that the subjective sense of self is discovered not merely in a person's relationship to other people but also with reference to those environmental settings in which daily life occurs. They define this aspect of the self as place-identity.

From a more biographical and interpretive perspective, Rowles (1983c) has argued that attachment to place on the part of senior adults can be thought of as consisting of three related types of "insideness": physical, social, and autobiographical. He particularly emphasizes the role of autobiographic insideness in fostering a sense of attachment to a place, or to a community, and in fostering a *located* sense of personal identity. Similarly, Rubinstein (1990) has described the differential relationship of key, thematically salient elements of personal identity to specific environmental locations or collections. Here, through an emphasis on the biographical perspective, the focus was on the current interpretation of past life events and current activities and the degree to which these might or might not have meaningful environmental correlates. However, Rubinstein found no necessary correlates between personal themes of older informants and their environmental representation.

The example of Mrs. Cohen strongly illustrates the salience of the biographical perspective for the understanding of the relationship of the older person to environmental meanings and affect. For example, the meaning of her home could only be narrated or explained to the interviewer in the context of the life course events and decisions she had made: the relative isolation she felt as a child; her marital and work history; her home as a solution to relational problems; the "golden age" of her life together with her beloved husband; as well as neighborhood and societal changes and her experience of what it means to be old personally and socially. Further, an additional layer of meaning has now been added that refers to her health status and the physical tasks necessary for continued independence.

Viewing Experiential Links between Person and Home

There are several ways of approaching the various processes that link person to place. In sum, these may be grouped as psychosocial and (auto)biographic (Rowles, 1983c; Rubinstein, 1989), temporal-processual (the environment through time; Werner, Altman, & Oxley, 1985), or spatial-processual (moves and residence transitions; Rowles, 1983c, 1987; Saile, 1985; Shumaker & Conti, 1985).

Thus, some experiential literature on the relationship of older person to place may be seen as reflecting this relationship from a temporal (time to time) or a spatial (space to space or "being left behind") perspective. Work in these areas appears to be largely recent, underdeveloped, and potentially significant. Certainly, there is a large literature from the mainstream perspective on residential moves by elders either in community context or to a long-term care facility, but unfortunately there is little from an experiential perspective (although cf. Redfoot, 1987). There is, however, a richer theoretical literature from the biographical and psychosocial perspectives.

The example of Mrs. Cohen speaks to many of the properties of the psychosocially based link between person and place. Rubinstein (1989) has distinguished psychosocial linking processes that are based in (1) the domestic order as socioculturally based; (2) the life course; and (3) bodily experiences. Viewed from this perspective, attachment is seen as conceptually disaggregated into several experiential components. The example of Mrs. Cohen shows most clearly how the home is imbued with meaning by reference to life course events and personal predilection. In later life, environmental meaning can be harvested with reference to prior life course events. Two aspects are suggestive in this context. Mrs. Cohen made reference to the pleasure she had from the array of colors and light in her living room; this represents a rather low level of psychological involvement or personalization. In contrast is her startling statement that she still sees the decrepit homes in her decaying neighborhood as they appeared years ago, despite acknowledging the poor objective environmental circumstances. These are separable components of attachment. Rubinstein has distinguished four distinctive, but increasingly intensifying, aspects of person-environment linkage based on the life course as an object of environmental meaning. Seeing the local environment in a way radically different from the way it really is (although acknowledging those "objective" circumstances) represents an extreme degree of intensification of the personal and of the life course experience in the environment and, as such, represents a form of environmental embodiment, or the subjective merging of environment and self that Rubinstein (1989) suggests is active for certain elders.

Further, an additional layer of meaning has been built atop life course meaning by reference to changes in bodily abilities. Mrs. Cohen has engaged in a process of environmental centralization, reducing the lived space of her home and the frequency of her forays into difficult spaces, such as the basement, and increasingly experiencing these moments consciously and as the object of careful scrutiny. We might hypothesize increasing reflection or reflective self-monitoring as a correlate of environmental centralization, controlling for cognitive abilities. Further, we might hypothesize an increased "hardening" or simplification of personal themes accompanying environmental centralization. These are topics for further exploration.

NOTE

Research by the author discussed in this chapter was supported by the National Institute of Aging "The Meaning and Function of Home for the Elderly"; the Commonwealth Fund "The Personal Surrounds of Frail Elders Living Alone," and the Retirement Research Foundation "Aging in Place: Older Persons' Assessment of Urban Neighborhood Resources." I am grateful to these organizations for their support of my research.

I would also like to thank the following for feedback on and input into the various papers of which I am an author or coauthor cited in this chapter: M. Powell Lawton, Pat Parmelee, Mark Luborsky, Maria Cattell, Janet Kilbride, and Sharon Nagy. Sharon Nagy did the interviews with, and wrote the original case account of, "Mrs. Cohen." This is a pseudonym, and other details of this case have been disguised to protect anonymity. I am grateful to Don Redfoot, Graham Rowles, and Edward Steinfeld, who have shared papers with me, and to Dr. Steinfeld for a discussion of some of the issues in this chapter.

REFERENCES

Agnew, J. (1981). Home ownership and identity in capitalist societies. In J. Duncan (Ed.), *Housing and identity: Cross-cultural perspectives* (pp. 60–97). London: Croom Helm.

Altman, I., & Chemers, M. (1980). *Culture and environment*. Monterey, CA: Brooks/Cole.

Altman, I., Rapoport, A., & Wohlwill, J. (1980). *Human behavior and the environment: Advances in theory and research: Vol. 4, Environment and culture*. New York: Plenum.

Bachelard, G. (1969). *The poetics of space*. Boston: Beacon.

Bauman, Z. (1978). *Hermeneutics and social science: Approaches to understanding*. London: Hutchinson.

Bollnow, O. (1967). Lived space. In N. Lawrence & D. O. O'Connor (Eds.), *Readings in existential phenomenology* (pp. 178–186). Englewood Cliffs, NJ: Prentice-Hall.

Boschetti, M. A. (1984). *The older person's emotional attachment to the physical environment of the residential setting*. Unpublished doctoral dissertation, University of Michigan.

Bourdieu, P. (1978). *An outline of a theory of practice*. Cambridge: Cambridge University Press.

Bourdieu, P. (1990). *The logic of practice*. Stanford, CA: Stanford University Press.

Buttimer, A. (1980). Home, reach and sense of place. In A. Buttimer & D. Seamon (Eds.), *The human experience of space and place* (pp. 133–148). London: Croom Helm.

Carp, F., & Carp, A. (1984). A complementary/congruence model of well-being or mental health for community elderly. In I. Altman, M. P. Lawton, & J. Wohlwill (Eds.), *Elderly people and the environment*. New York: Plenum.

Clark, M. (1972). Cultural values and dependency in later life. In D. Cowgill & L. Holmes (Eds.), *Aging and modernization* (pp. 263–274). New York: Appleton-Century-Crofts.

Cooper, C. (1974). The house as a symbol of home. In J. Lang, C. Burnette, W. Moleski, & D. Vachon (Eds.), *Design for human behavior: Architecture and the behavioral sciences* (pp. 130–146). Stroudsburg, PA: Dowden, Hutchinson and Ross.

Cooper, C. (1976). The house as a symbol of the self. In H. M. Proshansky, W. H. Ittelson, & L. G. Rivlin (Eds.), *Environmental psychology: People and their physical settings* (pp. 435–448). New York: Holt, Rinehart and Winston.

Crapanzano, V. (1985). *Tuhami: Portrait of a Moroccan*. Chicago: University of Chicago Press.

Csikszentmihalyi, M., & Rochberg-Halton, E. (1981). *The meaning of things: Domestic symbols and the self*. Cambridge: Cambridge University Press.

Dovey, K. (1978). Home: An ordering principle in space. *Landscape, 22*, 27–30.

Dovey, K. (1985). The concept of home. In I. Altman & C. Werner (Eds.), *Home environments: Vol. 8, Human behavior and the environment: Advances in theory and research*. New York: Plenum.

Duncan, J. (1981). From container of women to status symbol: The impact of social structure on the meaning of the house. In J. Duncan (Ed.), *Housing and identity: Cross-cultural perspectives* (pp. 36–59). London: Croom Helm.

Duncan, J. (1985). The house as symbol of social structure: Notes on the language of objects among collectivistic groups. In I. Altman & C. Werner (Eds.), *Home environments: Vol. 8, Human behavior and the environment: Advances in theory and research*. New York: Plenum.

Duncan, N. G. (1981). Home ownership and social theory. In J. Duncan (Ed.), *Housing and identity: Cross-cultural perspectives* (pp. 98–134). London: Croom Helm.

Eckert, J. K., & Murray, M. I. (1984). Alternative modes of living for the elderly: A critical review. In I. Altman, M. P. Lawton, & J. F. Wohlwill (Eds.), *Elderly people and the environment*. New York: Plenum.

Eliade, M. (1961). *The sacred and the profane*. New York: Harper and Row.

Frank, G. (1979). Finding the common denominator: A phenomenological critique of life history method. *Ethos, 7*, 68–94.

Frank, G. (1980). Life histories in gerontology: The subjective side to aging. In C. Fry & J. Keith (Eds.), *New methods in old age research: Anthropological alternatives* (pp. 155–176). Chicago: Center for Urban Policy, Loyola University of Chicago.

Frank, G., & Vanderburgh, R. (1986). Cross-cultural use of life history methods in gerontology. In C. Fry & J. Keith (Eds.), *New methods for old age research: Strategies for studying diversity* (pp. 185–212). South Hadley, MA: Bergin and Garvey.

Fry, C. (1990). The life course in context: Implications of comparative research. In R. Rubinstein (Ed.), *Anthropology and aging: Comprehensive reviews* (pp. 129–152). Dordrecht: Kluwer.

Fry, C., & Keith, J. (1982). The life course as a cultural unit. In M. W. Riley, R. D. Abeles, & M. S. Teitelbaum (Eds.), *Aging from birth to death: Sociotemporal perspectives*. Boulder, CO: Westview Press.

Fry, C., & Keith, J. (1986). *New methods for old age research: Strategies for studying diversity* (pp. 51–70). South Hadley, MA: Bergin and Garvey.

Geertz, C. (1973). Thick description: Toward an interpretive theory of culture. In C. Geertz (Ed.), *The interpretation of culture* (pp. 3–32). New York: Basic Books.

Geertz, C. (1984). ''From the native's point of view'': On the nature of anthropological understanding. In R. Shweder & R. A. Levine (Eds.), *Culture theory: Essays on mind, self and emotion* (pp. 123–136). Cambridge: Cambridge University Press.

Goffman, E. (1961). *Asylums: Essays on the social situation of mental patients and other inmates*. Garden City, NY: Doubleday Anchor.

Goffman, E. (1963). *Stigma: Notes on the management of spoiled identity*. Englewood Cliffs, NJ: Prentice-Hall.

Golant, S. (1984). *A place to grow old: The meaning of the environment in old age*. New York: Columbia University Press.

Gurwitsch, A. (1970). Problems of the life-world. In M. Natanson (Ed.), *Phenomenology and social reality* (pp. 185–207). The Hague: Martinus Nijhoff.

Gutman, G., & Blackie, N. (1986). *Aging in place: Adaptations and options for remaining in the community*. Burnaby, BC: Simon Fraser University, Gerontology Research Center.

Hallowell, A. I. (1955a). Cultural factors in spatial orientation. In A. I. Hallowell (Ed.), *Culture and experience* (pp. 184–202). New York: Schocken.

Hallowell, A. I. (Ed.). (1955b). *Culture and experience*. New York: Schocken.

Hallowell, A. I. (1955c). The Ojibwa self in its behavioral environment. In A. I. Hallowell (Ed.), *Culture and experience* (pp. 172–183). New York: Schocken.

Hallowell, A. I. (1955d). The self and its behavioral environment. In A. I. Hallowell (Ed.), *Culture and experience* (pp. 75–111). New York: Schocken.

Hardie, G. J. (1985). Continuity and change in the Tswana'a house and settlement form. In I. Altman & C. Werner (Eds.), *Home environments: Vol. 8, Human behavior and the environment: Advances in theory and research* (pp. 213–236). New York: Plenum.

Hartwigsen, G. (1987). Older widows and the transference of home. *International Journal of Aging and Human Development, 25*, 195–207.

Hayward, D. G. (1975). Home as an environmental and psychological concept. *Landscape, 20*, 2–9.

Heelas, P., & Locke, A. (1981). *Indigenous psychologies: The anthropology of the self*. New York: Academic Press.

Husserl, E. (1931). *Ideas: A general introduction to pure phenomenology* (W. R. B. Gibson, Trans.). New York: Macmillan.

Husserl, E. (1970). *The crisis of European sciences and transcendental phenomenology* (D. Carr, Trans.). Evanston, IL: Northwestern University Press.

Kalymun, M. (1983). Factors influencing elderly women's decisions concerning living room items during relocation. *EDRA: Environmental Design Research Association, 14*, 75–83.

Kastenbaum, R. J. (1981). Habituation as a model of human aging. *International Journal of Aging and Human Development, 12*, 159–170.

Kaufman, S. (1981). Cultural components of identity in old age: A case study. *Ethos, 9*, 51–87.

Kaufman, S. (1986). *The ageless self: Sources of meaning in later life*. Madison: University of Wisconsin Press.

Korosec-Serfaty, P. (1985). Experience and use of the dwelling. In I. Altman & C. Werner (Eds.), *Home environments: Vol. 8, Human behavior and the environment: Advances in theory and research* (pp. 65–86). New York: Plenum.

Kron, J. (1983). *Home-psych: The social psychology of home and decoration*. New York: Clarkson N. Potter.

Langness, L. L., & Frank, G. (1981). *Lives: An anthropological approach to biography*. Novato, CA: Chandler and Sharp.

Lauer, Q. (1965). *Phenomenology: Its genesis and prospect*. New York: Harper and Row.

Lawrence, R. J. (1985). Comparative analyses of homes. In I. Altman & C. Werner (Eds.), *Home environments: Vol. 8, Human behavior and the environment: Advances in theory and research* (pp. 113–132). New York: Plenum.

Lawton, M. P. (1980a). Environmental change: The older person as initiator and responder. In N. Datan & N. Lohmann (Eds.), *Transitions of aging* (pp. 171–194). New York: Academic Press.

Lawton, M. P. (1980b). *Environment and aging*. Monterey, CA: Brooks/Cole.

Lawton, M. P., Altman, I., & Wohlwill, J. F. (1984). Dimensions of environment-behavioral research: Orientation to place, design, process and policy. In I. Altman, M. P. Lawton, & J. F. Wohlwill (Eds.), *Elderly people and the environment*. New York: Plenum.

Lawton, M. P., & Nahemow, L. (1973). Ecology and the aging process. In C. Eisdorfer & M. P. Lawton (Eds.), *Psychology of adult development and aging* (pp. 619–674). Washington, DC: American Psychological Association.

Lawton, M. P., Windley, P. G., & Byerts, T. O. (1982). *Aging and the environment: Theoretical approaches.* New York: Springer.

Loyd, B. (1981). Women, home and status. In J. Duncan (Ed.), *Housing and identity: Cross-cultural perspectives* (pp. 181–197). London: Croom Helm.

Luborsky, M. (1990). Alchemists' visions: Cultural norms in eliciting and analyzing life history narratives. *Journal of Aging Studies, 4,* 17–30.

Marsella, A. J., DeVos, G., & Hsu, F. L. K. (1985). *Culture and self: Asian and western perspectives.* New York: Tavistock.

Merleau-Ponty, M. (1962). *The phenomenology of perception* (C. Smith, Trans.). London: Routledge.

Merleau-Ponty, M. (1970). *Themes from his lectures* (J. O'Neill, Trans.). Evanston, IL: Northwestern University Press.

Moos, R. H., & Lemke, S. (1984). Supportive residential settings for older people. In I. Altman, M. P. Lawton, & J. F. Wohlwill (Eds.), *Elderly people in the environment.* New York: Plenum.

Myerhoff, B. (1978). *Number our days.* New York: Simon and Schuster.

Myers, P. (1982). *Aging in place: Strategies to help the elderly stay in revitalizing neighborhoods.* Washington, DC: Conservation Foundation.

Norris-Baker, C., & Scheidt, R. J. (1989). Habituation theory and environment-aging research: Ennui to joie de vivre? *International Journal of Aging and Human Development, 29,* 241–257.

Ortner, S. (1984). Theory in anthropology since the sixties. *Comparative Studies in Society and History, 25,* 126–166.

Pollak, P. B. (1985). *Aging in place: Five housing alternatives for the elderly.* Monticello, IL: Vance.

Porteous, J. D. (1976). Home: The territorial core. *Geographical review, 66,* 383–390.

Pratt, G. (1981). The house as expression of social worlds. In J. Duncan (Ed.), *Housing and identity: Cross-cultural perspectives* (pp. 135–180). London: Croom Helm.

Proshansky, H., Fabian, A., & Kaminoff, R. (1983). Place-identity: Physical world socialization of the self. *Journal of Environmental Psychology, 3,* 57–83.

Rakoff, R. (1977). Ideology in everyday life: The meaning of the house. *Politics and Society, 7,* 85–104.

Rapoport, A. (1969). *House form and culture.* Englewood Cliffs, NJ: Prentice-Hall.

Rapoport, A. (1981). Identity and environment: A cross-cultural perspective. In J. Duncan (Ed.), *Housing and identity: Cross-cultural perspectives* (pp. 6–35). London: Croom Helm.

Rapoport, A. (1982a). Aging-environment theory: A summary. In M. P. Lawton, P. Windley, & T. Byerts (Eds.), *Aging and the environment: Theoretical approaches* (pp. 132–149). New York: Springer.

Rapoport, A. (1982b). *The meaning of the built environment.* Beverly Hills, CA: Sage.

Rapoport, A. (1985). Thinking about home environments: A conceptual framework. In I. Altman & C. Werner (Eds.), *Home environments: Vol. 8, Human behavior and the environment: Advances in theory and research* (pp. 255–286). New York: Plenum.

Redfoot, D. (1987). "On the separatin' place": Social class and relocation among older women. *Social Forces, 66,* 486–500.

Redfoot, D., & Back, K. W. (1988). The perceptual presence of the life course. *International Journal of Aging and Human Development, 27,* 155–169.

Reinharz, S., & Rowles, G. (1988). *Qualitative gerontology.* New York: Springer.

Relph, E. (1976). *Place and placelessness.* London: Plon.

Rochberg-Halton, E. (1984). Object relations, role models and cultivation of the self. *Environment and Behavior, 16,* 335–368.

Rose, D. (1987). *Black American street life: South Philadelphia, 1969–1971.* Philadelphia: University of Pennsylvania Press.

Rowles, G. D. (1978). *Prisoners of space? Exploring the geographical experience of older people.* Boulder, CO: Westview.

Rowles, G. D. (1980). Growing old "inside": Aging and attachment to place in an Appalachian community. In N. Datan & N. Lohmann (Eds.), *Transitions of aging* (pp. 153–170). New York: Academic Press.

Rowles, G. D. (1981). The surveillance zone as meaningful space for the aged. *Gerontologist, 21,* 304–311.

Rowles, G. D. (1983a). Between worlds: A relocation dilemma for the Appalachian elderly. *International Journal of Aging and Human Development, 17,* 301–312.

Rowles, G. D. (1983b). Geographical dimensions of social support in rural Appalachia. In G. D. Rowles & R. J. Ohta (Eds.), *Aging and milieu: Environmental perspectives on growing old* (pp. 111–130). New York: Academic Press.

Rowles, G. D. (1983c). Place and personal identity in old age: Observations from Appalachia. *Journal of Environmental Psychology, 3,* 299–313.

Rowles, G. D. (1984). Aging in rural environments. In I. Altman, M. P. Lawton, & J. F. Wohlwill (Eds.), *Elderly people and the environment.* New York: Plenum.

Rowles, G. D. (1987). A place to call home. In L. L. Carstensen & B. A. Edelstein (Eds.), *Handbook of clinical gerontology.* New York: Pergamon.

Rubinstein, R. L. (1987). The significance of personal objects to older people. *Journal of Aging Studies, 1,* 226–238.

Rubinstein, R. L. (1989). The home environments of older people: A description of the psychosocial processes linking person to place. *Journal of Gerontology: Social Sciences, 2,* S45–S53.

Rubinstein, R. L. (1990). Personal identity and environmental meaning in later life. *Journal of Aging Studies, 4,* 131–147.

Rubinstein, R. L. (1992). Anthropological methods in gerontological research: Entering the world of meaning. *Journal of Aging Studies, 6,* 57–66.

Rubinstein, R. L., Kilbride, J., & Nagy, S. (1992). *Elders living alone: Frailty and the perception of choice.* Hawthorne, NY: Aldine de Gruyter.

Rubinstein, R. L., & Parmelee, P. (1992). Place attachment among the elderly. In I. Altman & S. Low (Eds.), *Place attachment.* New York: Plenum.

Saegert, S. (1985). The role of housing in the experience of dwelling. In I. Altman & C. Werner (Eds.), *Home environments: Vol. 8, Human behavior and the environment: Advances in theory and research* (pp. 287–310). New York: Plenum.

Saile, D. (1985). The ritual establishment of home. In I. Altman & C. Werner (Eds.), *Home environments: Vol. 8, Human behavior and the environment: Advances in theory and research.* New York: Plenum.

Schutz, A. (1967). *The phenomenology of the social world* (G. Walsh & F. Lehnert, Trans.). Evanston, IL: Northwestern University Press.

Schutz, A. (1970). *Alfred Schutz on phenomenology and social relations.* Chicago: University of Chicago Press.

Sherman, E., & Newman, E. S. (1977). The meaning of cherished personal possessions for the elderly. *International Journal of Aging and Human Development, 8,* 181–192.

Shostak, M. (1981). *Nisa: The life and words of a !Kung woman.* New York: Vintage Books.

Shumaker, S., & Conti, G. (1985). Understanding mobility in America: Conflicts between stability and change. In I. Altman & C. Werner (Eds.), *Home environments: Vol. 8, Human behavior and the environment: Advances in theory and research* (pp. 237–254). New York: Plenum.

Shweder, R., & LeVine, R. (1984). *Culture theory: Essays on mind, self, and emotion.* New York: Cambridge University Press.

Spurling, L. (1977). *Phenomenology and the social world.* London: Routledge and Kegan Paul.

Starr, J. (1983). Toward a social phenomenology of aging: Studying the self process in biographical work. *International Journal of Aging and Human Development, 16,* 255–267.

Steinfeld, E. (1981). The place of old age: The meaning of housing for old people. In J. Duncan (Ed.), *Housing and identity: Cross-cultural perspectives* (pp. 198–246). London: Croom Helm.

Taylor, R., & Brower, S. (1985). Home and near home territories. In I. Altman & C. Werner (Eds.), *Home environments: Vol. 8, Human behavior and the environment: Advances in theory and research* (pp. 183–212). New York: Plenum.

Thomas, L. E. (1989). *Research on adulthood and aging: The human sciences approach.* Albany: SUNY Press.

Tilson, D. (1990). *Aging in place: Supporting the frail elderly in residential environments.* Glenview, IL: Scott, Foresman.

Tuan, Y. (1974). *Topophilia: A study of environmental perception attitudes and values.* Englewood Cliffs, NJ: Prentice-Hall.

Tuan, Y. (1977). *Space and place: The perspective of experience.* Minneapolis: University of Minnesota Press.

Turner, V. W. (1967). *The forest of symbols.* Ithaca, NY: Cornell University Press.

Turner, V. W. (1969). *The ritual process.* Harmondsworth, UK: Penguin.

Turner, V. W., & Bruner, E. M. (1986). *The anthropology of experience.* Urbana: University of Illinois Press.

Wagner, H. (1970). Introduction. *Alfred Schutz on phenomenology and social relations.* Chicago: University of Chicago Press.

Watson, L., & Watson-Franke, M. (1985). *Interpreting life histories: An anthropological inquiry.* New Brunswick, NJ: Rutgers University Press.

Weideman, S., & Anderson, J. (1985). A conceptual framework for residential satisfaction. In I. Altman & C. Werner (Eds.), *Home environments: Vol. 8, Human behavior and the environment: Advances in theory and research* (pp. 153–182). New York: Plenum.

Werner, C., Altman, I., & Oxley, D. (1985). Temporal aspects of home: A transactional perspective. In I. Altman & C. Werner (Eds.), *Home environments: Vol. 8, Human behavior and the environment: Advances in theory and research* (pp. 1–32). New York: Plenum.

Williams, B. (1988). *Upscaling downtown: Stalled gentrification in Washington, DC.* Ithaca, NY: Cornell University Press.

5

The Social Ecological Approach of Rudolf Moos

RICK J. SCHEIDT

Although three fourths of 20 million elderly householders owned their own homes in 1990 (Bureau of the Census, 1995), most of the remaining 5 million resided in some form of alternative housing. This includes planned housing serving the healthy elderly, supportive housing serving the moderately impaired, and housing environments for frail and handicapped individuals (Regnier & Pynoos, 1987). Rates of homeownership decline gradually for those over 65 years, from almost 80 percent for householders between ages 65 and 69 to 62 percent for those in their nineties (Bureau of the Census, 1995). About 10 percent of older individuals reside in "specialized living environments" that share a common mission of providing access to services for unrelated individuals and possess a distinctive layer of social organization not found in traditional community living (Moos & Lemke, 1985, 1994).

The most fruitful integrated model for understanding many determinants of the well-being of older residents of these group living facilities springs from the work of Rudolf Moos and colleagues of the Social Ecology Laboratory at Stanford University. For over two decades, Moos has systematically utilized a "social ecological approach" to assess the personal and environmental factors affecting the adaptation of elderly individuals within these settings. In brief, social ecology is "the multidisciplinary study of the impacts of physical and social environments on human beings. Its primary concern is with the enhancement of human environments to improve the quality of life" (Moos, 1976a, p. 31).

This chapter illustrates the usefulness of this approach for researchers and practitioners interested in housing for elderly populations. The research of Moos and his colleagues bears directly upon environment-behavior theory, as well as interventions designed to improve the quality of life of older residents of sheltered care environments. Discussion here is targeted primarily at readers less familiar with this approach and is divided into three primary sections. First, following an introduction to factors distinguishing this approach, the specific conceptual model guiding the research and the measures operationalizing the environmental domain of the model are described. Second, selected research is used to illustrate its theoretical and practical contributions to a few relevant issues capturing the attention of gerontological housing researchers. These include determinants of housing atmosphere or "social climate"; resident-facility matching; choice, control, and adaptation; as well as those related to improving environmental quality and resident adaptation through systematic intervention and evaluation. Readers seeking more comprehensive reviews of this approach are advised to see Moos's earlier reviews (1984, 1985), as well as his more recent book, *Group Residences for Older Adults* (Moos & Lemke, 1994). Last, I discuss the applicability of the approach for housing theory, research, and practice in more independent living environments.

THE SOCIAL ECOLOGICAL PERSPECTIVE

Environmental Origins

Research on behavioral ecology emerges from a longer, broader recognition by early behavioral theorists that human environments may exert significant influences on behavior (Barker, 1968; Brunswik, 1955; Lewin, 1935; Murray, 1938). Owing to their efforts, as well as those of earlier gerontological researchers (Kleemeier, 1959), the study of the ecology of aging has thrived over the past 35 years. As Lawton (1985) notes, the " 'discovery' of environment by behavioral scientists led to enthusiasm over the possibilities of using gerontological knowledge in designing housing, institutions, and even neighborhoods for older users" (p. 450).

Despite the quick recognition that there are a number of ways to define environments, problems associated with environmental classification still remain (Lawton, 1989, in press). Nonetheless, gerontologists have researched the effects of social environmental influences on older residents in various forms of housing for several years. This is particularly true for planned housing and neighborhoods (Lawton, 1975, 1985).

Interestingly, while Moos's work has had a powerful impact on research in the ecology of aging, the major influences affecting the development of Moos's social ecological perspective arose outside of mainstream gerontology. They emerged "from a clinical perspective rather than from a perspective of social action or of environmental or social psychology. This background leads me to a certain focus on human environments, on how they should be measured, and on the practical implications which follow" (Moos, 1976b, p. 313).

Specifically, Moos notes that person-environment (P-E) research conducted in the 1970s produced results that convinced him that a social ecological perspective was necessary for an adequate understanding of social functioning. Among the most notable were outcomes showing that person X setting interactions accounted for substantial variation among individuals in real-life settings; there was an awareness of an apparent upper limit to the accuracy of behavioral prediction afforded by individual difference and background variables in studies of personnel prediction, violent behavior, and runaway behavior from correctional institutions; psychiatric and correctional program outcome studies showed postinstitutional behavior significantly influenced by the immediate community settings in which people reside; and studies showed that long-term group care settings had significant impacts upon child residents (Moos, 1976b).

Moos has been consistently generous in acknowledging the contribution of psychologists and others to the development of his approach (Insel & Moos, 1974; Moos, 1979; Moos & Lemke, 1994). He is well steeped in the history of thinking regarding human contexts (Moos, 1976a), and his approach attempts to utilize earlier contributions to thinking about environments while redressing specific shortcomings.

Distinguishing Features

There are five distinguishing features of the social ecological approach:

1. Social ecology "attempts to understand the impact of the environment from the perspective of the individual" (Moos, 1976a, p. 28). This goal distinguishes social ecology from the broader study of "human ecology," directing its focus upon individuals as opposed to entire communities or larger human populations (Insel & Moos, 1974). The respect for perceptions of the individual locates the approach paradigmatically within a transactional perspective, where " 'the environment is brought into the person' " (Lawton, 1989). In other respects, which become apparent in its later development, the approach more closely typifies both "organismic" and "interactionist" worldviews (Altman & Rogoff, 1987), particularly in its methodological assumptions (Scheidt, 1992).

2. Social ecology "attempts to synthesize the study of the physical and social environments" where "the concern is with the basic unity of the milieu" (Moos, 1976a, p. 28). Moos believes that physical and social environments exert mutual impact on one another and are inextricably related. That is, research on the objective physical environment, historically within the domain of human ecology, is incomplete without an adequate accounting of social regulatory mechanisms occurring within physical spaces.

3. Social ecology "emphasizes individual adaptation, adjustment, and coping," where "assessments of the environment must precede assessments of the impact of these environments on human functioning" (Moos, 1976a, p. 29). Though the approach emphasizes both human adaptation and environments, greater emphasis is given to environments, specifically to their stressful, limiting, selecting, releasing, and challenging attributes.

4. Social ecology has "a practical applied orientation" aimed at helping individuals "by providing more accurate and complete information about existing environments and environmental choices . . . to enhance constructive change" (Moos, 1976a, p. 31). The specific interventive goal here is to maximize congruence between individual preferences and environmental resources. This value led Moos to focus specifically on older adults whose physical limitations or illnesses may necessitate housing choices that may limit their functioning and personal growth.

5. Social ecology has "an explicit value orientation in that it is concerned with promoting maximally effective human functioning" (Insel & Moos, 1974, p. 180); "it is not simply an approach for science" but "a humanistic approach by which to benefit mankind" (Moos, 1976a, p. 31). The approach attempts to redress what Moos terms "an environmental crisis in human dignity," to increase the amount of control that individuals have over their environments and to provide information to environmental planners, designers, administrators, and policy makers seeking alternatives to the role of "social control agent."

Overall, these features are totally consistent with the defining features and guiding values characterizing thinking and research in the ecology of aging (Scheidt & Windley, 1985), including (a) the holistic focus on the mutual and interdependent relations between individuals, environmental contexts, and behavior (Willems, 1977); (b) the efforts of older individuals to orchestrate congruence between internal and external needs, preferences, and resources; (c) research-guided intervention at both individual and environmental levels to bring this about; and (d) a healthy interdisciplinary eclecticism marked by a tendency for researchers "to borrow concepts, methods, and hypotheses freely, with little sense of preciousness about boundaries between disciplines" (Willems, 1973, p. 207).

The Graying of Social Ecology

After conducting research for several years in other classes of microenvironmental domains (e.g., treatment environments; total institutions; educational environments; community environments), Moos focused his conceptual approach on older individuals in selected specialized living environments. This was inevitable, perhaps, given the values of the approach and the increased needs of a vulnerable segment of older Americans for supportive housing.

In the late 1970s, he targeted three setting categories varying by level of care provided: skilled and intermediate care nursing facilities providing 24-hour professional nursing care, meals, and assistance with tasks of daily living, as well as personal care; residential care facilities providing personal care, and assistance with activities of daily living (ADL) tasks but not nursing care; and congregate apartments offering regular meals but only minimal or occasional health, administrative, and personal care services (Lemke & Moos, 1987). These subgroups have "evolved naturally" in response to society's attempts to respond to the needs of elderly who "are frail, indigent, or otherwise less able to maintain an independent household" (Moos & Lemke, 1985, p. 865).

Moos translated the broad conceptual features of the social ecological approach into a rather specific integrative framework that has been usefully applied in these as well as several other settings (Moos, 1979, 1985; Moos & Lemke, 1994).

The Integrative Framework

Figure 5.1 shows the conceptual model Moos developed to order relations among program resources and outcomes. The influence of objective program characteristics (panel I) and personal factors (panel II) on resident adaptation (panel V) is mediated by both social climate (panel III) and resident's coping responses (panel IV). This model, along with similar earlier versions, comprises the conceptual keystone of Moos's research, guiding the generation of hypotheses, the construction of measures, and comprehensive program evaluations, and serves as an essential framework for organizing research results (Moos & Lemke, 1984b).

Considerable effort has been directed at defining and measuring the objective features (panel I) and the appraised culture (panel III) of the program environment. Objective features include physical and architectural resources, policy and program resources, and aggregate characteristics of residents. Social climate features include specific features defining relationship, personal growth, and system maintenance and change dimensions (Moos & Lemke, 1984b, 1994). In addition to individual sociodemographic characteristics, the personal system is composed of "personal resources such as health status, cognitive and functional ability, and self-esteem" (Moos & Lemke, 1985, p. 868), including personal preferences for specific features of residential facilities (Moos & Lemke, 1994). The environmental (panels I and III) and personal systems affect each other through selection and allocation, as "most environments admit new members selectively, and people usually have some voice in choosing the environments they wish to enter" (Moos & Lemke, 1985 p. 868).

Residents' coping responses and adaptive behaviors (indexed by adjustment, activity level, and use of program services) may affect and be affected by personal and environmental factors. For example, the appraisal of activity level and group cohesion (social climate dimension) in a setting may be affected by personal characteristics such as resident age and functional health or by environmental factors such as availability of special activity areas or perceptual consensus that residents are active and involved with one another. Or, one's use of a coping skill may change either the personal or environmental system, as in the case of socially proactive residents who may experience higher self-esteem (personal system change) or find that complaints bring about changes in the environment (Moos & Lemke, 1985). Adaptive outcomes may influence future adaptation by way of their influence on the personal system or contribute to

Figure 5.1
A Model of the Relationship between Environmental and Personal Factors and Resident Stability and Change

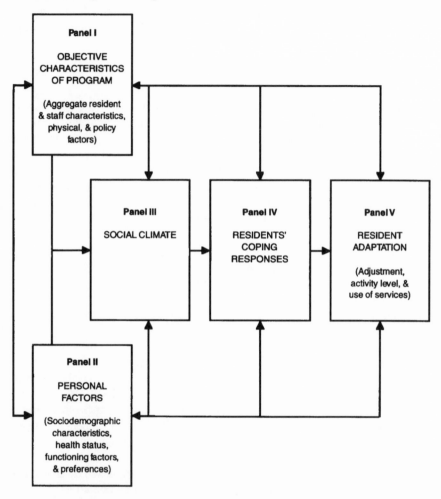

Source: Moos & Lemke, 1994, p. 8. Reprinted with permission.

defining features of the environmental system, for example, where health outcomes contribute to defining the aggregate characteristics of the environment (Moos & Lemke, 1985, p. 868).

Not surprisingly, given the premises of the approach and the historical neglect of the area, Moos focused primary attention on the environmental system. His research on this component alone is arguably the most valuable contribution to date of the social ecological approach. Others have proposed alternative models to describe the impact of person-environment transactions on the adaptive functioning of older individuals in traditional community and supportive housing environments, most notably Carp and Carp (1984), Lawton and Nahemow (1973), and Kahana (1982). (See Lawton in this volume for a consideration of these theories.) However, over the past 20 years, Moos has produced the most complete holistic articulation of environmental components and measures and has investigated in prolific fashion interactions among them, as well as other domains of the integrated framework.

An appreciation for numerous possibilities of ways of conceptualizing environments was gained through explorations of diverse literatures: "In this search I found myself as Alice in Wonderland, fascinated by new areas which I did not fully understand. I found relevant work in the fields of history, geography, meteorology, human ecology, cultural ecology, anthropology, sociology, political science, architecture, urban planning, and so forth'' (Moos, 1976b, p. 316).

The Multiphasic Environmental Assessment Procedure

This theoretical excursion resulted in the formulation of four domains of environmental resource variables and an umbrella procedure—the Multiphasic Environmental Assessment Procedure (MEAP)—for measuring each. These domains are: physical and architectural features, policy and program factors, suprapersonal factors, and social-environmental factors. The domains roughly correspond to the boundaries of the four separate disciplines of architecture and design; sociology and social psychology; housing research on aggregate characteristics of older residents; and social ecology, respectively (Moos & Lemke, 1985).

Dimensions of the procedure were developed using six conceptual and empirical criteria: meaningfulness, applicability, distribution, discrimination, interrelatedness of items, and independence of scales. The initial version of the MEAP was developed using a representative sample of 93 residential settings drawn from five California counties:

> Facilities were identified from directories of licensed skilled nursing, intermediate care, and community care facilities, from telephone directories and from listings of HUD-funded apartments for the elderly. They were selected to represent the range of ownership types, size, and location. Within this sample, three facility subtypes were defined: skilled nursing facilities (SNFs), independent apartments (APTs), and an intermediate category that we have termed residential care facilities (RCs). In order to ensure that facilities were relevant to the study's purposes, three general criteria were set: each facility had to have a minimum of ten residents, these residents had to be predominantly elderly, and each facility had to offer at least a meal plan. (Moos & Lemke, 1984b, p. 165)

A second phase added 169 facilities from geographically representative regions in 20 states, yielding a combined normative group of 262 community facilities (Moos & Lemke, 1994; Timko & Moos, 1991a).

Each of the four dimensions "is conceptually unified by a common functional implication for residents," with items representing "opportunities or environmental resources for a given area of functioning" (Moos & Lemke, 1985, p. 872). Items were constructed to apply to the full range of facilities types and to discriminate among facilities. Overlap between dimensions was minimized by combining dimensions with high intercorrelations (Moos & Lemke, 1984b, p. 166). Measures of each of the four environmental components may be administered separately, or the MEAP may be administered in its entirety. A fifth measure, the Rating Scale, covers evaluative judgments of the facility by outside observers and is not usually discussed as a formal part of the MEAP (Moos, Lemke, & David, 1987). Before discussing the practical and research uses of the MEAP, I offer a brief description of each environmental domain. Readers interested in further information about the conceptual and psychometric features of the MEAP are advised to see Moos and Lemke (1984a, 1996) and the separate publications within each section below.

The Physical and Architectural Features (PAF) Checklist

The PAF was designed to respond to the need for a method to assess the impact of physical and design features of sheltered care environments on the functioning of older residents (Moos & Lemke, 1980). In its current form, the PAF uses 153 items to assess eight distinct physical environmental resources. To assess the ease of accessibility of residents to community services, the Community Accessibility dimension measures the proximity of a facility to these services. Physical Amenities and Social-Recreational Aids assess the presence of physical features that add convenience and comfort. Three dimensions— Prosthetic Aids, Orientational Aids, Safety Features—assess facility features that aid residents in tasks of daily living and in negotiation of the facility environment. Allowance for space for resident and staff functions is assessed by Staff Facilities and Space Availability. Most items are assessed using a yes/no format relying on direct observation.

The Policy and Program Information Form (POLIF)

In response to Moos's belief that assessments of organizational and policy features of these settings are either too comprehensive and qualitative or too narrowly quantitative, the POLIF was constructed to allow "for a quantitative measurement of a facility's policies" and to capture "some of the richness and complexity of the setting" (Lemke & Moos, 1980, p. 96). The information regarding its nine dimensions is gathered from the administrator or a reliable staff member using 130 items. The degree to which behavioral expectations are imposed on residents is measured by two dimensions—Expectations for Functioning and Tolerance for Deviance. The balance between individual freedom and institutional order and stability is assessed by four domains, including the degree to which policies permit residents to select their own patterns of daily routine (Policy Choice); the extent of formal structures allowing residents influence in the facility (Resident Control); clarity of communication regarding policies and programs (Policy Clarity); and amount of privacy for residents (Resident Privacy). Finally, a third set of dimensions taps the extent of Available Health Services, Daily Living Assistance, and Social-Recreational Activities within the facility (Moos & Lemke, 1994; Timko & Moos, 1991a).

The Resident and Staff Information Form (RESIF)

The RESIF was designed to tap six aspects of sheltered care environments that are a function of their residents and staff. It is premised on the belief that the aggregate of members' attributes partly defines group subculture, which, in turn, may influence individual behavior. It is also based on evidence indicating that "settings tend to become homogeneous through selection and social allocation" and that this homogeneity, which may vary across settings, can produce "direct and indirect impacts on the quality of life in a setting" (Lemke & Moos, 1981, p. 234). Information for the RESIF's 69 scored items is drawn from residents' medical records and staff records (Timko & Moos, 1991a).

Staff Resources taps the resources available from staff, including their experience, training, and diversity. Resident Social Resources assesses the current status of residents with respect to demographic variables that facilitate social competence (e.g., marital status, education), while Resident Heterogeneity measures the extent of sociodemographic diversity among residents. Current functioning of residents is assessed using three dimensions: Resident Functional Abilities to perform daily functions and extent of handicapping in performing these; Resident Activity Level, indicating the degree of involvement in self-initiated activities; and Activities in the Community, measuring rate of participation in activities outside of the facility.

The Sheltered Care Environment Scale (SCES)

This novel scale is based on the assumption that "each environment has its own unique personality that gives it unity and coherence" (Lemke & Moos, 1987, p. 20) and that the traits comprising this environmental personality or "social climate" can be readily appraised by tapping members' perceptions of them (Moos et al., 1979). In fact, the SCES is the only component of the MEAP that draws upon residents' perceptions of the facility environment and can be usefully administered to staff as well. Several years of research by Moos and colleagues in other types of settings has yielded evidence of three common, underlying dimensions of social climate: relationship dimensions, assessing the degree to which residents are involved in the environment and mutually supportive of one another; personal growth or goal orientation dimensions, assessing the directions in which personal development tends to occur in the environment; and system maintenance and change dimensions, measuring the degree to which the environment is orderly, clear in its expectations of residents, and responsive to change. The revised version of the SCES has 63 items measuring seven dimensions beneath these three conceptual umbrellas. Specific descriptions of each dimension are found in Lemke and Moos (1987, p. 24) and in Moos and Lemke (1994). Two relationship dimensions are Cohesion, measuring how helpful and supportive staff members are toward residents and how involved and supportive residents are with each other, and Conflict, assessing the extent to which residents express anger and are critical of each other and the facility. Personal growth is represented by two measures: Independence, how self-sufficient residents are encouraged to be in their personal affairs and how much responsibility and self-direction they exercise, and Self-exploration, the extent to which residents are encouraged to express their feelings and concerns openly. Three dimensions comprise system maintenance and change: Organization, how important order and organization are in the facility, the extent to which residents know what to expect in their daily routine, and the clarity of rules and procedures; Resident Influence, the extent to which residents can influence the policies and rules of the facility and are free from restrictive regulations; and Physical Comfort, the extent to which comfort, privacy, pleasant decor, and sensory satisfaction are provided by the physical environment.

Investigation of the qualities of the SCES indicate that it assesses the "actual, agreed-on qualities of a setting," not simply respondent characteristics, that there is a core of consensual reality in environmental reports that are "relatively stable across subgroups of individuals" and seem to be independent of respondents' personality characteristics (Lemke & Moos, 1987, p. 28). Staff and resident ratings of the same facility social climate show moderate agreement overall, ranging from 0.17 to 0.54. As ratings differ across facility types, it is wise to obtain views of both groups when employing the SCES (Lemke & Moos, 1987). An investigation (Smith & Whitbourne, 1990) of the construct validity of the SCES indicated moderate to high levels of reliability and validity for conflict, self-exploration, and organization. Data for resident influence, cohesion, physical comfort, and independence yielded contradictory results. However, Lemke and Moos (1990) claim that these researchers misinterpreted the intent of the SCES, testing its validity as a measure of differences among individuals within a facility as opposed to its intended use as a discriminator of social climate perceptions across facility types.

THE MODEL AT WORK: ILLUSTRATIVE ISSUES

The MEAP resides at the center of much of the research generated for the past 15 years within the broader integrated conceptual framework (Figure 5.1). In this section, I illustrate the application of the model (and the MEAP) to selected housing issues of relevance to those interested in group living environments, as well as more traditional housing arrangements of elderly individuals. Similar to Timko and Moos (1991a), for convenience, I organize the discussion into issues of primary relevance for research and for practice, recognizing that overlap here is clearly intrinsic to the social ecological approach. Given the conceptual goals of the chapter, I devote less attention to issues of application;

rather, I offer a brief overview of practical uses of the social ecological frame-work and the MEAP and offer relevant sources for the reader interested in more detailed accounts. There are numerous comprehensive reviews of previous re-search utilizing the model (Moos & Lemke, 1984b, 1985, 1994), and the reader is urged to see these sources for a more extensive view. I illustrate just a few of the many issues and applications occupying the model in recent years.

Theoretical Applications

Theoretical applications are well illustrated by two issues: determinants of social climate and resident-facility matching processes. The selection of these issues is based on their central value to the conceptual framework, as well as to long-standing issues within environment-behavior research. Clearly, the model has relevance for other, no less important issues as well. These include institutional relocation of elderly residents (Lemke & Moos, 1984), appraisal and coping processes (Moos & Swindle, 1990), and multiple environmental determinants of adaptation (Moos, 1987). The final section of this chapter will deal with the value of some of this work for research on more traditional forms of housing for the elderly.

Determinants of Social Climate

Initial research on Moos's sample of specialized living environments for the elderly focused largely on the descriptive data revealed by each separate instru-ment. Thus, early findings gathered with each scale indicated notable differences among the three types of residential settings in both objective environmental characteristics and social climate. Differences on these dimensions were also related to other characteristics associated with settings, including size, staffing, cost, and profit-nonprofit status. (See citations for each scale or Timko and Moos [1991a] for an overview of these differences.)

Moos focused his immediate attention on the significant variability in social climate found among the three types of facilities. For instance, RCs and APTs were lower than SNFs on conflict but higher on organization and physical com-fort. SNFs and RCs were lower than APTs on independence and self-disclosure, but no differences among the three types emerged for cohesion and resident influence. Consistent with previous research on group living facilities showing the importance of perceived social atmosphere on factors such as residents' life satisfaction (Harel, 1981), staff treatment of residents (Holland, Konick, Buffum, Smith, & Petchers, 1981), and residents' morale (Kahana, Liang, & Felton, 1980), these findings led Moos and colleagues to examine the determinants of social climate. Other environmental domains assessed by the MEAP were hy-pothesized as having major causal influence on social climate in these facilities. Figure 5.2 displays the causal model hypothesized to represent these relations. Note that this model brings causal ordering to the domains comprising panel I in Figure 5.1, with the addition of Institutional Context (level of care, ownership,

Figure 5.2
A Model of the Determinants of Social Climate in Group Residential Facilities

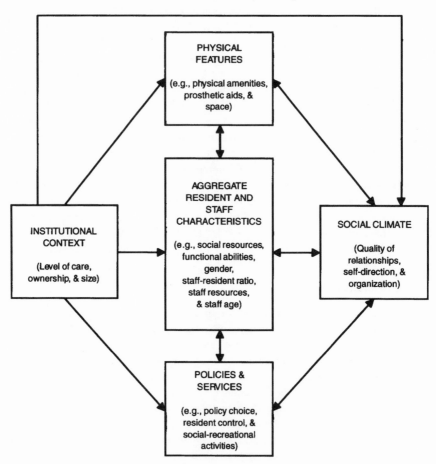

Source: Moos & Lemke, 1994, p. 130. Reprinted with permission.

and size) as a contextual influence on all four environmental domains. At the time, relations between features of sheltered care settings and resident functioning had received much research attention (e.g., Carp, 1978–1979; Lawton, 1975), but few studies had focused on 'how physical, policy, and human aggregate factors might influence the social environments in facilities'' (Moos & Igra, 1980, p. 88).

Early test of this model on the initial sample of 90 California congregate housing facilities for the elderly produced a complex and interesting pattern of results (Moos & Igra, 1980). Facility type (Institutional Context in earlier research) was strongly related to each social climate dimension. Perceived degree of cohesion, independence, self-exploration, organization, resident influence, and physical comfort were highest in APTs, followed by RCs and then by nursing homes (NHs). However, almost all of the influence of facility type on social climate was shared with physical, policy, and human aggregate dimensions, with little prediction occurring directly. All 14 dimensions taken together explained substantial variation in the social climate in these facilities, ranging from 22 percent for self-exploration to 56 percent for independence. Architectural and policy factors accounted for more unique variance than did type of facility and resident and staff characteristics. Third, taken two or three at a time, environmental dimensions explained considerable variation in most social climate variables (with the exception of self-exploration). Those facilities displaying more democratic policies and residents with higher functional health had greater effect on social climate than facilities possessing either of these qualities alone. The predictive advantage was even greater for these facilities if they possessed richer architectural features or a lower level of care.

Overall, the findings supported the key supposition that the four environmental dimensions influence the social climate in specialized living environments for the elderly. More specifically, combinations of these factors were related to particular social climate dimensions. For example, social climates described as more cohesive and higher in resident influence and physical comfort are more likely to be found in facilities with more physical amenities, better social-recreational aids, and more architectural choice and space. Residents have more policy choice and control and are functionally healthier in these places. Interestingly, results indicated that there was less emphasis on independence and resident influence in facilities with better staffing, an issue with implications for later research. Also, similarity of residents' characteristics or "resident homogeneity" was of little relevance for predicting facility social climate, leading Moos to comment that "easily available objective information about a facility may provide very little information about the actual experiences of residents and their quality of life" (Moos & Igra, 1980, p. 96), prompting a call for a broader search for salient influences of social climate.

Interventive implications emerged for all three domains of environmental predictors of the MEAP. First, the fact that policy and program factors predicted larger proportions of unique and shared variance in most of the social climate dimensions is potentially good news, since these factors are usually easier to modify than the built environment. Moos and Igra (1980) suggest that increasing environmental choice and control and enriching social-recreational activities should help to increase cohesion, independence, and possibly organization, influence, and physical comfort also. Second, information about the objective physical and architectural environment may be useful for making comparisons among settings and for planning long-term change. And third, information about aggregate characteristics of residents may be used to inform new residents about the kinds of people they will encounter in a facility.

In 1990, Timko and Moos revisited this model, interested specifically in the extent to which the environmental domains predicted two aspects of setting social climate—interpersonal support, represented by the SCES dimensions of cohesion and conflict, and self-direction, indexed by independence and resident influence. This study was prompted by research indicating that facilities with supportive relations and self-direction are associated with higher quality of care and resident functioning (Harel, 1981; Holland et al., 1981; Kahana, Liang, & Felton, 1980). Timko and Moos (1990) asked two basic questions: To what extent are supportive, self-directed social climates determined by physical features, policies and services, and aggregate resident and staff characteristics? To what extent do these two aspects of social climate work at cross-purposes to one another (where efforts to create supportive environments may unintentionally undermine residents' feelings of control and increase dependency on staff)?

An expanded sample of 244 facilities (127 NHs, 55 RCs, 62 APTs) from 20 states was surveyed on the MEAP. Both residents and staff perceptions of social climate were assessed in order to determine possible differences in determinants for the two groups. There were 25 residents and 11 staff members on average in each facility.

Among the large number of findings, there was significant staff-resident agreement on each of the four dimensions of the social climate, and this agreement was quite consistent across the three types of social settings. Comparisons of determinants of resident-staff views showed similarities and differences. On interpersonal support, there was agreement that a more comfortable physical environment is associated with greater cohesion and that having residents with more social resources decreases conflict. Differences were related to the presence of separate staff facilities. For instance, among residents, the presence of staff facilities was associated with increased cohesion; however, among staff, separate staff facilities increased conflict. Among staff, having more middle aged staff was related to reduced conflict; among residents, having greater autonomy and fewer residents was associated with reduced conflict. As to self-direction, there was agreement that greater physical comfort is independently related to increased resident influence. Staff and resident data showed agreement in that higher resident influence and independence was predicted by greater resident social resources, and policies that promoted autonomy were associated with more resident influence. However, only residents' reports showed separate staff facilities contributing to independence; also, a higher staff-resident ratio was related to lower independence and resident influence only among residents.

Once again, the findings supported the general features of the Moos and Igra (1980) model of the determinants of social climate. The four environmental attributes explained substantial variation in the four dimensions of the SCES used here, ranging from 14 percent for the staff's assessment of cohesion to 39 percent for residents' assessment of independence. From the perspective of both residents and staff, facilities providing a higher level of care have more conflict and less independence. This supports previous research indicating that residents' dissatisfaction is likely to increase in institutions lacking privacy and requiring conformity, leading to increased friction with residents and dependency upon staff (Langer & Avorn, 1982), as well as research indicating that a greater desired mix of privacy and support is likely to be obtained by older persons in noninstitutional housing (Lawton, 1981).

Although the data are correlational in nature, Timko and Moos offer thoughtful interventive suggestions. They emphasize that among both residents and staff improvement of the physical comfort of a facility will help to underscore cohesion and resident influence in the eyes of both groups. Interestingly, they suggest that when staff and residents' perceptions disagree, managers would do well to focus on concerns of the residents who obviously must spend more time in these ''home'' settings. Consistent with other research on autonomy and control in institutional settings (Langer & Rodin, 1976; Schulz, 1976), residents will be more likely to remain active and socially engaged if they feel they exercise control over their environments, though administrators are cautioned against providing an environment of choice and control that may exert excessive demands on less functionally healthy residents (Lawton, 1981). Finally, though aggregate staff and resident characteristics are difficult to modify, Timko and Moos urge use of this information to educate both groups. For example, knowing that a high staff-resident ratio decreases residents' perceptions of independence and influence, staff might be taught that overassistance encourages dependence; similarly, as residents' social resources predicted social climate consistently, staff might be sensitized to differing levels of resident social competence, and in larger facilities, more contact and communication among residents, as well as staff and residents, might be encouraged.

In order to develop a typology of social climates of group residential facilities, Timko and Moos (1991b) cluster analyzed social climate dimensions of 121 NHs, 50 RCs, and 64 APTs. They examined the relations between type of social climate to facility level of care, ownership, and size and to aggregate resident characteristics. In addition, they examined the relations between type of social climate and resident adaptation (assessed by measures of activity level, community integration, and utilization of health services). (See Segal and Moyles [1988] for an alternative typology of sheltered care environments.)

Six distinct clusters of facilities emerged from the clustering procedure: supportive, self-directed (34 facilities); supportive, well-organized (45 facilities); open conflict (52 facilities); suppressed conflict (30 facilities); emergent-positive (42 facilities with average or above average scores on all SCES dimensions); and unresponsive (32 facilities of average or below average scores on the seven SCES dimensions). Each level of care was represented in each social climate type, with the exception of APTs, which do not appear in the suppressed conflict type. Most of the NHs fell into the four clusters of open conflict, suppressed conflict, emergent-positive, and unresponsive. One fourth of RCs fell into the supportive, self-directed cluster, with the rest falling across the other five types. The APTs were distributed in the supportive, well-organized cluster and the supportive, self-directed and open conflict clusters. As for ownership type, more than half of the 88 nonprofit facilities were located in the supportive, self-directed and supportive, well-organized clusters. On the other hand, almost half of the for-profit facilities were in the open conflict and suppressed conflict clusters, with about 39 percent among the emergent-positive and unresponsive clusters. About half of the 23 public facilities fell into the open conflict group. Among findings for facility size, supportive, self-directed and supportive, well-organized facility types had significantly more residents than the suppressed conflict and unresponsive clusters.

Type of social climate was also related to resident characteristics. Interestingly, residents' social resources and gender were related to social climate type, but functional ability was not. Those in supportive, self-directed facilities had more social resources than those in open conflict, suppressed conflict, and emergent-positive facilities. Resident adaptation was better among those in supportive, well-organized, supportive, self-directed, and emergent-positive clusters. Residents in more supportive social climates had higher rated well-being, were more active in the community and in the facility, and used fewer health services.

Timko and Moos suggest that interventions that target physical, policy, and service factors may modify conditions in particular clusters of facilities, reducing, for instance, the conflict and enhancing independence, organization, and physical comfort in emergent-positive social climates, or increasing cohesion and resident influence in unresponsive and conflict social climate types. Larger, nonprofit facilities may be easier to target in this regard, as well as facilities with more women residents and those with more social resources. Moreover, they suggest that the social climate typologies may help "to match specific sets of residents with particular kinds of social climates. Better methods of resident-facility matching are likely to enhance resident adaptation to facilities over the short and long term. Future research can focus on identifying combinations of resident characteristics and social climate configurations that promote residents' health and well-being" (Timko & Moos, 1991b, p. S168).

To illustrate other uses of the MEAP and the social ecological framework shown in Figure 5.1, the area of resident-facility matching will be considered.

Person-Environment Matching Processes

How do older individuals come to reside in various types of specialized living environments? Are there ways in which the "fit" or congruence between residents and features of these environments might be maximized to enhance individual adaptation? These questions lie at the heart of the social ecological framework and spring from one of the most long-standing interests within the ecology of aging—understanding the person-environment interactions affecting positive and negative adaptive outcomes in the later years (Scheidt & Windley, 1985).

Moos sees two major approaches as useful for examining person-environment matching. One perspective is represented in Lawton and Nahemow's (1973) competence-press model. It assumes that competent older adults are more adaptable and can meet the demands posed by a wide array of environmental situations; less competent individuals, on the other hand, function adequately only in a narrower range of environment settings, their behavior shaped by environmental factors to a larger extent than is the case with more competent elderly adults. Adaptation (positive emotion and behavior) is experienced when level of competence is matched within reasonable limits to the demands of the environment (Lawton, 1982). (However, see Lawton [1989] for a modified version of this "environmental docility" hypothesis.) The other perspective is represented in Moos's own approach, focusing on environmental preferences of residents in addition to their needs and resources. It proposes that older people may achieve suitable congruence with their environments if they are "enabled" to follow their preferences in selecting environments (Moos, 1987, p. 233).

Recent research with the MEAP and other dimensions of the model have revealed interesting results regarding the degree to which residents' characteristics are matched with facility resources (Timko & Moos, 1991a). Moos's model assumes that "a variety of personal and social forces help determine who seeks to live in a group setting and which particular residence they choose" (Timko & Moos, 1991a, p. 121). Moos has used the RESIF to assess some of these, including need (health status, need for services), predisposing (age, living alone), and enabling (financial resources) factors. Moos and colleagues showed that selection into the three types of settings was determined largely by functional abilities (need) rather than sociodemographic (predisposing, enabling factors). NH residents were the most impaired, with lesser impairment found among residents of RCs and, least impaired, those in APTs, indicating "a relatively good process of matching older people's functional and health status to different levels of services" (Timko & Moos, 1991a, p. 122). However, selection within the three types of settings occurred largely on the basis of enabling and predisposing factors. Residents' need for services is only moderately related to the features of their specific facility.

> We have concluded that there are two distinct resident-facility matching processes. One process is guided by residents' functional ability and need for services, which are the strongest determinants of the type of facility residents enter and the level of care they receive. The other process reflects predisposing and enabling factors that enable more privileged residents to live together in more homogeneous settings and to obtain access to richer staff resources and services. There is relatively little evidence for a matching process within a given level of care such that residents who need more services are placed in better staffed facilities. (Timko & Moos, 1991a, p. 123)

The MEAP has also been used to examine how resident characteristics might be used to improve the match between residents and facilities (Timko & Moos, 1991a). Previous research has shown that experimental interventions designed to enhance residents' sense of personal control and autonomy in long-term care facilities had positive effects on their psychological well-being, activity, level, and health status (Rodin & Langer, 1977; Schulz & Hanusa, 1978). Timko and Moos (1989) examined how adaptation of residents in group living facilities was affected by "naturally occurring" levels of personal choice and control (POLIF dimensions). They examined the degree to which these relations were mediated by clarity of facility policies (a RESIF dimension) and SCES dimensions of independence, resident influence, and organization. Finally, they examined the degree to which residents' functional abilities moderated the influence of these predictors on residents' adaptation (defined by rated resident well-being, community integration, and reliance on facility services). This last goal sought to reaffirm previous research on this issue and to address existing theories regarding the interaction between functional health and person-environment transactions (Carp, 1978; Lawton, 1985). All data were gathered from the expanded sample of 244 facilities (127 NHs, 55 RCs, 62 APTs).

In general, residents of sheltered care settings adapted better in facilities with more policy choice and resident control, thus extending results of previous short-term intervention studies to facilities exhibiting long-standing levels of personal control. The influence of choice and control on adaptation was partially mediated by policy clarity and facility social climate; and policy clarity, independence, resident influence, and organization had an independent impact on adaptation, as well (Timko & Moos, 1989, p. 649). In addition, policy clarity and the three social climate dimensions mediated most of the relationship between choice and control and adaptation, suggesting the need for researchers to consider a wide range of policies and social climate dimensions when studying adaptation in these sheltered care environments. Functional ability moderated the impact of the environmental dimensions on resident adaptation. Facilities whose policies promoted personal control and independence showed better resident adaptation (less use of services) for moderately and highly functional residents but not among those with poorer functional health. Timko and Moos interpret the last findings as supporting the models of person-environment congruence of Carp (1978), Lawton (1985), and Sherman (1974).

Similar issues of improving older resident-environment matching were addressed by Lemke and Moos (1989), who conducted an individual-level analysis of 1,492 residents in 42 facilities (9 NHs, 6 RCs, 18 APTs, plus 9 VAs [Veterans facilities]). The study was conducted to understand more about the personal and facility factors influencing activity involvement (in-house formal and informal activities; community activities) of older residents of group facilities. Selected dimensions from each of the MEAP components (including the Background Information Form [BIF]) were assessed. Most relevant here are results bearing upon existing models of person-environment fit. Interactions between personal and facility characteristics were examined in light of Sherman's (1974) threshold model predicting that more impaired elderly individuals are more affected by the availability of environmental resources, while the same resources have little impact on more capable elderly. Evidence was also sought for Lawton's (1985) prediction that environmental resources may serve as demands for more impaired elderly, leading to negative adaptation in some cases. Consistent with Lawton's model, results showed that residents with below average functioning were less likely than their healthier counterparts, particularly in large facilities, to initiate activity in settings with more autonomy. Consistent with Sherman's (1974) threshold model, however, supportive environmental features (staffing level, staff richness, services) enhanced participation in formal activities among more impaired residents but had minimal influence on more competent residents. Lemke and Moos (1989) interpret the results as supporting a compensatory model where environmental resources may help impaired individuals function more effectively. Overall, "a given environmental factor can be either a resource or a demand, depending on its level, the context in which it occurs, and how it is appraised" (Lemke & Moos, 1989, p. S147).

Overview of Practical Uses

As indicated above, research conducted within the social ecological framework using the MEAP or its separate components has demonstrated several diverse practical uses. These range from using the SCES at the individual clinical level to generate "environmental diagnoses" (Moos & Fuhr, 1982) to using the MEAP to define the structure and process of the quality of care for older residents of facilities in the normative sample.

The MEAP and the social ecological framework have uses in both formative and summative program evaluation, including assessing program implementation, facilitating and monitoring environmental change, and designing and evaluating program environments (Timko & Moos, 1991a).

The MEAP may be administered in a four-step program to develop and monitor program changes in group living environments: (1) environmental assessment, including both staff and resident perspectives; (2) feedback of the results to program administrators and staff; (3) planning and instituting change; and (4) reassessing the environment to determine the efficacy of these changes. According to Timko and Moos (1991a), this paradigm has been successfully implemented in at least two long-term care settings (Hatcher, Gentry, Kunkel, & Smith, 1983; Wells, Singer, & Polgar, 1986), improving staff-resident relations, and residents' sense of self-confidence and perceived competence. Also of aid here, it is possible to develop individual MEAP profiles for facilities, comparing scores to those of residents, staff, and facilities comprising the normative sample, or, as illustrated above, to compare staff and residents' perceptions of the social climate using the SCES (Timko & Moos, 1990). These uses are illustrated by three studies. Thompson and Swisher (1983) used the MEAP to evaluate a single rural life-care center, comparing SCES profiles of 38 elderly residents and 17 staff members. The authors attribute the harmonious perceptions of the facility offered by the elderly residents to a selection process favoring a population with homogeneous financial and health characteristics.

In the second study, Stein, Linn, and Stein (1987) compared SCES ratings of 301 residents and 231 nursing staff from ten (presumably Florida) community nursing homes ranging from "poor" to "good" in quality of care. Regardless of quality of the homes, staff ratings were more favorable than resident ratings on cohesion, independence, self-exploration, and resident influence. Residents perceived themselves as having less control and influence than did the staff. Staff in better-quality homes also viewed the social climate more favorably than did staff in poorer homes. And in agreement with outside experts who rated home quality, residents in poorer homes rated their facilities less favorably than those in better homes. Interestingly, overall discrepancy between staff-resident ratings did not vary by quality of homes. As to practicability of the findings, the authors state: "Though it would seem that better quality institutions are moving in the right direction in providing social climates that can promote health, it is still true that the [low] mean ratings for the factors given by both staff and residents strongly suggest there is much more work needed in these areas" (Stein, Linn, & Stein, 1987, p. 45).

Finally, in an attempt to develop British norms for the MEAP, as well as to compare results to the normative U.S. sample, Benjamin and Spector (1990) assessed four facilities (short-stay psychogeriatric ward; long-stay ward at a British psychiatric hospital; and two bungalows at a residential care home). Among the findings was evidence that called into question the British Department of Health and Social Services recommendations for assessing residents' needs for easy access to community facilities. Despite the lack of obstacles to community resources, community access was a low priority for these residents. And in contrast to findings obtained by Moos and Lemke (1984a) on American samples, British residents expressed lower preferences for physical amenities, social, prosthetic, and orientational aids, and safety features. The authors believe that additional information regarding the physical environment (a well-marked building, a map of community resources, staff and resident photographs) might rectify these views.

As this last study illustrates, the MEAP may be used to identify design and program preferences among current and potential older populations (Moos, Lemke, & David, 1987) and to improve these aspects of the residential environment. Moos and colleagues have modified items in the POLIF and the PAF to assess preferences for ideal design and program features. Two studies have compared design and program preferences of congregate apartment residents with those of samples of older community residents and gerontological experts in the field (Brennan, Moos, & Lemke, 1988, 1989). Results were varied and indicate that designers and program planners must not be presumptive regarding similarities among their own preferences, current APT residents, and potential users. For instance, while older community and APT residents held similar preferences for physical and architectural features of congregate facilities, their service and policy preferences differed somewhat. The latter preferred greater privacy but fewer supportive services and formal organizational structures. Experts' views differed from both groups of older people, endorsing lower expectations for functioning, higher levels of policy clarity and choice, and resident control. They also preferred more physical design features than did the older people.

These preference measures have several possible applications in both preoccupancy and postoccupancy phases of program development; facilitating selection of more satisfying residential settings; guiding preliminary programming plans; monitoring and, if necessary, modifying service packages and policies; and examining congruence between residents' views of actual and preferred features of physical and program environments (Brennan, Moos, & Lemke, 1989, p. 55). (See also Moos, Lemke, and David [1987] for further discussion of these issues.)

POTENTIAL EXTENSIONS TO OTHER HOUSING ISSUES

As the foregoing discussion indicates, most research conducted to date utilizing the MEAP and the broader model has focused on older residents of specialized living environments. The approach has potential, however, for informing research in other housing domains as well. I offer a few examples here of some of the areas that might make ready use of the social ecological approach.

Multiple Environmental Contexts

Following Bronfenbrenner's (1979) model of multiple social environmental influences on human development, Moos (1987) examined the manner in which cross-situational influences of "mesosystems" (two or more environmental settings occupied by the individual), as well as "exosystems" (influential settings not directly occupied by the individual), affect person-environment match between students and learning environments and between patients and treatment environments. In the case of learning environments, results indicated that continuities between school and home social climates (mesosystems) were associated with better academic self-concept and more enthusiasm for school (p. 240) and that differences in the perceived work climate of teachers (exosystems) affected the social climate of their classrooms (p. 240).

The recognition of the embeddedness of these multiple environmental influences should alter the typically held view that group living facilities are "closed systems" where older residents are exposed only to residential programs (Moos & Lemke, 1985, p. 885): "In reality, the residential setting is but one of the multiple environmental 'microsystems' in which the person functions. The influences emanating from other enduring microsystems, such as extended family and peer networks, may have a stronger effect on individual's morale and well-being than the characteristics of the residential setting."

Some of Moos's more recent work has implications for understanding possible interactions among multiple contextual influences, though not directly targeted at older populations and intended only to represent social contextual factors. To articulate ongoing environmental systems (from life events and transitions) within the adaptation model, Moos, Fenn, and Billings (1988) developed a Life Stressors and Social Resources Inventory (LISRES) that assesses the extent to which factors associated with personal (e.g., physical health) and social contexts (e.g., work, family, marriage, friends) may serve as potential stressors or resources. The inventory was developed on small samples of depressed, alcoholic, arthritic, and healthy adults. Interestingly, a "home/neighborhood" domain assessed with six items is represented among the nine stressors but, like "physical health," was not among the seven parallel summary indices of social resources. Thus, the inventory does not assess the extent to which the physical milieu serves as a resource as well as a stressor. Parallel stress/resource assessments of physical environmental dimensions common to multiple contexts would seem a feasible task.

Little research has examined such meso- and exosystem influences on the adaptation of older residents to specialized living environments nor, as Moos suggests, to the ways in which residential programs may affect other settings (e.g., family environments) that older residents may occupy. Knowledge of these possibly mutual causal influences is critical to more fully informed program evaluation and the recognition that an intervention program is but "one (indeed, a temporary one) of the multiple environmental microsystems or specific settings that influence personal growth and maturation" (Moos, 1984, p. 17).

Other Housing Contexts

It may be possible to extend the technology of the MEAP or its various components to explore adaptation of older residents in other forms of supportive housing, especially where the social, architectural, and policy milieu contribute to a relatively distinct sense of community. For instance, the approach may be extended to naturally developing or planned retirement communities, life care communities (illustrated by the Thompson and Swisher study cited above), and alternative planned housing. Share-a-Home, which provides some services to moderately independent residents who live in separate bedrooms, possesses some of the same "push" (declining independence) and "pull" (social motivation) factors characterizing the group living environments studied by Moos and colleagues (Lawton, 1985; Streib, Folts, & Hilker, 1984). Expanding the range of housing types may be useful for examining variations in environmental supports (security versus autonomy issues), a wider variety of possible matches between environmental and individual characteristics, and adaptation to "accommodating" versus "constant" environments. In addition, features of the MEAP, particularly the SCES, the RESIF, and adapted versions of the POLIF and PAF, might well be applied to other forms of housing, including condominiums, cooperatives, hotels, and mobile home parks.

Blake (1987), for example, used the MEAP to assess ten boarding homes in

New Jersey that housed deinstitutionalized chronically mentally ill, as well as frail elderly, residents. He found that facilities had few prosthetic and orientational aids and afforded little privacy. The POLIF revealed serious deficiencies in public policy for boarding homes; high expectations for resident functioning were "coupled with low tolerance for deviance, unclear policies, and little opportunity for resident input and control" (p. 48). RESIF findings revealed these homes to be institutional in character, despite their lower numbers of residents, indicating the need for better qualified staff. Residents rated the boarding homes high on dimensions of staff-resident relations and organization but low in conflict, independence, and resident influence. According to Blake, the reliability and validity of these social climate ratings are questionable, given the probable fears of many residents to offer negative opinions and difficulties understanding some of the questions.

Cast more broadly, the social ecological model might be also focused on more naturally evolving housing environments and the surrounding milieu, including urban and rural neighborhoods, housing tracts, and small communities. Indeed, Scheidt and Windley (1985, 1987), applying community-level assessments of social climate across 18 small Kansas communities, found reliable differences in social climate associated with varying profiles of psychological well-being among 1,000 elderly rural residents. Although the MEAP is designed to assess components of more supportive environments, it would seem reasonable to adapt the technology to milieus hosting more independently housed elderly.

Environmental Matching: Aging in Place versus Relocation

The social ecological model has potential for enriching our understanding of "theoretical approaches to residential decision making" (Lawton, 1985, p. 452), including decisions to move or to remain in place. Also, if applied to the broader housing environment, the approach could offer an accounting of the impact of rapidly changing environments upon those who "age in place" in other housing contexts. These are rather natural issues for the approach, given its applicability to issues of person-environment congruence.

Although they have used the MEAP in a study of intrainstitutional relocation of nursing home residents (Moos & Lemke, 1994), little research exists that uses the MEAP to assess interinstitutional relocation.

Most older Americans elect not to move. Seventy-five percent of all older Americans own their homes, and only 2 percent of them move on a yearly basis (Callahan, 1992). As Lawton (1985) notes, "[T]he fact that remaining in place is by far the most frequent decision made by older people should lead us to look more closely at the complex of factors that contribute to residential immobility" (p. 452).

Among this complex of factors, transactional researchers have determined that many older residents elect to remain in their homes and neighborhoods, because they have formed strong attachments to place (Fogel, 1992; Rowles 1987; Rubinstein, 1989; Scheidt & Norris-Baker, 1990). Elements of the environment, both current and remembered, possess psychological meanings that bind individuals to their current milieus. Although the social ecological approach has had relatively little to say about environmental attachment (or, more broadly, about affective "terms of the organism"), it might be applied usefully by those interested in the ways in which psychologically represented environments influence decisions to "age in place" versus to relocate.

For example, Howell (1980) posits that older individuals utilize cognitive and affective experiences garnered in past environments as templates to guide their interactions with new environments: "What if the transaction between aging people and whatever their current environment is were not merely what we observe as 'adaptive' accommodation but rather were sets of responses to their nonrandom histories of interactions with environments?" (Howell, 1980, pp. 425–426).

She suggests combining a focus on historical experience with the contemporary emphasis of the social ecological model: "To argue that current context, as perceived and interacted with, is a function of both the measurable attributes (physical and social) of the presenting scene [Moos & Lemke, 1980] and the person-place-event history of the respondent is to provide a basis for better explanation and prediction of environment and aging behaviors" (p. 426).

At times, Moos has operationally defined adaptation in his model as the degree of incongruity between ratings of the actual (or current) environment and the desired (ideal) environment. Such comparisons might be made between former and current residential environments, as well, affording greater articulation of particular environmental features affecting residential satisfaction in models of residential decision making, such as that of Wiseman (1980). This includes knowledge of factors influencing Wiseman's various forms of residential relocation (such as amenity moves, "environmental push" moves, and assistance moves). To illustrate, we still know little about subjective factors influencing return migration or urban migration of empty-nest suburbanites, motives influencing local moves to retirement communities, or why some older individuals may elect to remain in place despite low housing satisfaction and a wish to move (Lawton, 1985).

At a broader level, of course, the point is that the interactionist paradigm employed by Moos may be enriched, as Howell's suggestion indicates, if it remains open to the possible contributive influences of housing research generated by other paradigms.

REFERENCES

Altman, I., & Rogoff, B. (1987). World views in psychology: Trait, interactional, organismic, and transactional perspectives. In D. Stokols & I. Altman (Eds.), *Handbook of environmental psychology* (pp. 7–40). New York: John Wiley & Sons.

Barker, R. (1968). *Ecological psychology: Concepts and methods for studying the environment of human behavior.* Stanford, CA: Stanford University Press.

Benjamin, L. C., & Spector, J. (1990). Environments for the dementing. *International Journal of Geriatric Psychiatry, 5,* 15–24.

Blake, R. (1987). The social environment of boarding homes. *Adult Foster Care Journal, 1,* 42–55.

Brennan, P. L., Moos, R. H., & Lemke, S. (1988). Preferences of older adults and experts for physical and architectural features of group living facilities. *Gerontologist, 28,* 84–90.

Brennan, P. L., Moos, R. H., & Lemke, S. (1989). Preferences of older adults and experts for policies and services in group living facilities. *Psychology and Aging, 4,* 48–56.

Bronfenbrenner, U. (1979). *The ecology of human development: Experiments by nature and design.* Cambridge: Harvard University Press.

Brunswik, E. (1955). Representative design and probabilistic theory in a functional psychology. *Psychological Review, 62,* 193–218.

Bureau of the Census. (1995, January). *Statistical brief: Housing of the elderly.* U.S. Department of Commerce (SB/94–95), Washington, DC.

Callahan, J. (1992). Aging in place. *Generations, 26,* 5–6.

Carp, F. M. (1978). Effects of the living environment on activity and use of time. *International Journal of Aging and Human Development, 9,* 75–91.

Carp, F. M. (1978–1979). Effects of the living environment on activity and use of time. *International Journal of Aging and Human Development, 9,* 75–91.

Carp, F. M., & Carp, A. (1984). A complementary/congruence model of well-being or mental health for the community elderly. In I. Altman, M. P. Lawton, & J. F. Wohwill (Eds.), *Elderly people and the environment* (pp. 279–336). New York: Plenum Press.

Fogel, B. S. (1992). Psychological aspects of staying at home. *Generations, 26,* 15–19.

Harel, Z. (1981). Quality of care, congruence, and well-being among institutionalized aged. *Gerontologist, 21,* 523–531.

Hatcher, M., Gentry, R., Kunkel, M., & Smith, G. (1983). Environmental assessment and community intervention: An application of the social ecology model. *Psychosocial Rehabilitation Journal, 7,* 22–28.

Holland, T. P., Konick, A., Buffum, W., Smith, M., & Petchers, M. (1981). Institutional structure and resident outcomes. *Journal of Health and Social Behavior, 22,* 433–444.

Howell, S. C. (1980). Environments as hypotheses in human aging research. In L. Poon (Ed.), *Aging in the 1980's: Psychological issues* (pp. 424–432). Washington, DC: American Psychological Association.

Insel, P. M., & Moos, R. H. (1974). Psychological environments: Expanding the scope of human ecology. *American Psychologist, 29,* 179–188.

Kahana, E. (1982). A congruence model of person-environment interaction. In M. P. Lawton, P. G. Windley, & T. O. Byerts (Eds.), *Aging and the environment: Theoretical approaches* (pp. 97–121). New York: Springer.

Kahana, E., Liang, J., & Felton, B. (1980). Alternative models of person-environment fit: Prediction of morale in three homes for the aged. *Journal of Gerontology, 35,* 584–595.

Kleemeier, R. W. (1959). Behavior and the organization of the bodily and the external environment. In J. E. Birren (Ed.), *Handbook of aging and the individual* (pp. 400–451). Chicago: University of Chicago Press.

Langer, E. J., & Avorn, J. (1982). Impact of the psychosocial environment of the elderly on behavior and health organization. In R. Chellis, J. Seagle, & B. Seagle (Eds.), *Congregate housing for older people*. Lexington, MA: Lexington Books.

Langer, E. J., & Rodin, J. (1976). The effects of choice and enhanced personal responsibility for the aged: A field experiment in an institutional setting. *Journal of Personality and Social Psychology, 37*, 191–198.

Lawton, M. P. (1975). *Planning and managing housing for the elderly*. New York: Wiley-Interscience.

Lawton, M. P. (1981). Community supports for the aged. *Journal of Social Issues, 37*, 102–115.

Lawton, M. P. (1982). Competence, environmental press, and the adaptation of older people. In M. Lawton, P. Windley, & T. Byerts (Eds.), *Aging and environment: Theoretical approaches* (pp. 33–59). New York: Springer.

Lawton, M. P. (1985). Housing and living environments of older people. In E. Shanas & R. Binstock (Eds.), *Handbook of aging and the social sciences* (pp. 450–478). New York: Van Nostrand Reinhold.

Lawton, M. P. (1989). Behavior-relevant ecological factors. In K. W. Schaie & C. Schooler (Eds.), *Social structure and aging: Psychological processes* (pp. 57–77). Hillsdale, NJ: Lawrence Erlbaum.

Lawton, M. P. (in press). Environmental taxonomy: Generalizations from research on the elderly. In T. Wachs & S. Friedman (Eds.), *Assessment of the environment across the life span*. Washington, DC: American Psychological Association.

Lawton, M. P., & Nahemow, L. (1973). Ecology and the aging process. In C. Eisdorfer & M. Lawton (Eds.), *The psychology of adult development and aging* (pp. 619–674). Washington, DC: American Psychological Association.

Lemke, S., & Moos, R. (1980). Assessing the institutional policies of sheltered care settings. *Journal of Gerontology, 35*, 96–107.

Lemke, S., & Moos, R. (1981). The suprapersonal environments of sheltered care settings. *Journal of Gerontology, 36*, 233–243.

Lemke, S., & Moos, R. H. (1984). Coping with intra-institutional relocation: Behavioral change as a function of residents' personal resources. *Journal of Environmental Psychology, 4*, 137–151.

Lemke, S., & Moos, R. (1987). Measuring the social climate of congregate residences for older people: Sheltered Care Environment Scale. *Psychology and Aging, 2*, 20–29.

Lemke, S., & Moos, R. H. (1989). Personal and environmental determinants of activity involvement among elderly residents of congregate facilities. *Journal of Gerontology: Social Sciences, 44*, S139–S148.

Lemke, S., & Moos, R. H. (1990). Validity of the Sheltered Care Environment Scale: Conceptual and methodological issues. *Psychology and Aging, 5*, 569–571.

Lewin, K. (1935). *A dynamic theory of personality: Selected papers*. New York: McGraw-Hill.

Moos, R. H. (1976a). Conceptualizations of human environments. In R. Moos (Ed.), *The human context: Environmental determinants of behavior* (pp. 3–35). New York: John Wiley & Sons.

Moos, R. H. (1976b). Evaluating and changing community settings. *American Journal of Community Psychology, 4*, 313–326.

Moos, R. H. (1979). Social-ecological perspectives on health. In G. Stone, F. Cohen, N. Adler, & Associates (Eds.), *Health psychology: A handbook* (pp. 523–547). San Francisco: Jossey-Bass.

Moos, R. H. (1984). Context and coping: Toward a unifying conceptual framework. *American Journal of Community Psychology, 12*, 5–25.

Moos, R. H. (1985). Creating healthy human contexts: Environmental and individual strategies. In J. Rosen & L. Solomon (Eds.), *Prevention in health psychology* (pp. 366–389). Hanover, MA: University Press of New England.

Moos, R. H. (1987). Person-environment congruence in work, school, and health care settings. *Journal of Vocational Behavior, 31*, 231–247.

Moos, R. H., Fenn, C. B., & Billings, A. G. (1988). Life stressors and social resources: An integrated assessment approach. *Social Science Medicine, 27*, 999–1002.

Moos, R. H., & Fuhr, R. (1982). The clinical use of social-ecological concepts: The case of an adolescent girl. *American Journal of Orthopsychiatry, 52*, 111–122.

Moos, R. H., Gauvain, M., Lemke, S., Max, W., & Mehren, B. (1979). Assessing the social environments of sheltered care settings. *Gerontologist, 19*, 74–82.

Moos, R., & Igra, A. (1980). Determinants of the social environments of sheltered care settings. *Journal of Health and Social Behavior, 21*, 88–98.

Moos, R. H., & Lemke, S. (1980). Assessing the physical and architectural features of sheltered care settings. *Journal of Gerontology, 35*, 571–583.

Moos, R. H., & Lemke, S. (1984a). *Multiphasic Environmental Assessment Procedure (MEAP)*. Stanford, CA: University Medical Center.

Moos, R. H., & Lemke, S. (1984b). Supportive residential settings for older people. In I. Altman, M. P. Lawton, & J. Wohlwill (Eds.), *Elderly people and the environment* (pp. 159–190). New York: Plenum Press.

Moos, R. H., & Lemke, S. (1985). Specialized living environments for older people. In J. Birren & K. W. Schaie (Eds.), *Handbook of the psychology of aging* (pp. 864–889). New York: Van Nostrand Reinhold.

Moos, R. H., & Lemke, S. (1994). *Group residences for older adults: Physical features, policies, and social climate.* New York: Oxford University Press.

Moos, R. H., & Lemke, S. (1996). *Evaluating residential facilities: The Multiphasic Environmental Assessment Procedure.* Thousand Oaks, CA: Sage Publications.

Moos, R. H., Lemke, S., & David, T. C. (1987). Priorities for design and management in residential settings for the elderly. In V. Regnier & J. Pynoos (Eds.), *Housing the aged: Design directives and policy considerations* (pp. 179–205). New York: Elsevier.

Moos, R. H., & Swindle, R. W. (1990). Person-environment transactions and the stressor-appraisal-coping process. *Psychological Inquiry, 1*, 30–32.

Murray, H. (1938). *Explorations in personality.* New York: Oxford University Press.

Regnier, V., & Pynoos, J. (Eds.). (1987). *Housing the aged: Design directives and policy considerations.* New York: Elsevier.

Rodin, J., & Langer, E. (1977). Long-term effects of a control-relevant intervention with the institutionalized aged. *Journal of Personality and Social Psychology, 35*, 897–902.

Rowles, G. D. (1987). A place to call home. In L. Carstensen & B. A. Edelstein (Eds.), *Handbook of clinical gerontology.* New York: Pergamon Press.

Rubinstein, R. L. (1989). The home environments of older people: A description of the psychosocial processes linking person to place. *Journal of Gerontology: Social Sciences, 44,* S45–S53.

Scheidt, R. J. (1992, November). Organicism and housing contexts: Lessons from the work of Rudolf Moos. In P. Windley (Chair), *Environment and aging theory: A focus on housing.* Symposium conducted at the 45th annual meeting of the Gerontological Society of America, Washington, DC.

Scheidt, R. J., & Norris-Baker, C. (1990). A transactional approach to environmental stress among older residents of rural communities. *Journal of Rural Community Psychology, 11,* 5–30.

Scheidt, R. J., & Windley, P. G. (1985). The ecology of aging. In J. Birren & K. W. Schaie (Eds.), *Handbook of the psychology of aging* (pp. 245–260). New York: Van Nostrand Reinhold.

Scheidt, R. J., & Windley, P. G. (1987). Environmental perceptions and patterns of well-being among older Americans in small rural towns. *Comprehensive Gerontology, 1,* 24–29.

Schulz, R. (1976). Effects of control and predictability on the physical and psychological well-being of the institutionalized aged. *Journal of Personality and Social Psychology, 33,* 563–573.

Schulz, R., & Hanusa, B. (1978). Long-term effects of control and predictability-enhancing interventions: Findings and ethical issues. *Journal of Personality and Social Psychology, 36,* 1194–1201.

Segal, S. P., & Moyles, E. W. (1988). Sheltered care: A typology of residential facilities. *Adult Foster Care Journal, 2,* 118–134.

Sherman, S. R. (1974). Leisure activities in retirement housing. *Journal of Gerontology, 29,* 325–335.

Smith, G. C., & Whitbourne, S. K. (1990). Validity of the Sheltered Care Environment Scale. *Psychology and Aging, 5,* 228–235.

Stein, S., Linn, M., & Stein, E. (1987). Patients and staff assess social climate of different quality nursing homes. *Comprehensive Gerontology, 1,* 41–46.

Streib, G., Folts, W., & Hilker, M. (1984). *Old homes, new families: Shared living for the elderly.* New York: Columbia University Press.

Thompson, B., & Swisher, M. (1983). An assessment, using the Multiphasic Environmental Assessment Procedure (MEAP), of a rural life-care residential center for the elderly. *Journal of Housing for the Elderly, 1,* 41–56.

Timko, C., & Moos, R. H. (1989). Choice, control, and adaptation among elderly residents of sheltered care settings. *Journal of Applied Social Psychology, 19,* 636–655.

Timko, C., & Moos, R. H. (1990). Determinants of interpersonal support and self-direction in group residential facilities. *Journal of Gerontology: Social Sciences, 45,* S184–S192.

Timko, C., & Moos, R. H. (1991a). Assessing the quality of residential programs: Methods and applications. *Adult Residential Care Journal, 5,* 113–129.

Timko, C., & Moos, R. H. (1991b). A typology of social climates in group residential facilities for older people. *Journal of Gerontology: Social Sciences, 46,* S160–S169.

Wells, L., Singer, C., & Polgar, A. (1986). *To enhance quality of life in institutions: An empowerment model in long-term care: A partnership of residents, staff, and families.* Toronto: University of Toronto Press.

Willems, E. P. (1973). Behavioral ecology and experimental analysis: Courtship is not enough. In J. R. Nesselroade & H. Reese (Eds.), *Life-span developmental psychology: Methodological issues* (pp. 195–217). New York: Academic Press.

Willems, E. P. (1977). Relations of models to methods in behavioral ecology. In H. McGurk (Ed.), *Ecological factors in human development* (pp. 21–35). New York: North-Holland.

Wiseman, R. F. (1980). Why older people move: Theoretical issues. *Research on Aging, 2,* 141–154.

6

The Evolving Concept of Behavior Settings: Implications for Housing Older Adults

CAROLYN NORRIS-BAKER

Like Lawton and Nahemow's (1973) concept of competence and press, and Proshansky's formulation of place identity, behavior setting theory and its extensions have provided seminal theoretical constructs for environmental psychology by attempting to address the complexity of people's interactions with their surroundings (Stokols, 1995, p. 824). Despite this status, behavior settings rarely have been considered as a conceptual or methodological approach for examining housing issues for older adults. Roger and Louise Barker (1961) did report descriptive comparisons of the psychological ecology of community settings for older residents of a county seat in Kansas and a market town in Yorkshire, but these data are now more than 40 years old. The lack of use of behavior settings may stem at least partially from characteristics of the major research programs that have contributed to the development of the theory—the focus on public settings in behavior setting surveys (excluding individual dwellings), a frequent orientation toward the community as a whole, or to groups such as children rather than older adults, and the use of resource-intensive methods to collect information. Although the large body of behavior setting research provides relatively little empirical information specifically focused on housing (with the exception of Bechtel's [1977, 1982] work on military bases) or on older adults (see Barker & Barker, 1961; Norris-Baker & Scheidt, 1994; Scheidt & Norris-Baker, 1990; Windley & Scheidt, 1982), behavior setting theory suggests many concepts applicable to the residential needs of older adults, especially when the definition of housing includes not only the physical dwelling unit but the context in which it is embedded. This broad definition encompasses the entire physical and social context, including neighborhood characteristics and services such as shopping, recreation, health care, and transportation (Bylund, 1985).

To illustrate the potential of behavior setting theory for planning, designing, and managing housing environments for older adults, let us consider what we might observe if we dropped in late one morning on a resident of a continuing care retirement community. We meet Mrs. B at 11:30 A.M. as she is leaving her apartment in the independent living section of the community. She walks down the corridor and through an enclosed walkway to a lobby area in front of the dining room in the central building. There, other residents are gathering and socializing, waiting for the dining room to open its doors for the noon meal. Mrs. B joins in the socializing with her friends, and when the dining room opens at 11:45 A.M., they go in and take their seats for the meal. After the meal has been served and eaten, some residents linger over coffee to chat, while others leave more quickly. Mrs. B finishes her coffee and walks from the dining room into the lobby and then down the corridor toward the health-care unit where her husband is recuperating from a hip fracture. As she enters the health-care unit just after 1:00 P.M., she passes through a portion of the activity room where a staff member is working with some residents on a craft activity. Mrs. B enters the alcove area of the activity space designated for physical therapy, greets her husband and the aide who is working with him, and becomes involved in learning how to assist her husband with his exercises. After half an hour, Mrs. B leaves the therapy area and goes through the area where staff and several residents are decorating the activity room for the Halloween party that will be held later that afternoon. She pauses to help hang up some decorations and then walks back through the corridors to her apartment. She enters, completes toileting and hygiene activities in the bathroom, and goes into the living room, where she relaxes in her easy chair for an hour, reading. Then she is off to the meeting room in the central building, where she is responsible for leading the women's Bible study group, which meets each Wednesday from 3 to 4 P.M. At 4 P.M., she walks down the corridor to the health-care unit again and joins her husband in the activity room as the annual Halloween party for neighborhood children is beginning.

The mental images that undoubtedly accompany reading this description of Mrs. B's afternoon are drawn not only from experiences with the appearances of residential environments for older adults but also from an understanding of the kinds of activities that occur and are expected as a part of eating a congregate meal or attending a Bible study. If we list the physical environments in which we observed Mrs. B, they include the entry, bathroom, and living room of her apartment, the corridors of the retirement community, the lobby at the entrance to the dining room, the dining room, and the meeting room in the central building, and the activity/therapy room of the health-care unit. However, we also can describe the behavior settings in which she participated and the potentially rich set of information and characteristics that can be associated with each, including its space and time boundaries, its members, their roles, and routine programs of action. Since Mrs. B is always in a behavior setting, moving seamlessly from one to another throughout the day, we would have observed her in settings with descriptive labels such as: corridors, congregate noon meal, corridors, weekday craft program, individual physical therapy session, party decorating, corridors, own dwelling, corridors, Wednesday afternoon women's Bible study, corridors, and annual Halloween party. Having labeled the probable behavior settings in which Mrs. B participated, let us consider the formal definition of a *behavior setting*, how its concepts and theory evolved over time, and how behavior settings may be useful for understanding issues involving housing older adults.

BEHAVIOR SETTINGS

The concept of the behavior setting was initially proposed by Roger G. Barker and his associates to describe and measure the ecological environment of behavior using a unit consisting of an interaction between behaving persons and things, time, and the immediate environment. Many of the key definitions for behavior settings have appeared repeatedly over the past 40 years, so only selected references providing substantial information about the theory and its development are provided as citations here (Barker, 1968, 1987; Barker & Associates, 1978; Bechtel, 1977; Schoggen, 1989; Wicker, 1987). According to Barker (1990), ideas that contributed to development of the theory were threefold: the indigenous inhabitants of communities, where behavior settings (not labeled as such) were basic facts of life of the town, research that suggested a child's behavior could be predicted better from place of occurrence than from personality, and the ideas of ''deep thinkers'' such as Heider's theories of perception and Lewin's theories of dynamic unity (pp. 510–512).

The behavior setting is defined as ''a standing pattern of behavior and a part of the milieu which are synomorphic and in which the milieu is circumjacent to the behavior'' (Barker & Wright, 1955, p. 45). Standing patterns of behavior are behaviors that tend to be extraindividual; that is, the behavior will continue even if the individuals in the setting change. Synomorphy of behavior and milieu is the fit that exists between a behavior pattern and the physical and temporal surroundings that provide its context. Thus, if we consider Mrs. B participating in the congregate noon meal behavior setting, standing patterns of behavior probably would include residents eating and conversing with one another, and staff serving and clearing dishes. These patterns would have continued unchanged when Mr. B stopped coming because of his hip fracture, when Mrs. B invited a friend to lunch, or when an individual member of the wait staff resigned. The physical and social structure of the environment ''fit'' and support the standing patterns of behavior—the tables seat small numbers of people to facilitate social interaction and provide appropriate surfaces for serving and eating a meal, tables are spaced so that wait staff can move between them with trays, dishes and silverware are provided for eating, and so forth.

Colleagues and associates of Barker have provided additional insights into the definition and usefulness of the behavior setting. As Gump (1969) notes, behavior settings are not intended as a constructed abstraction. The unit is ''a

naturally occurring one that places people in the position of components contributing behavior to setting maintenance and in the position of individuals
whose life spaces are partly formed by the settings' attributes'' (p. 203). They
are a part of the real world, with clear time and place loci. Wicker (1979/1983)
observed that behavior settings can be seen as the ''most immediate of human
environments''—small-scale social systems composed of people and physical
objects that are configured in such a way as to carry out a routine program of
actions within specifiable place and time boundaries (p. 9). Behavior settings
are highly interdependent, and everyone is always in one, moving seamlessly
from one setting to another throughout the day. Thus, entering a setting reflects
a choice between two or more settings, although the opportunities for choice
among settings may vary. ''The fundamental significance of behavior settings
. . . comes from their position within the topographical hierarchy of entities ranging from cell, to organ, to person, to behavior setting, to institution (in some
cases), and to community. Within this included-inclusive series, behavior settings are proximal and circumjacent to people (people are components of behavior settings), and behavior settings are proximal and interjacent to institutions
and communities (they are components of institutions and communities)'' (Barker & Associates, 1978, p. 287). Thus, relationships exist between settings and
communities and between settings and individuals.

Wicker's amendments to behavior setting theory have attempted to incorporate this larger social and physical environmental context, as well as a temporal
one that can be described in terms of the life cycles of settings, and relationships
between people and settings (Wicker, 1987, 1992; Wicker & King, 1988). Although a behavior setting observed over a short period of time may seem a
stable phenomenon in comparison with behavior, Wicker and his colleagues
have developed a framework of four temporal stages: preconvergence (prior to
its founding), convergence (initial organization and beginning operation), continued existence (highly variable in duration), and divergence (disintegration of
the setting and reallocation of its resources). Wicker (1992) also suggests that
at certain stages of behavior settings, such as their founding or when crises
occur, setting participants may not have the interchangeability that Barker's
conceptualization proposes, and the personal motivation and cognition of individuals may play roles in the course of the behavior setting's existence. These
modifications and extensions of Barker's theory that incorporate the larger physical, social, and policy environments, processes involved in the creation and
disintegration of settings, and individual variations in leadership into the theory
all make behavior setting theory more useful for conceptualizing housing issues
for older adults.

Behavior Setting Survey

Research involving behavior settings typically required the use of the behavior
setting survey to systematically and quantitatively obtain information about behavior settings. The behavior setting survey is an inventory of the town's (or

institution's) ecological environment in terms of behavior settings (Barker, 1987). It uses a variety of methods to develop a comprehensive inventory and description of all the behavior settings in a particular community or institution during a stated period of time. Since some kinds of settings may be annual events, preference in conducting the survey was for the use of a year as the time frame. Within such a framework, setting frequency may range from once (such as the annual Halloween party Mrs. B attended), to very infrequently, to periodically every month or week (such as the Bible study Mrs. B conducted, to daily (congregate noon meals), or even continuously (the corridors of the retirement community). According to Barker's longtime associate Phil Schoggen (1988b), the main purpose of completing a behavior setting survey of a community is not to account for all of the living time of each resident but to describe the resources, opportunities, and obligations the community provides for its residents (p. 377). The methods employed to complete behavior setting surveys include direct observation of behavior, searches of archives such as newspapers, membership rosters, and organizational records, and interviews with informants (Bechtel [1977] adapted the survey process to a questionnaire and interview technique). The survey process should exhaust all possible sources of information to ensure a comprehensive survey. The comprehensive nature of a behavior setting survey necessarily limits the size of the institution or community with which it can be used. Perkins, Burns, Perry, and Nielsen (1988) point out that too large a community may limit the settings that are sampled, and no comprehensive taxonomy would be developed. If, however, the residents of a community are known, then the population can be defined and sampled.

When all the behavior settings in the survey frame have been identified, each is described in terms of multiple indices, including its number of occurrences, duration, number of participants and occupancy time among subgroups of the population, leadership, spatial independence, behavior objects, molar actions, temporal contiguity, and behavior mechanisms (Barker, 1968; Barker & Schoggen, 1973). In addition, characteristics of the community's molar environment are measured, such as the Ecological Resource Index (providing a single estimate of the relative extents of parts of the community in terms of the number, occurrence, and duration of behavior settings). The descriptive information can be used to classify behavior settings using many schema—in fact, Barker (1968) believed that behavior settings could be classified in as many ways as they had discriminable attributes. This flexibility is a great asset for the potential application of behavior setting theory to the rapidly changing and diverse environments involved in housing older adults. The potential for specific uses of the varied measures that can be derived from behavior setting surveys will be considered in a later section of the chapter.

Limitations of the Focus on Public Behavior Settings

An important critique of behavior setting theory by community psychologists has been that although the theory "provides a methodologically comprehensive approach to characterizing human environments . . . eliminating nonpublic and other 'unofficial' settings has important theoretical and practical implications" (Perkins et al., 1988, p. 359). According to Schoggen (1988b), the task of describing all the behavior settings in all the homes of even a small community like "Midwest" probably would require methods and procedures different from those developed to study a community's public settings, as well as extensive resources. However, it is important to recognize what is omitted by the conceptually and pragmatically driven need to focus on public behavior settings. The yearlong behavior settings surveys completed in Midwest, Kansas, and Yoredale, England, did not account for 77 percent and 81 percent of the waking person-hours of time of their residents (Barker & Schoggen, 1973).

As Perkins and his colleagues (1988) observed, "For certain groups the loss of information is striking. . . . Nonpublic settings may be particularly important to the behavioral opportunities of specific groups not greatly involved in the commercial, educational, and administrative tasks characteristic of public settings (e.g., the retired, homebound, unemployed, disabled, and psychiatrically impaired" (p. 359–360). Older adults are disproportionately represented in these groups, and the constraints and opportunities offered by home behavior settings may become more crucial as people grow older. It also is possible, however, that as people grow older and mobility is restricted, the influence of the neighborhood increases, perhaps making it as important as the home (Carp, 1986). Regardless of the relative importance of these home versus public settings, other methods provide alternatives to gather information about individual activities and participation in behavior settings within and outside the home. Perkins and his colleagues suggest, "From the perspective of individual residents, the most meaningful definition of the community can be understood using the 'activity range' concept developed by Wright. (See Gump and Adelberg, 1978). An individual's activity range comprises the number and kinds of settings he or she enters, i.e., his or her personal community" (Perkins et al., 1988, p. 360). Time budget methods also provide a good way to document the activity ranges of residents, including the occupancy time in public and private settings for any particular population subgroups (Schoggen, 1988b).

Behavior Setting Dynamics

Behavior settings differ greatly in the variety and stability of their standing patterns and in the strength of their maintenance forces (Barker, 1987). "One source of the stability . . . is a balance between many independent forces that bear upon them. Some of the forces issue from the larger community, some are intrinsic to the setting itself, and some originate within the individuals who populate the setting (pp. 161–163). Whereas Barker's concept "highlights the impact of environmental forces, more recent conceptualizations of behavior settings have emphasized both the psychological processes within setting inhabitants (Wicker) [sic] and the reciprocal nature of human-setting and group-setting transactions (Stokols, 1981; Stokols & Shumaker, 1981)'' (Fuhrer, 1990, p. 528). As Wicker (1990) states, if we maintain an open systems perspective, we must consider not only ''behavior setting dynamics, but person-setting dynamics and setting-organization dynamics'' (p. 497). His amendments to behavior setting theory incorporate a dynamic and developmental approach to setting programs that reflect continuous negotiation between participants and accommodate differentiation in person-setting relationships (Wicker, 1992).

Newer directions in behavior setting theory also have begun to consider behavior settings as cultural phenomena—the possibility that some behavior settings may embody the core values of a culture and thus be particularly susceptible to cultural change (Welz, 1984), as well as denotative and connotative meanings that may be imposed on settings (Fuhrer, 1990). ''Any behavior setting, in being used as a cultural entity and in having effects on people, operates via certain denotative and connotative meanings'' (p. 528). Objects communicating denotative meanings may ''represent important contextual determinants of the actions of setting members and impose meanings on settings through the use of cognitive schemes'' (p. 528), while complex connotative meanings may be associated with personal and collective experiences, beliefs, and evaluations shared within a group or culture. The personal and cultural meanings of behavior settings are relevant for housing issues involving older adults for several reasons. First, place identity and place attachment (which might mean attachment to a behavior setting itself rather than its surrounding milieu) are important dimensions in the lives of many older people. Second, relocation issues, whether from one community to another or from home to long-term care facility, necessarily involve adjustments in opportunities for behavior setting involvement as well as the potential loss of access to behavior settings that hold personal and/or cultural meaning. Third, changes in a community that lead to the loss of highly valued settings such as those associated with a church or school may threaten the sense of self and embodiment of home for some older residents. Thus, considering the role of behavior settings as vessels for embodying culture and identity may help inform planning and housing policies that deal with community change.

DESCRIPTIVE AND TAXONOMIC APPLICATIONS OF BEHAVIOR SETTING THEORY

Behavior setting theory incorporates physical properties, human components, and the setting program and can be applied at levels from a single room to community scale. It is able to incorporate complex indices of person-environment transactions and to reflect suprasetting contextual and historical factors and change over time. These characteristics suggest many potential applications of the theory to housing older adults, especially when housing is defined to include the context of an individual's dwelling unit, be it a single-family home or a double-bedded room in a long-term care facility.

Classifications and Analyses for Describing the Community

As noted earlier, there are as many ways to classify behavior settings as dimensions on which they can be scaled. In view of this diversity, and the complexity of measuring some of the indices, only a few examples of indices and classifications will be discussed. Barker (1968) used two systems of classification—genotype (based on the interchangeability of leaders in different settings and intended to describe the varieties of behavior available to residents) and an authority system based on five sources of authority (business, churches, government, schools, and voluntary associations). Genotype classification results in a reduction of categories by a factor of about three to five (Bechtel, 1981). Other studies have developed functional classification schemes and/or used demographic and role variables (Bechtel, 1981, 1982; Bechtel & O'Reilly, 1982; Price & Blashfield, 1975). Price and Blashfield (1975) employed factor and cluster analysis using 43 of Barker's descriptive setting attributes, which yielded nine factors including adult members and targets, religion versus government, young performers, young members and targets, female members and targets, business, duration of behavior settings, adolescent members and targets, and male members and targets. On the basis of these analyses of small-town data, age and sex appear to interact with role positions to produce types.

Bechtel (1981) analyzed behavior setting survey data from eight military installations/communities in Alaska with a complex set of overlapping programs that classified both variables and objects. He also found demographic and role data the most important variables in classifying behavior settings. However, in contrast to Barker's five authority categories, his analyses indicated work, social, living, minority groups, and children as functional classifications for settings. Bechtel and O'Reilly (1982) introduced performers (versus nonperformers) as well as function and demographics into their classification of survey data from two studies, one in Alaska (Bechtel, 1981) and one of six small communities in Kansas that had experienced many changes as a result of the construction of a flood-prevention dam and reservoir (Harloff, Gump, & Campbell, 1981).

Analyses of 30 setting variables, using the same technique Bechtel had employed in previous studies, identified age, number of performers, and duration of settings as central principles for classification. In the midwestern towns, "aged, who were fewer in number [than children,] defined their own behavior setting types" (Bechtel & O'Reilly, 1982, p. 115). Although the samples of settings used in these classification studies were far from representative, the recurring importance of age and performance suggests that behavior survey methods could be useful in understanding the segregated and integrated ways in which a population such as older adults participate in their communities, whether that community is an institution or a town.

As Schoggen (1983) points out, "Behavior setting surveys of whole communities are especially well suited to the task of describing the position occupied by members of particular population subgroups within the public arena of the town'' (p. 152). Clearly, if resources are available to gather the information, these data provide comprehensive descriptions on which different communities can be classified and compared in terms of the needs and preferences of older adults. These applications could range from descriptions of and contrasts among small towns that are naturally occurring retirement communities to studies of resident opportunities for involvement and control in continuing care retirement communities. Another potential application is to the issues of migration. For example, Longino's (1990) research indicated that retired migrants often fail to develop business and family relationships and thus do not become integrated into their new community. They form ties primarily with other migrants, ''perpetuating their separateness'' (p. 393). Since a strength of behavior setting surveys is the ability to focus on issues of segregation and integration, they could be useful in exploring transition processes for migrants as well as some of the impacts on the host community.

In terms of design, the classification studies contradict the idea that designers/ researchers must discover the behavior settings and then shape their designs to fit the settings. Rather, the key ''seems to be to design for variations with no rigid function but being conscious that people sort themselves into leaders and followers and into integrated or non-integrated age groups on a purely local basis. Flexibility would seem to be the key design variable'' (Bechtel & O'Reilly, 1982, p. 115).

Behavior Settings as Cultural Phenomena in the Community

Much of the attention to classifying behavior settings was completed within the traditional Barkerian paradigm and thus did not incorporate more recent amendments such as issues involving life cycles, suprasetting contexts, and the roles of connotative and denotative meaning for settings as cultural phenomena. Behavior settings in a community are part of the essence that contributes to and shapes the experience and meaning of home in terms of the neighborhood, the community, and the regional culture (Norris-Baker & Scheidt, 1994). Rivlin (1987) argues that four neighborhood domains combine to create strong attachments to place: the ways in which personal needs (ranging from shopping to religious activities) are met, the degree to which those services are concentrated in the neighborhood, the strength of affiliation and shared values with residents of the neighborhood, and the extension of these patterns over time. Behavior setting theory focuses at a scale and with measures that directly address these issues. The differences between the experiences of different cohorts (young-old having had more mobility and perhaps less time to develop affiliations with settings than the old-old) and the trend toward homogenizing environments (e.g., fast-food franchises) raise questions about the processes by which affiliations with settings develop and how expectations about the availability of opportunities for setting participation may differ among older adults.

The questions of ''fit'' between older individuals and community may involve behavior setting theory as well. For example, Hummon (1986) suggests that each of us has an image of ourselves appropriated from community imagery—a community identity as a city person, suburbanite, small-town person, or country person. While Feldman (1995) has found that a significant minority (10 to 12 percent) rejected such identification as meaningless, such bonds to types of settlements appear to be transferable—and could perhaps be conceptualized in terms of behavior settings that hold essential denotative and connotative meanings related to that identity. Thus, behavior setting theory can be introduced into questions of place identity—what characteristics of settings facilitate the sense of "feeling at home" in one's community and region as well as one's dwelling unit. Hummon's (1995) research suggests that these three identities are not nested, and we must look simultaneously at multiple loci of attachment and the ways in which social, spatial, and psychological factors shape these attachments. In Toyama's (1988) study of the outcomes of relocating to housing for the elderly in Sweden, he found that residents who adjusted more positively had been able to recreate an interior similar to their former homes and find a parallel in rooms and therefore in daily routine (perhaps approximating the idea of a behavior setting?). Behavior settings, as cultural phenomena that integrate aspects of the social, psychological, and spatial environments, seem well suited to help advance our understanding of attachment, especially at the levels of community and region, and how the costs of relocations and loss of access to settings might be minimized for older adults who experience such problems.

BEHAVIOR SETTING SURVEYS AND SPECIFIC HOUSING-RELATED ISSUES

In addition to global classifications strategies, many measures derived from behavior setting surveys may be useful in understanding more discrete issues related to housing older adults. In order to explore this potential, let us return to the example of Mr. and Mrs. B and consider some possible uses of information from a behavior setting survey of the retirement community. Such an example provides a microcosm of the issues that also might be considered in any institution or in a town or community small enough for a form of behavior setting survey to be completed. Focusing on this type of small community with well-defined boundaries and known residents also responds to some of the methodological concern raised by Perkins and his colleagues (1988).

Availability, Diversity, and Focus of Settings

Researchers may complete analyses of the distributions of measures such as occupancy times, action patterns, and populations across the total setting survey or subgroupings of settings, focusing on specific needs and expectations of the older adult clientele. Roger and Louise Barker (1961) used this strategy in describing the community lives of older residents of small towns in Kansas and

Yorkshire, making intergenerational and international comparisons between the range of settings entered, depth of penetration (from stranger to leader), and exposure time in the settings and to action patterns. Today, one useful measure could be that of *habitat size*, which describes the number of settings convenient in time, place, and access that exist within the boundaries of the survey (Barker, 1987). If such a measure were targeted on the kinds of settings perceived necessary to a high quality of life in residential environments for aging (whether in a community or an institution), cross-sectional and longitudinal comparisons between survey sites are possible. In the example of the retirement community, the strategic plan might require a certain level of habitability for commercial, service, and health-care settings within the boundaries of the facility. If habitat size changed markedly, the retirement community might consider whether changes in the types or hours of such settings within the facility were needed to satisfy resident expectations. It might also be possible to monitor the extent to which the entire habitat and its component settings were used by residents of the community. Measures of habitat could be focused at the individual resident level as well, assessing needed access to particular settings, patterns of use, and degree of involvement, for example.

Another possible measure is *welfare*, which documents whether a setting exists for a certain age group. Although this measure was developed for use with settings involving children, it could as easily be applied to other age groups such as older adults. Settings may be classified as not concerned with participants of the specified age group, serving members of that age (most of the settings in which Mrs. B participated), serving them in other settings (the office of the director of the retirement community), instigating and supporting other settings that serve the age group (meetings of the board of directors and perhaps other community service organizations), or having that age group serve other members of the setting (the Halloween party for neighborhood children).

Participation in Behavior Settings

The potential to use behavior setting data to profile age, sex, and performer/nonperformer characteristics of settings already has been mentioned; such measures might be valuable in targeting particular types of settings as well. Penetration levels measure how central a participant's performance is to the setting, using six zones from the status of an onlooker to being the single leader. The behavior settings in which Mrs. B participated all were predominantly populated by people over 65. Her penetration levels varied across the entire scale from an onlooker in the weekday craft program to a single leader in the Bible study. Measures of penetration also may address issues of role opportunities, transitions, and losses and of leadership and control—all highly relevant to older adults and their housing choices.

A related scale measures *pressure*, or the degree to which forces outside a behavior setting act to draw a person into a setting or to encourage avoidance.

Like welfare, this was a scale developed initially for studying children but useful for issues involving older adults. Its potential for applications might be highest for issues involving relocation and adaptations to transitions in housing and community situations.

If knowledge about participation in behavior settings and the characteristics of those settings is combined with other information, such as individual behavioral or clinical data, behavior settings can be used to place the individual within the larger temporal-social-physical environmental context, to predict behaviors, and to analyze intersetting differences in behavior. Examples of research that included a focus on person-setting relationships in well-defined institutional settings include the program of research conducted by Willems, Vineberg, LeCompte, Halstead, and their colleagues at a rehabilitation hospital (Willems & Halstead, 1978) and a study of a large community residence for women with mental disorders (Perkins & Perry, 1985), which focused the behavioral demands settings placed on the residents. Although neither study population was elderly, the clinical and behavioral issues involved are highly relevant for the more supportive residential environments in which many older adults reside. Another potential arena for application is that of the single dwelling unit (especially single-family homes or apartments), in which characteristics of behavior settings within the home might best describe the temporal-social-physical environmental context in which an older person resides and the demands that are created.

Autonomy and Independence versus Dependency

Autonomy, independence, and control are issues that undergird much of the research on environments and aging and on housing issues in particular. Pynoos and Golant (1995) cite the work of Barker (1968), along with Moos and Lemke (1994) and Jaffe and Howe (1988), when they conclude, "The quality of relationships between the sponsor [or manager] and the elderly residents are dependent on the policies and practices of the facility which, in turn, are related to the dependency of the residents and the size of the facility" (p. 314). Autonomy can assess how decisions are made and the extent of the control over decisions that can be exercised within the setting. Decisions can include those about behavior setting programs and schedules, who can be admitted as members, and fees for participation. Such decisions may be made within the setting (Mrs. B decided to cancel Bible study when her husband was in the hospital), within the community (a local bank provides a free transportation service to events at the town's cultural/community center), or at a great distance, such as state and federal policies regulating admission procedures for the constellation of behavior settings in the health-care unit.

We know that social and physical milieus of highly institutional environments such as many nursing homes may lead to a loss of autonomy and control and even learned helplessness; however, "if . . . programs were in place to strengthen residents' sense of their own competence, nursing homes might be more favorable settings for aging, and some residents might return to the community'' (Carp, 1987, p. 347). While Carp uses the word ''programs,'' substituting the term ''behavior settings'' highlights the potential of *setting* characteristics such as pressure and autonomy as well as activity patterns to enhance competence. Again, research strategies that obtain data for both individuals and settings can be useful in monitoring individual changes in independence as well as the degree to which behavior settings support independent or self-initiated activity. The research conducted by Willems and his colleagues demonstrated that independence was strongly setting specific within the rehabilitation institution, and in home and community settings after discharge (Norris-Baker, Stephens, & Willems, 1982; Willems & Halstead, 1978).

Finally, the *richness* of a behavior setting provides a summative index that may be useful for issues of independence and control. It measures the range of occupants' ages and leadership to the varieties of behavior. The greater the range of occupant groups, higher the penetration levels, and greater the behavior mechanisms and action patterns, the higher the richness index of the setting. This index can be determined for an individual behavior setting, for a group or classification of settings, or for the community or institution as a whole.

BEHAVIOR SETTING THEORY: DESIGN INTERVENTIONS

Behavior setting theory can be linked to the concept of ecological diagnosis and intervention—that is, a problem may be better understood and a more appropriate intervention devised if the problem is evaluated in terms of the ecological environment in which it is situated. Since each setting is linked to many others within a nested ecological hierarchy (Barker, 1968, 1987), the consequences of changes in one setting (whether intentional or not) may appear not only in that setting but in other, related settings. The process by which change occurs in settings and the roles of individual people—whether solely as components or taking more active roles as change agents—creates questions about whether changes in settings can be intentional and whether it is possible for insiders (participants) to engage in intervention. Perkins (1988), in his critique of setting theory, maintains that settings are not self-modifying but rather are '' 'tools' which people invent, refine, borrow, and ultimately *use* in order to satisfy their needs'' (p. 389). Wicker's amendments to setting theory also recast the influences that key performers may have in settings, especially in periods of creation or crisis (Wicker, 1987, 1992). Barker's stance on the role of interventionists is clear—he espouses one general principle: ''Behavior-setting experts and those who actually create, alter, and choose them must be outsiders, that is, people who are not yet creatures of the settings they will deal with'' (Barker, 1987, p. 1427). This issue continues unresolved, but it is certain that insider and outsider perspectives on a setting may differ greatly.

Behavior Setting Boundaries

Boundaries of behavior settings—"where the behavior stops"—are obvious when the spatial boundaries (such as walls) exactly correspond to the setting boundaries (Bechtel, 1977, 1982). However, when spatial and setting boundaries are not contiguous—that is, a setting either includes multiple rooms or spaces, or multiple settings overlap in a single room—boundary problems may occur. Solutions to boundary problems involve ecological diagnosis and interventions that may focus on design, management, or a combination of the two. In the case of a setting that spans multiple rooms (such as a dwelling or perhaps a special-care unit for people with dementia), connections between the physical spaces must support the standing patterns of behavior. In the retirement community where Mrs. B lives, the congregate meal setting probably includes the physical spaces of both the lobby area where people gather and the dining room itself, but problems do not occur because there is synomorphy between the patterns of behavior and the milieu.

Frequently, boundary problems result from ambiguous or overlapping behavior settings. Bechtel (1977, 1982) advocates creating boundaries where they are lacking in order to help define social groups and spaces. This strategy has proved successful in settings ranging from offices in a military installation to conflicts between physical and occupational therapies in a health-care setting. It is important, however, that the new or modified boundary function for all perceptual dimensions that may be impacted by the overlapping settings—for example, the partitions in an office landscape do not create an auditory boundary, nor does white noise create a visual one. Large "generic" activity or social spaces, as are found in many residential environments and long-term care settings, are likely locales for setting boundary problems. For example, when Mrs. B visited the health-care unit, she traversed both the craft program and party decorating settings to reach physical therapy. Although some settings may welcome on-lookers, the programs of others may be disrupted. In addition, many settings have criteria for admission and needs for privacy (e.g., counseling and physical therapy settings, Mrs. B's Bible study) that make infringements on setting boundaries unacceptable. Employing behavior setting theory, rather than focusing on the physical environment alone, may help identify and solve such boundary problems. Occupancy time and duration also may impact setting boundary problems. Using the activity room as an example, a religious service conducted there on Sundays would not create any boundary problems with physical therapy because occupancy times do not overlap.

Behavioral Focus Points

Another concept with potential for use in ecological diagnosis and community design is that of a *behavioral focal point*. This is the behavior setting that is most accessible to the largest number of various kinds of people in any geographical area or community domain—a combination of several complementary functions that will attract more people jointly than they would separately (Bechtel, 1977). Potential focal points can be diagrammed for a community or institution and enhanced by making these settings as rich as possible, locating necessary and well-attended functions nearby, and having as few visible barriers as possible. In some cases, seating to accommodate appropriate numbers of community residents may facilitate the setting's function as a behavioral focal point. The concept of establishing or enhancing existing behavioral focal points is directly applicable to the planning and design of new residential environments for older adults, as well as to existing institutional environments and communities.

Optimizing Setting Size

Behavior setting theory and its extensions also address questions about the optimal sizes of behavior settings and the consequences of fewer than optimal numbers of participants (understaffing) or greater than optimal participants (overstaffing) (Barker & Associates, 1978; Barker & Schoggen, 1973; Schoggen, 1983, 1988a; Wicker, 1983, 1987; Wicker, McGrath, & Armstrong, 1972). Research comparing the two communities in Kansas and England found that in "Midwest," which was relatively understaffed, residents spent more time per person in public settings, more frequently assumed roles of responsibility in the community's behavior settings, and engaged in more actions of leadership. Children, adolescents, and people over age 65 assumed more responsibilities than in the better staffed "Yoredale," suggesting that the quality of life may have been different for these groups in the two towns (Barker & Barker, 1961; Schoggen, 1983).

Settings that are understaffed have many possible consequences for those who participate in them. These settings exert more pressure on potential participants to enter and take part. Participants tend to take more responsibility for the setting functioning, are less sensitive to and less evaluative of individual differences among members, perceive themselves as having greater functional importance and identity (in terms of what they can do in the setting), and may experience greater insecurity because they need to perform more challenging tasks with fewer backup resources (Schoggen, 1988a).

According to Barker (1979), "For those who are able to cope, the more difficult actions lead to greater hardiness, to more experience of success and failure, and to enhanced self-esteem and self-confidence" (p. 79). These kinds of outcomes might be seen as desirable in some residential environments or communities, especially for the young-old, who are relatively healthy, active, and independent. However, attempting difficult actions may have negative effects for those who find themselves "spread so thin that they have to perform at or near the limits of their abilities and energies just to keep up" (Wicker, 1983, p. 73). They may experience "reduced stamina and vigor, higher morbidity and mortality, more experience of failure, and lower self-regard and self-esteem'' (Barker, 1979, p. 79). This is less likely to occur in planned housing environments (except perhaps in the case of staff) than in naturally occurring retirement communities and small towns that are declining, where human and financial resources are limited (Norris-Baker & Scheidt, 1996; Scheidt & Norris-Baker, 1990, 1993). Furthermore, the duration of the behavioral effects of undertaffing is unclear (Perkins et al., 1988). Some of the satisfactions that may be derived from understaffing, such as increased feelings of challenge and involvement, may disappear if the situation is long lasting (Wicker, 1987). Within the framework of housing issues for older adults, the most applicable concept is that of optimizing setting size so that there are appropriate amounts of both resources and opportunities for participation. Intentional understaffing of settings to increase pressure and encourage involvement and responsibility among residents seems inadvisable, given the lack of knowledge about its long-term consequences for older adults. Where understaffing and underpopulation are endemic, such as very small communities, perhaps residents should be encouraged to reduce the settings they are maintaining and reallocate the setting resources to better support the functioning of those settings that remain.

CONCLUSION

There are many reasons that behavior setting theory has been relatively underutilized in studying housing issues for older adults. The dominant methodology is costly and at times cumbersome, and applications have been primarily case studies of diverse communities and institutions. Thus, we lack a broad base of normative data with which new information can be compared. Innovative techniques for collecting data and reducing its costs are essential if the theory is to be useful in the current social and political climate. Although Bechtel's (1977, 1982) work started to develop alternative methods, much more work is needed. The most appropriate situations in which to apply behavior setting theory today may be in well-bounded community and institutional environments. The extensions and amendments to the theory have created new possibilities for studying person-setting and community-setting relationships, all of which are vital to the well-being of older adults in today's diverse housing environments.

Behavior setting theory is evolutionary, and therein lies its great potential for understanding issues associated with housing older adults. As Barker (1968) believed about his original ideas, and Wicker stated about the more recent framework he proposed, behavior setting theories are only beginning steps that must be advanced by researchers who ''think new thoughts'' and are ''open to ideas from other fields'' (Wicker, 1987). Likewise, the ways in which we conceptualize and study housing issues for older adults may be advanced by considering what new thoughts and ideas might be gained from behavior setting concepts and theory.

REFERENCES

Barker, R. G. (1968). *Ecological psychology: Concepts and methods for studying the environment of human behavior.* Stanford, CA: Stanford University Press.

Barker, R. G. (1979). The influence of frontier environments on behavior. In J. Steffen (Ed.), *The American West* (pp. 61–92). Norman: University of Oklahoma Press.

Barker, R. G. (1987). Prospecting in environmental psychology: Oskaloosa revisited. In D. Stokols & I. Altman (Eds.), *Handbook of environmental psychology* (Vol. 2, pp. 1413–1432). New York: Wiley.

Barker, R. G. (1990). Recollections of the Midwest Psychological Field Station. *Environment and Behavior, 22,* 503–513.

Barker, R. G., & Associates. (Eds.). (1978). *Habitats, environments, and human behavior.* San Francisco: Jossey-Bass.

Barker, R. G., & Barker, L. S. (1961). The psychological ecology of old people in Midwest, Kansas, and Yoredale, Yorkshire. *Journal of Gerontology, 16,* 144–149.

Barker, R. G., & Schoggen, P. (1973). *Qualities of community life: Methods for measuring environment and behavior applied to an American and an English town.* San Francisco: Jossey-Bass.

Barker, R. G., & Wright, H. F. (1955). *Midwest and its children.* New York: Harper & Row.

Bechtel, R. (1977). *Enclosing behavior.* Stroudsburg, PA: Dowden, Hutchinson & Ross.

Bechtel, R. (1981). *Classification of behavior settings.* In A. Osterberg, C. Tiernan, & R. Findlay (Eds.), *Design research interactions* (pp. 101–109). Washington, DC: Environmental Design Research Association.

Bechtel, R. (1982). Contributions of ecological psychology to the evaluation of environments. *International Review of Applied Psychology, 31,* 153–167.

Bechtel, R., & O'Reilly, J. (1982). Classification of behavior settings. In P. Bart, A. Chen, & G. Francescato (Eds.), *Knowledge for design* (pp. 112–116). Washington, DC: Environmental Design Research Association.

Bylund, R. (1985). Rural housing: Perspectives for the aged. In R. Coward & G. Lee (Eds.), *The elderly in rural society: Every fourth elder* (pp. 129–150). New York: Springer.

Carp, F. M. (1986). Neighborhood quality perception and measurement. In R. J. Newcomer, M. P. Lawton, & T. O. Byerts (Eds.), *Housing an aging society: Issues, alternatives, and policy* (pp. 127–140). New York: Van Nostrand Reinhold.

Carp, F. M. (1987). Environment and aging. In D. Stokols & I. Altman (Eds.), *Handbook of environmental psychology* (Vol. 1, pp. 329–360). New York: Wiley.

Feldman, R. (1995, March). Maintaining continuity of place attachment with residential mobility. In R. Feldman & E. Freid (Chairs), *Functions and dysfunctions of place attachment.* Symposium conducted at the meeting of the Environmental Design Research Association, Boston, MA.

Fuhrer, U. (1990). Bridging the ecological-psychological gap: Behavior settings as interfaces. *Environment and Behavior, 22,* 518–537.

Gump, P. V. (1969). Intra-setting analysis: The third grade classroom as a special but instructive case. In E. P. Willems & H. L Raush (Eds.), *Naturalistic viewpoints in psychological research* (pp. 202–220). New York: Holt, Rinehart & Winston.

Gump, P., & Adelberg, B. (1978). Urbanism from the perspective of ecological psychologists. *Environment and Behavior, 10,* 171–191.

Harloff, H., Gump, P., & Campbell, D. (1981). The public life of communities: Environmental change as a result of the intrusion of a flood control, conservation, and recreational reservoir. *Environment and Behavior, 13,* 685–706.

Hummon, D. (1986). City mouse, country mouse: The persistence of community identity. *Qualitative Sociology, 9* (1), 3–25.

Hummon, D. (1995, March). Place attachment: Observations on multiple ties to home, community, and region. In R. Feldman & E. Fried (Chairs), *Functions and dysfunctions of place attachment.* Symposium conducted at the annual meeting of the Environmental Design Research Association, Boston, MA.

Jaffe, D. J., & Howe, E. (1988). Agency-assisted shared housing: The nature of programs and matches. *Gerontologist, 28,* 318–324.

Lawton, M. P., & Nahemow, L. (1973). Ecology and the aging process. In K. W. Schaie & C. Schooler (Eds.), *Social structure and aging: Psychological processes* (pp. 57–78). Hillsdale, NJ: Erlbaum.

Longino, C. F. (1990). Retirement migration streams: Trends and implications for North Carolina communities. *Journal of Applied Gerontology, 9,* 393–404.

Moos, R. H., & Lemke, S. (1994). *Group residences for older adults: Physical features, policies, and social climate.* New York: Oxford University Press.

Norris-Baker, C., & Scheidt, R. (1991). A contextual approach to serving older residents of economically-threatened small towns. *Journal of Aging Studies, 5,* 333–346.

Norris-Baker, C., & Scheidt, R. (1994). From ''Our Town'' to ''Ghost Town''? The changing context of home for rural elderly. *International Journal of Aging and Human Development, 38* (3), 99–120.

Norris-Baker, C., & Scheidt, R. (1996). Aging survivors: The mental health of older residents of declining rural communities. In A. G. Parks (Ed.), *Aging and mental health: Aging in the Heartland* (pp. 15–33). Dubuque, IA: Kendall/Hunt.

Norris-Baker, C., Stephens, M. A. P., & Willems, E. P. (1982). Negotiability and everyday behavior in housing for the physically disabled: A case study. In P. Bart, A. Chen, & G. Francescato (Eds.), *Knowledge for design* (pp. 380–392). Washington, DC: Environmental Design Research Association.

Perkins, D. (1988). Alternative views of behavior settings: A response to Schoggen. *Journal of Community Psychology, 16,* 387–391.

Perkins, D., Burns, T., Perry, J., & Nielsen, K. (1988). Behavior setting theory and community psychology: An analysis and critique. *Journal of Community Psychology, 16,* 355–372.

Perkins, D., & Perry, J. (1985). Dimensional analysis of behavior setting demands in a community residence for chronically mentally ill women. *Journal of Community Psychology, 13,* 350–359.

Price, R., & Blashfield, R. (1975). Explorations in the taxonomy of behavior settings: Analyses of dimensions and classifications of settings. *American Journal of Community Psychology, 3,* 335–351.

Pynoos, J., & Golant, S. (1995). Housing and living arrangements for the elderly. In R. H. Binstock & L. K. George (Eds.), *Handbook of aging and the social sciences* (pp. 303–324). San Diego: Academic Press.

Rivlin, L. (1987). The neighborhood, personal identity, and group affiliation. In I. Altman

& A. Wandersman (Eds.), *Neighborhood and community environments* (pp. 1–34). New York: Plenum.

Scheidt, R., & Norris-Baker, C. (1990). A transactional approach to environmental stress among older residents of rural communities. *Journal of Rural Community Psychology, 11*, 5–30.

Scheidt, R., & Norris-Baker, C. (1993). The environmental context of poverty among older residents of economically-endangered Kansas towns. *Journal of Applied Gerontology, 12*, 335–348.

Schoggen, P. (1983). Behavior settings and the quality of life. *Journal of Community Psychology, 11*, 144–157.

Schoggen, P. (1988a). A behavioral settings approach. In G. Albee, J. Joffee, & L. Dusenbury (Eds.), *Prevention, powerlessness, and politics* (pp. 433–440). Newbury Park, CA: Sage.

Schoggen, P. (1988b). Commentary on Perkins, Burns, Perry, and Nielsen's "Behavior setting theory and community psychology: An analysis and critique." *Journal of Community Psychology, 16*, 373–386.

Schoggen, P. (1989). *Behavior settings: A revision and extension of Roger G. Barker's ecological psychology.* Stanford, CA: Stanford University Press.

Stokols, D. (1981). Group x place transactions: Some neglected issues in psychological research on settings. In D. Magnusson (Ed.), *Toward a psychology of situations: An interactional perspective* (pp. 393–415). Hillsdale, NJ: Lawrence Erlbaum.

Stokols, D. (1995). The paradox of environmental psychology. *American Psychologist, 50*, 821–837.

Stokols, D., & Shumaker, S. (1981). People in places: A transactional view of settings. In J. Harvey (Ed.), *Cognition, social behavior, and the environment* (pp. 441–488). Hillsdale, NJ: Erlbaum.

Toyama, T. (1988). *Identity and milieu: A study of relocation focusing on reciprocal changes in elderly people and their environment.* Stockholm, Sweden: Department for Building Function Analysis, The Royal Institute of Technology.

Welz, G. (1984). Behavior settings in a changing cultural context. *Man-Environment Systems, 14* (5–6), 233.

Wicker, A. (1983). *An introduction to ecological psychology.* New York: Cambridge University Press. (Original work published 1979)

Wicker, A. (1987). Behavior settings reconsidered: Temporal stages, resources, internal dynamics, context. In D. Stokols & I. Altman (Eds.), *Handbook of environmental psychology* (Vol. 1, pp. 613–653). New York: Wiley.

Wicker, A. (1990). The Midwest Psychological Field Station: Some reflections of one participant. *Environment and Behavior, 22*, 492–498.

Wicker, A. (1992). Making sense of environments. In B. Walsh, K. Craik, & R. Price (Eds.), *Person-environment psychology* (pp. 157–192). Hillsdale, NJ: Lawrence Erlbaum.

Wicker, A., & King, J. (1988). Life cycles of behavior settings. In J. McGrath (Ed.), *The social psychology of time: New perspectives* (pp. 182–200). Newbury Park, CA: Sage.

Wicker, A., McGrath, J. E., & Armstrong, G. E. (1972). Organization size and behavior setting capacity as determinants of member participation. *Behavioral Science, 17*, 499–513.

Willems, E. P., & Halstead, L. S. (1978). An ecobehavioral approach to health status and health care. In R. G. Barker & Associates (Eds.), *Habitats, environments, and human behavior* (pp. 169–189). San Francisco: Jossey-Bass.

Windley, P., & Scheidt, R. (1982). An ecological model of mental health among small town rural elderly. *Journal of Gerontology, 37,* 235–242.

7

Theory and Research on Housing for the Elderly: The Legacy of Kurt Lewin

PATRICIA A. PARMELEE

Perhaps the single greatest contribution Kurt Lewin made to the study of human behavior was his promulgation of the formula $B = f (P, E)$: Behavior is a function of the person and the environment. That simple dictum, revolutionary in a time when psychologists regarded the organism itself as the primary locus of causation of behavior, set the stage for and guided much of the development of the field now known as environment-behavior studies. During the past several decades, that discipline has evolved rapidly, drawing from the ranks not only of psychologists but of geographers, architects and designers, urban planners, sociologists, anthropologists, and others interested in the ways in which humans interact with the physical world.

Perhaps because of its rapid and multidisciplinary development, the study of environment-behavior relationships has also progressed decidedly self-consciously, closely and continuously scrutinizing its concepts, methods, and underlying assumptions. Although this self-reflective trend spans all foci within the field, it has been especially notable within environmental gerontology. For example, in a review of research on design of special residential environments for older people, Parmelee and Lawton (1990) noted a lull in research during the preceding decade and suggested that the field stood conceptually and methodologically at a crossroads. We cited a number of factors, including changing policy and practice in housing for the elderly, as contributors to that lull but strongly asserted that conceptual and methodological advances were needed to revitalize the study of environment and aging. In particular, we pinpointed transactional models of person-environment (P-E) relations and methodologies that complement such models as especially promising approaches.

This chapter is a second step in the process of evaluating and redirecting environmental gerontology toward more transactional frameworks. Its primary aim is to make some suggestions for how we may fine-tune the trend toward transactional research to yield a more complete understanding of person-environment relationships—and hence of housing needs, preferences, and behavior in late life. The central premise of this chapter is that conceptually the field would benefit markedly from a return to and rethinking of Kurt Lewin's B = f (P, E) formula and, more generally, the theoretical tenets of his field theory. In particular, his concept of life space, the psychological field in which behavior is based and takes place, is offered as an exemplar of transactional thought and, hence, as an ideal guide for research on housing and home for older persons.

In pursuing this thesis, it will first be helpful to review briefly the transactional worldview and its parallel in application, contextualism. We shall then examine Lewin's basic conceptual tenets and how they exemplify the transactional perspective. Particular attention will be given to three issues: the holistic focus of the life space on interpersonal and sociocultural as well as physical environmental elements, its subjective nature, and the roles of past, present, and future in shaping the life space and, hence, behavior. With respect to each of these points, representative research will be presented and recommendations made for continued "transactionalization" of the study of housing for older persons.

TRANSACTIONALISM AND CONTEXTUALISM IN ENVIRONMENT-BEHAVIOR RELATIONSHIPS

The unique qualities of the transactional approach to P-E relationships are perhaps best illustrated by contrast with interactionism, the conceptual paradigm that has dominated much of environment-behavior research since its inception. Altman and Rogoff (1987) described interactionism as seeking to predict and control behavior by "treat[ing] psychological processes, environmental settings, and contextual factors as independently defined and operating entities" (p. 15). As Parmelee and Lawton (1990) point out, this approach deals basically with P-E stimulus-response relationships, examining the effects of "discrete aspects of person and environment in order to predict some hypothesized outcome" (p. 477). To be sure, this perspective recognizes the multiplicity of personal and environmental factors that may converge to produce a given behavior. However, the interactional view is inherently reductionistic, assuming that discrete elements of the P-E system can be isolated and measured separately and that the effects of one predictor (or set of predictors) can be clearly distinguished from that of another (or others). Similarly, the assumed causal dynamic is usually linear, from personal characteristics, environmental features, and the interaction between the two, to overt behavior. Finally, although change over time is acknowledged, time is treated separately from psychological processes and assumed to operate as a result of the preexisting characteristics of person and environment rather than of any mutual influence between the two. In short, the interactional approach exemplifies the translation of traditional physical scientific methods and models to behavioral phenomena.

The transactional perspective, in contrast, emphasizes "changing relations among psychological and environmental aspects of holistic unities. . . . The transactional whole is not composed of separate elements but is a confluence of inseparable factors that depend upon one another for their very definition and meaning" (Altman & Rogoff, 1987, p. 24). Thus defined, transactionalism essentially views the relationship between an individual and his or her environment as an open system. This perspective rejects the notion that one can separately identify elements of the P-E system or that the relationships among persons and environments can be understood in any but a longitudinal context. Thus, person-environment systems cannot be reduced to their component parts; rather, one must study the whole. That whole is, however, something of a moving target in that it naturally evolves over time and with changing extrasystem circumstances. Thus, change is not something that happens to P-E systems but an intrinsic part of them.

The transactional perspective translates theoretically and methodologically to contextualism (Stokols, 1987). According to Stokols, the contextual approach dictates viewing psychological processes "in relation to the spatial, temporal, and sociocultural milieu in which they occur" (p. 42); supplementing focused, short-term analyses with more molar studies of the temporal and environmental context of behavior; acknowledging the situational specificity of behavior simultaneously with the search for general laws, and carefully considering the external and ecological validity of research findings. Specifically, contextual analysis demands examination not only of the central predictor(s) of interest but also of an array of other situational variables presumed to affect the targeted outcome. Similarly, outcomes should be assessed broadly and within different contexts to ascertain the generality versus situation specificity of findings.

Altman and Rogoff cited Kurt Lewin's field theory as an exemplar of transactional thinking, primarily on the basis of his elaboration of the concept of life space as the psychological "field" in which behavioral processes are played out. Similarly, as we shall see, Lewin was a vocal proponent of many of the tenets of contextualism cited by Stokols. The remainder of this chapter examines in-depth how Lewin's notion of life space can operate as a guide for developing more transactional, contextual models of older persons' relationships with their living spaces. As a foundation for that analysis, it will be helpful first to review the concept of life space and some general tenets of Lewin's field theory.

LEWIN'S FIELD THEORY AND THE CONCEPT OF LIFE SPACE

The impetus for Lewin's development of field theory lay in the contrast of his own basic philosophy of science, based on a Galilean physical scientific approach, with the more Aristotelian perspective held by his contemporaries in the field of psychology (Lewin, 1931). Decrying the emphasis on classification, abstraction, and generalization that he felt dominated the psychology of his day, Lewin argued cogently for a scientific psychology that stressed process rather than state and the "pure" over the "average" case. The Aristotelian approach led, said Lewin, to an artificial focus on gross structural similarities rather than on shared processes that may underlie ostensibly very different classes of phenomena. In particular, he contended that psychology was severely limited by its emphasis on common, regularly recurring events to the exclusion of individual differences and apparent exceptions to the rule: "The fact that lawfulness and individuality are considered antitheses . . . makes it appear hopeless to try to understand the real, unique, course of an emotion or the actual structure of a particular person's personality. It thus reduces one to a treatment of these problems in terms of mere averages" (1931, p. 155). Instead, Lewin argued, the search for lawfulness of behavior has to be grounded in a thorough understanding of the individual case and the factors relevant in each such case. If each case is understood in-depth, he suggested, apparent contradictions or exceptions will be resolved and the truly universal laws of behavior will emerge. "[G]eneral laws and individual differences are merely two aspects of one problem; they are mutually dependent on each other and the study of the one cannot proceed without the study of the other" (Lewin, 1951, p. 243).

This emphasis on thorough analysis of each situation under study uncovers a second and, to Lewin, even more limiting consequence of adherence to the Aristotelian model. Aristotelian physics emphasized the tendency of objects toward perfection and assumption of their "natural" place in the order of things. As a result, Lewin argued, psychology wrongly came to focus on the individual himself or herself as the primary locus of behavior, to the exclusion of external factors. In contrast, Lewin strongly maintained that to understand the causes of behavior, one must examine that behavior in situ and as a whole: "[T]he transition seems inevitable to a Galilean view of dynamics, which derives all its vectors not from single isolated objects, but from the mutual relations of the factors in the concrete whole situation, that is, essentially, from the momentary condition of the individual and the structure of the psychological situation. The dynamic of the processes is always to be derived from the relation of the concrete individual to the concrete situation, and, so far as internal forces are concerned, from the mutual relations of the various functional systems that make up the individual" (1931, p. 174; emphasis omitted).

The phrase "the momentary condition of the individual and the structure of the psychological situation" constitutes a first definition of what Lewin called the life space. His conceptualization of life space as the whole of the psychological situation, including both person and environment, was quite unique at the time and in several respects foreshadowed (or perhaps more accurately, helped shape) current notions of transactionalism. Thus, it will be helpful briefly to examine several general features of this conception before turning to those most pertinent to the present question of housing for the elderly.

A first important quality of the life space is its holistic form: It consists of "a totality of coexisting facts . . . [that] have the character of a 'dynamic field' in so far as the state of any part of this field depends on every other part of the field" (Lewin, 1951, p. 25). This definition underscores, first, Lewin's impatience with psychology's reductionistic approach, his metaphorical insistence that "[i]t is technically impossible to describe the movement of the sun by describing the movement of every ion contained in it" (1951, p. 244). For Lewin, the life space was the single cause of behavior and, hence, the only appropriate unit of analysis for behavioral research.[1]

A second point—quite radical given the dominance at the time of linear causal notions and of stimulus-response models emphasizing the organism's reactive response to the environment—was the notion of mutual influence between person and environment. Lewin insisted that changes in the environment necessarily result in changes in the person, and vice versa. Thus, his emphasis on dynamics takes on a dual meaning, referring to his focus not only on process rather than structure but also on an ever-changing system in which even minor perturbations of individual or environmental states can lead to large-scale changes in the life space as a whole. Lewin did acknowledge the concept of equilibrium at the level of the system as a whole (e.g., 1935, p. 58) but emphasized within the life space constant movement and change as the individual pursues goals and responds to external forces.

Lewin's conception of the P-E system as a unitary, fluid, mutual interchange between the individual and his or her surroundings neatly illustrates the notion of "changing relations among . . . inseparable factors" to which Altman and Rogoff (1987) referred in their explication of the transactional perspective. Similarly, the focus of the contextual perspective on studying behavioral processes within the larger temporal and environmental circumstances in which they occur harkens directly to Lewin's emphasis on the environment, broadly defined, as an integral aspect of the psychological life space. Stokols's (1987) call for recognition of situationally specific behaviors as variants of more general, lawful processes also draws directly from Lewin's critique of Aristotelian science. Thus, the transactional perspective and its application to contextual analysis owe much to Lewin's expatiation of the life space and its dynamic.

The influence of Lewin's concept of life space is also readily apparent in the general environment and aging literature. With respect to the more specific question of housing for the elderly, however, transactional concepts and the Lewinian notions that shaped them are less immediately apparent. This is attributable to a number of considerations, primary among them the area's strong multidisciplinary character as well as its very applied (rather than theory-based) focus. Thus far, these characteristics have proven assets for the discipline. But as Parmelee and Lawton (1990) have suggested, the study of housing for older people may well have reached the limits of understanding that can be provided by an interactional approach; continued progress may well depend on development of more transactional perspectives. Therefore, the remainder of this chapter examines how Lewinian notions may be applied to research and conceptualization in housing for older people to lend conceptual depth to existing knowledge. In particular, three aspects of Lewin's conceptualization of life space merit special attention: its inclusion of social as well as personal and physical environmental factors, its subjective nature, and its temporal range. To illustrate Lewin's thinking on these three points and their relevance to the study of housing for the elderly, it will be helpful to examine them more closely with reference to conceptual models and empirical data that illustrate each.

SOCIAL ASPECTS OF THE LIFE SPACE

Lewin explicitly designated the ''E'' in his definition of the life space as including all aspects of the individual's milieu. In particular, he argued that ''the social aspect of the psychological situation is at least as important as the physical'' (1951, p. 241). Thus, from a Lewinian point of view, in order fully to understand transactions between older persons and their physical environments, we must explicitly factor in social processes as coequal influences on behavior.

Despite Lewin's clear and equal emphasis on the social as well as the physical milieu, subsequent translations of the formula B = f (P, E) have tended to emphasize physical over social environmental elements strongly. This is quite understandable on pragmatic grounds. First, whereas there is a strong tradition of behavioral research on interpersonal processes, the physical world was long neglected as an influence on behavior. As a result, there was not only much ''catching up'' to be done in the study of P-E relationships but also a need to differentiate environment-behavior studies from other, related disciplines (see, e.g., Altman, 1976; Epstein, 1976; Singer & Baum, 1981). Thus, the study of physical environmental processes developed parallel to, rather than in transaction with, our considerable knowledge of interpersonal processes in old age. Additionally, from an applied perspective, physical rather than social environmental questions are clearly more proximal to the design of housing for the elderly or other special populations. Early in the life of the discipline, there were numerous purely physical environmental issues to be clarified, and application of a truly transactional model at that point could well have beclouded rather than clarified understanding of basic environmental processes in late life. But as the field has matured, it has become clear that unless we follow Lewin's admonition to examine interpersonal aspects of the residential context, we can develop only a limited understanding of even the proper design and siting of housing for older persons.

This is not to say that social aspects of the life space have been ignored in environmental gerontology but that their incorporation has been somewhat piecemeal. On the one hand, macrolevel work—for example, research on neighborhoods—has often included interpersonal factors as integral aspects of P-E transactions and strong determinants of neighborhood usage patterns and residential satisfaction. But more microlevel work on individual housing and environmental behavior has tended to neglect social elements from the P-E equation. Representative of the latter trend are early studies of person-environment fit, including much of the work of Lawton and his colleagues on environmental docility (Lawton, 1982; Lawton & Nahemow, 1973). This and similar models, and hence the empirical work they have generated, have tended to focus on functional competencies, usually couched in terms of activities of daily living (ADL) or Instrumental Activities of Daily Living (IADL) performance, in relation to the service environment of congregate housing, nursing homes, or other special residential facilities. Although a parallel literature exists on interpersonal processes in such environments, there was until recently little effort to integrate the two foci. Similarly, the large literature on design of housing for the aged (e.g., Carstens, 1985; Hiatt, 1991; Regnier & Pynoos, 1987) focuses on the interface of persons with the physical structure and amenities of dwellings as a primary point of intervention for increasing resident autonomy and comfort. Although such amenities as space for socializing and design for privacy have been addressed, there has been little in-depth attention to social dynamics in special housing.

To be sure, these lines of research and theory offer excellent insights into the intricacies of P-E relations as well as important guidelines for facility design and planning. Person-environment fit models, in particular, have moved the study of housing needs and utilization much further toward the kind of situational specificity that Lewin argued was the only true means of identifying general principles of behavior. These models thus offer important conceptual guides to our understanding of how persons interact with physical space and the organizational context of planned housing. Nonetheless, from a Lewinian viewpoint, to the extent that they deemphasize social processes as part of the P-E system, they paint an incomplete picture of the causes of behavior.

On the other hand, research on interpersonal relationships has been a cornerstone of social gerontology from its inception, and at least a portion of this literature places social processes in environmental context. A good example is research on neighborhood age density. The pioneering work of Rosow (1967), Rosenberg (1970), and others (e.g., Teaff, Lawton, Nahemow, & Carlson, 1978) clearly demonstrated the importance of neighborhood-based social relationships and thus, more generally, the role of interpersonal processes in the P-E equation. Replications in congregate housing for the elderly of Festinger, Schachter, and Back's (1950) work on functional proximity and friendship formation (e.g., Lawton & Simon, 1968; Nahemow & Lawton, 1975) further demonstrated the interplay of social and physical environmental characteristics and processes. Recent elaborations of this general research thrust have shown the complex interplay of characteristics of the person and the social and physical environmental contexts in determining the effects of age segregation on satisfaction and well-being of older persons (Lawton, Moss & Moles, 1984; Usui & Keil, 1987).

Several ongoing research programs have tried to capture explicitly the mutual influences of the person, others in his/her life space, and environmental factors in single models. One exemplar of this approach is the work of Rudolf Moos and his colleagues (reviewed in Moos & Lemke, 1985; Moos, Lemke, & David, 1987) in describing the physical and social environments of long-term care settings. For example, the Multiphasic Environmental Assessment Procedure expressly includes not only physical environmental variables such as location, neighboring amenities, and physical prosthetics but also such macrolevel social variables as social cohesion and the extent to which the organizational structure affords opportunities for resident independence. Environments are characterized in terms of overall pattern of such characteristics, which may then be related to characteristics of and outcomes to individual residents (e.g., Lemke & Moos, 1989). A second excellent example of how the social milieu may be factored into the P-E equation is the work of Frances Carp (1975; Carp & Carp, 1980), demonstrating the interplay of individuals' level of sociability with the social environment in predicting outcomes of a move to planned housing.

   Although these and similar studies are an excellent step toward integrating social environmental factors with more traditional P-E foci, they remain somewhat interactional in their clear differentiation of elements of the system and paths of influence. In a more purely transactional vein, several recent studies have explicitly examined the meaning of social relationships in environmental context. One excellent example is Kalymun's (1985) description of how multigenerational families allocate space, which highlights the parallel nature of social and spatial processes within families. Another is Shields's (1988) anthropological study of nursing home life, in which she deftly integrates diverse notions of dependency and the sick role, staff social roles, and institutional totality to depict the strained social atmosphere in facilities that are dually but paradoxically defined as both home and hospital. On a more general level, Rowles's (1983, 1984) notion of social insideness, which stresses the interrelationship of patterns of social relationships with older persons' sense of place, is an excellent attempt to acknowledge the intimate interplay among the individual, the residential environment, and other persons in it.

   This focus—the merger of social and environmental meaning such that interpersonal relationships are interpreted in physical context, and vice versa—is a promising area for continued study, particularly in special housing for the elderly. It has long been known that relationships among residents of nursing homes and congregate housing facilities are fewer and more distant than neighborhood ties of elderly living in "everyday" community settings (Noelker & Poulshock, 1980; Tesch & Whitbourne, 1981). Several recent studies elucidate the dynamic of this phenomenon. For example, Stephens, Kinney, and McNeer's (1986) work in nursing homes clearly indicated that physical and cognitively impaired individuals are actively ostracized by more able residents. Sheehan's (1986) and Kaye and Monk's (1987) research in congregate housing settings illustrated a similar pattern of isolation and lack of support for residents who are functional or demographic minorities. But whereas these studies indicate a primary role of family in providing informal support in congregate housing, a similar study in a retirement community indicated that neighbors may be preferred over relatives for supportive assistance (Sullivan, 1986).

These studies appear to be tapping a true confluence of personal, interpersonal, and environmental factors that together produce a phenomenon unique to long-term care settings. In contrast with the benefits of social ties with neighbors in noninstitutional settings (Cantor, 1979; Rosow, 1967), the negative social connotations of sheltered care settings (Mathews, 1979; Piper & Langer, 1986) may lead to a very different social dynamic. Social psychological theory and research on interpersonal bases of self-esteem (e.g., Novak & Lerner, 1968; Tesser & Campbell, 1980) suggests that we actively avoid associating with persons who are undesirable targets for social comparison. Extrapolating to special housing for older persons, it may be that the combination of negative environmental meaning and other residents' physical and cognitive frailty renders social avoidance more beneficial to self-esteem than social integration. That is, more able individuals may actively distance themselves socially and emotionally from other residents in order to avoid the kind of self-labeling based on physical and social cues that may lead individuals to assume "mindlessly" that they, too, are frail and dependent (Piper & Langer, 1986).

Another relevant focus for research on social elements of the life space is the question of how changes in the social composition of the residential environment affect the older individual, and vice versa. Perhaps most intensively studied in this vein is the phenomenon of aging in place, whereby both physical and social aspects of the residential milieu change as residents as a group grow older and less able. For example, in a 10- to 12-year follow-up of five planned housing sites, Lawton, Moss, and Grimes (1985) found that an increase in the average age of residents was accompanied by a decrease in social activity and interaction. Thus, changes in the social fabric of the residential environment may immediately affect the individual's social life space. On the other hand, in a study of retirement communities, Streib, Folts, and LaGreca (1985) discussed how changes in the person—specifically, declining health of individual residents—threaten the larger social environment in terms of the community's continuing capacity for self-governance. In a similar vein, Cuba's (1992) analysis of migrants' perspectives on change in a resort community highlights how individuals' life spaces and activities shape the social climate of the town and, conversely, how changes in the social and physical residential environments affect individuals' perceptions and use of local resources. Presumably, gentrification—influx of younger, more affluent residents into physically and demographically older, poorer neighborhoods—similarly affects the life space of older persons, although this is at this point a regrettably understudied issue.

Inasmuch as these kinds of studies tap the intersection of personal, social, and environmental factors in late life, they represent fertile ground for continued, more transactional research. A similar tack might be taken with many substantive issues using a number of existing conceptual frameworks. The primary concern, following Lewin's dictum, is simply that research on P-E transactions in late life explicitly includes social processes as a coequal element of the life space. Although promising starts have been made, a truly transactional perspective on interrelationships among the person, the physical environment, and the social milieu has yet to be clearly elaborated.

A second major issue in incorporating the social life space into the study of environment and aging is the need to consider broader cultural and subcultural factors as well as immediate interpersonal processes. Lewin clearly defined the social life space as including not only immediate interpersonal factors but larger sociocultural processes as well. Yet there has been little explicit consideration of larger cultural influences on environmental behavior in late life. Such influences may be quite marked or very subtle. For example, though there has been little direct research on the phenomenon, it appears that three- (and even four-) generation households are much more common and more acceptable among some American subcultures than others. Such arrangements likely have profound effects on functional and social life of older and younger family members alike.

It has recently been suggested (Rubinstein & Parmelee, 1992) that one of the prime dynamics of P-E relationships at any point in the life cycle is the juxtaposition of collective and personal definitions of the life course, space and place, and interpersonal processes. The notion here is that much of the meaning that we attach to environments is culturally defined in terms of prevailing social norms, mores, and meanings. Yet while we think, feel, and act toward the physical environment within this broader cultural framework, our own unique experiences color that framework to yield highly individualized personal meanings. Thus, as Altman and his colleagues (Altman & Gauvain, 1981; Gauvain, Altman, & Fakim, 1983) have pointed out in their insightful analyses of the meaning of home, culture shapes the form and many functions of housing space. But within that context, persons define and use their homes in gloriously idiosyncratic ways that reflect their personal life experiences and sense of place. Similarly, the physical environment can be a rich medium for expression and transmission of collective tradition (Jacobi & Stokols, 1983). Thus one finds a dialectic tension between collective or cultural meaning, transmitted through socialization and more or less similar for all individuals within the culture, and the personal meaning that environments come to bear through direct and intimate transaction with specific physical aspects of the life space.

At present, the cultural embeddedness of physical environmental processes, and hence of design and use of special housing, is an unspoken assumption rather than a topic of overt study. With the exception of a few qualitative studies of specialized residential environments for older people (e.g., Hochschilds, 1973; Shields, 1988), we have tended to focus more on individual transactions with and specific social relationships within the physical environment; the sociocultural dynamics that give those transactions their basic form are only peripherally acknowledged.

This tendency to stress individual over cultural context is itself uniquely American, reflecting our value of what Sampson (1977) has called "rugged

individualism.'' This value in fact underlies our emphasis on continued autonomy and independence for older persons, and the negative connotations of nursing homes and other assisted living environments. Similarly, our concern with
"overhousing" or "underutilization" of housing by older people (Lane & Feins,
1985) is based on cultural norms for the "appropriate" use of residential space.
To be sure, the gerontological research culture is, like any open system, dynamic
and evolving. Today's emphasis on independence and diversity in aging contrasts sharply with very early work that tended, like society in general, toward
a normative view of the aged as "poor dears": infirm, passive, and in need of
interventive assistance. Thus, general sociocultural beliefs biased scientific inquiry toward an overly general treatment of aging and environment. In Lewin's
terms, Aristotelian methods of classification based on structural similarities—in
this case, age—led to deemphasis of the individual case and hence of the diversity of the aging process and its effects on P-E transactions. Our ongoing
shift toward a more positive emphasis on diversity and normal aging further
illustrates the Lewinian view of change—in this case, in the collective life space
of the discipline—as both internally and externally generated: Our substantive
biases have been shaped by (among other things) the changing characteristics
of the American population as a whole and older persons as a group, our own
developing knowledge base, and perhaps even the personal realization that, as
a colleague once mused, "We're rapidly becoming the people we study."

In sum, cultural influences more or less tacitly shape not only the general
dynamics and specific form of P-E transactions in late life but also our very
conception of them. At this point, it would serve us well to focus more overtly
on the cultural dynamics that color P-E relationships in old age, as well as our
own thinking about them, and to incorporate those dynamics explicitly into our
research paradigms.

THE ROLE OF PHENOMENOLOGY

The role of objective versus subjective or phenomenological environment has
been a controversial topic for years. The objectivists argue, on the one hand,
that environmental features are real and measureable physical entities and should
be treated as such in scientific investigation of their association with human
behavior (e.g., Brunswik, 1956; Wohlwill, 1975). The subjectivists (e.g., Gibson,
1960; Jessor & Jessor, 1973) riposte with the observation that objective environmental characteristics are too distal—that is, they are too removed from the
immediate psychological experience of the observer. According to this view,
subjective interpretations of those objective characteristics are more immediately
predictive of behavior.

Lewin grappled with this dilemma at length (e.g., 1936, chap. 5), but his
conclusion was clear and consistent: The life space is phenomenological, a subjectively experienced psychological environment. In fact, he referred to elements
of the life space external to the individual as quasi-physical and quasi-social to

underscore their abstraction from objective reality as a function of their psychological significance. Several factors influenced Lewin's reasoning on this question. First, referring repeatedly to the literature on psychophysics, he noted that perception is notoriously nonveridical, subject to distortion not only by basic perceptual processes but also by personal idiosyncrasies and motivational states. Thus, because they are unlikely to be perfectly perceived, objective characteristics of the environment are more or less irrelevant; rather, it is the subjective perception and interpretation of objective circumstances that shape behavior. Lewin therefore maintained that while it is incumbent upon the investigator to represent the situation as objectively as possible, that representation must reflect psychological rather than physical reality: "Even when from the standpoint of the physicist the environment is identical or nearly identical for a child and for an adult, the psychological situation can be fundamentally different. The same is true for the environment of . . . men of different personality. Further, a physically identical environment can be psychologically different even for the same man in different conditions. . . . [T]he situation must be represented in the way in which it is 'real' for the individual in question" (1936, pp. 24–25).

A second consideration is Lewin's emphasis on the relevance of variables at the given moment. We have already noted the dynamic quality of the life space as Lewin conceptualized it. Because the life space is constantly changing, the relevance of a given objective environmental feature to behavior can be equally ephemeral. Regardless of its presence or objective qualities, if an element of the environment is not important psychologically, it is not part of the life space at that moment and hence does not affect behavior. For example, the presence of a good public transit system may be a central factor in housing satisfaction of older persons who do not drive or are mobility impaired; but for the older person who never uses public transit, psychologically, the transit system does not exist.[2]

Thus, according to Lewin, "what is real is what has effects" (1936, p. 19), and our understanding of the life space must be based in an understanding of subjective representations of external stimuli rather than their objective qualities. But Lewin's "subjectification" of the environment was not limited to the ostensible failings of human perception and attention vis-à-vis objective reality. Rather, he regarded reality—or at least its psychological representation—as a continuum, ranging from relatively veridical cognitive representations of objective circumstances to the wildest of "unreal" fantasies. Lewin wrote extensively on *unreality* or *irreality* (he used the terms interchangably) as one dimension along which regions of the life space may vary. Lewin defined the "plane of reality" as the subjectively perceived representation of the current objective environment. In addition, however, he hypothesized that the life space includes varying levels of unreality: aspects of the psychological environment that are ideal or imagined and have little basis in objective circumstances but nonetheless are psychologically important and therefore influence behavior: "The psychological environment of the adult shows a rather marked differentiation into strata of various degrees of reality. The plane of reality is characterized briefly as the plane of 'facts' to which an existence independent of the individual's own wishes is ascribed. . . . The more unreal planes are those of hopes and dreams, often of ideology. . . . In a plane of unreality 'one can do what he pleases' " (1951, p. 103).

Lewin argued strongly that unreal or irreal aspects of the life space are just as important and influential a part of the life space as more "reality-based" elements. Indeed, the "wishes" that constitute goals account in Lewinian dynamics for much of the person's locomotion within and, as a result, for changes in the life space. Specifically, because Lewin conceptualized the life space as a topographical analog to "real" space, behavioral options are determined by one's location at a given time and by the contiguity of adjacent regions with one's present location. Thus, as persons move from one region to the next, the behavioral possibilities available to them are altered. In this way, unreality—in this case, goals or plans for the future that the individual is actively pursuing— can shape the present life space. (We shall return to this rather disconcerting implication that "the future causes the present" shortly.) Again, environmental gerontology has accepted and pursued these premises only to a limited extent. With quite good reason, many investigators have preferred objective, physically measurable qualities of the environment as predictors of outcomes to the individual. Those outcomes in turn were measured either objectively, in terms of functional status or social contacts, or subjectively, in terms of satisfaction with one's surroundings and one's life overall. The latter class of variables represents a laudable attempt to integrate objectivist and subjectivist views by specifying the links between objective environmental features and individuals' perceptions of them. Thus, older persons' apparent contentment with the status quo, even when it is objectively substandard or departs from basic design principles, is well documented (Brennan, Moos, & Lemke, 1988; Duffy, Bailey, Beck, & Barker, 1986; Lawton & Hoover, 1979). Particularly interesting in this vein is the work of Carp and her colleagues (Carp & Carp, 1982; Carp & Christensen, 1986) on objectively, easily measured technical environmental assessments that can be related reliably to subjective satisfaction and well-being.

Recent research on the phenomenology of residential environments moves even closer to a true Lewinian view of life space as the psychologically experienced environment. A series of studies have examined the meaning of living environments to older persons, particularly with respect to factors that promote their attachment to place (O'Bryant, 1982; Rowles, 1983, 1984; Rubinstein, 1989). Perhaps the most striking of these analyses is Rubinstein's (1989, 1990) work on personal identity and environmental meaning. For example, he describes processes of attachment to home in which home becomes an extension or representation of self. In its more intense form, Rubinstein suggests, this attachment may lead to a blurring of the psychological distinction between self and environment, in some cases to the extent that the individual believes himself or herself unable to survive without the home. He further suggests (1990) that P-E relationships may play out distinct, idiosyncratic "themes" of personal identity that suffuse an individual's transactions with the home environment. My own exploratory work in nursing homes (Rubinstein & Parmelee, 1992) similarly suggests that the process and outcome of adjustment to institutional life depend on the meaning one attaches to the environment, in terms of willingness to recognize the institution as just that and to judge it within that framework. This implies that even in assessing basic outcomes such as housing satisfaction, we need to be sensitive to the embeddedness of evaluations in a context of personal and sociocultural meaning.

This focus on the phenomenological meaning of environment is particularly important because it highlights the idiosyncrasy of the life space and hence of P–E relations in late life. With systematic investigation, we may well find that subjective factors are significant contributors to explanation of a number of common P-E transactions, for example, geographic mobility, adjustment to institutionalization, or even basic design preferences.

TIME AS A FACTOR IN PERSON-ENVIRONMENT RELATIONSHIPS

Perhaps the most worrisome aspect of the concept of life space for Lewin was its time frame. On the one hand, he insisted that behavior was a function of the current psychological environment: "Neither the past nor the future but only the present situation can influence present events" (1936, pp. 34–35). At the same time, Lewin repeatedly acknowledged the role of the past in shaping the current life space: "The properties of the 'life space' of the individual depend partly upon the state of that individual as a product of his history, partly upon the nonpsychologic—physical and social—surroundings" (1951, p. 62). "Their past history thus plays a great part in determining the import of things for the person" (1936, p. 23). "The behavior of an individual does not depend entirely on his present situation. His mood is deeply affected by his hopes and wishes and by his views of his own past" (1951, p. 75).

To resolve this dilemma, Lewin (1936) distinguished historical causality— the documentation of causal sequences in terms of circumstances and chains of events that led up to the situation in question—from systematic causality, the contemporaneous and lawful dynamics by which a specific event takes place. In elaborating this distinction, he differentiated the psychological situation into longer-term historical influences, which he termed the *life situation*, and specific contemporary circumstances that make up the momentary situation. This differentiation in turn affords the opportunity to examine the interrelations of long-term and immediate aspects of the life space, that is, the extent to which life situation influences momentary situation—and hence, behavior—in a given instance.

There is some controversy over the role of the future as an element of the life space, based in Lewin's argument against Aristotelian concepts of teleology (see, e.g., Altman & Rogoff, 1987). However, both Lewin's own words, quoted above, as well as our previous discussion of irreality indicate clearly that he incorporated futurity as an aspect of the current psychological environment. To be sure, Lewin seems to have struggled a bit in coming to terms with the fact that if the life space incorporates the psychological future, one has essentially a situation in which "the future causes the present." Nonetheless, his reasoning leaned consistently toward the belief that individuals' expectations and desires for the future affect present perceptions and goals: "The clarification of the problem of past and future has been much delayed by the fact that the psychological field which exists at a given time contains also the views of that individual about his future and past. The individual sees not only his present situation; he has certain expectations, wishes, fears, daydreams for his future" (1951, p. 53). Specifically, Lewin distinguished the fact of having a goal, which is an aspect of the present situation, from the content of the goal, which is an anticipated future event:

> The goal as a psychological fact undoubtedly lies in the present. It really exists at the moment and makes up an essential part of the momentary life space. On the other hand, the "content" of the goal . . . lies as a physical or social fact in the future. . . . The nature of the expectation and character of what is expected, in so far as they act as psychological conditions at the moment, naturally do not depend upon whether or not the event comes to pass. In either case the person strives toward a goal which exists psychologically in the present life space. (1936, p. 37)

By this reasoning, Lewin deftly managed to acknowledge the temporal diffuseness of the life space, encompassing at least indirectly (and sometimes directly) both past and future, without sacrificing the basic tenet that life space as it affects behavior is a momentary and contemporary construct. One may perhaps argue with the convolution of his reasoning, but the bottom line is clear and difficult to dispute: The present life space is but a temporary manifestation, a cross section cut from the ongoing flow of the uninterrupted psychological field. It is shaped by the past and even the future, but the behavior of the individual depends on the situation as it exists now.

Extrapolating to the current issue, this implies that we cannot fully understand P-E processes in old age (or, for that matter, at any life stage) unless we cast a careful eye to persons' unique past experiences as influences on the current behavioral arena. The present life space is similarly shaped by goals and expectations for the future. Our definition of *transactionalism* clearly embraces these implications. Yet, as with the study of the social life space, it has taken us a while to incorporate them into theory and research. Much of the early work in the field was appropriately cross sectional, examining outcomes such as adjustment to institutionalization or attachment to neighborhood at a single point in time in order to identify the basic dimensions of given phenomena and factors that are relevant to them. This has changed as the field has matured, thanks again in large part to the pioneering work of Carp (1975), S. Sherman (1975), and others who conducted early longitudinal studies of adjustment to special housing for the elderly. These and similar studies are exemplary not just by their longitudinal focus but by their astute targeting of identifiable change events such as residential relocation. This strategy offers a unique opportunity to examine explicitly differential dynamics of persons in environments in response to a single, objectively defined event. Thus, such research has been invaluable in delineating individual and contextual factors that shape adjustment to environmental change.

More recent work has looked at more "normative" developmental processes such as the phenomenon of aging in place discussed earlier. The dynamic here is one of mutual influence of person and environment as both change over time. For example, Lawton, Moss, and Grimes (1985), in a follow-up of five planned housing facilities for the aged, documented not only how individual aging places some residents at risk of undersupport but also the macrophenomenon of aging in place as the demographic characteristics of residents change over time. At a different level, the shift in design and planning emphases from construction of special facilities to adaptation of existing housing highlights long-term changes not only in individual needs but also in preferred housing form and function. An interesting sidelight here is the multiplicity of paths that lead to restored P-E congruence, in that persons may choose to modify the physical environment by adding needed features, to change the social life space through mechanisms such as shared housing (Pynoos, Hamburger, & June, 1990), or to pursue other tactics targeted to specific areas of the life space.

These kinds of research strategies are quite useful in describing the dynamic of life space changes, but they are limited by their prospective status. Of course, there is no fault to be found with prospective study; it is rightly the backbone of longitudinal method. But by beginning from some arbitrary contemporary baseline—usually defined by when we, the researchers, first got our hands on the respondents—we essentially define out of the P-E equation all aspects of the life space that are historical in nature. Of course, it is difficult to deal empirically with the past because of basic methodological problems with retrospective reports. However, fear of methodological contamination may be leading us to deprive ourselves of a rich class of explanatory variables.

When we ignore people's past, whether it be objective circumstances or their subjective representations of them in the current life space, we are saying that where and what a person was before we encountered her are irrelevant to her current behavior. For some phenomena, that may well be the case. But particularly for person-environment transactions, which are rooted in individuals' perceptions and interpretations of their physical surroundings, that assumption is likely fallacious.

In this vein, environmental gerontology might be well served by the experience of other disciplines. For example, there is a sizable literature on the effects of residential mobility on children's and adults' subsequent mental health (for reviews, see Brett, 1980; Stevens & Cvetkovich, undated). It makes sense to incorporate this sort of retrospective analysis in studies of, for example, postretirement migration or effects of neighborhood gentrification on elderly residents. Familiarity and expectations for the future have been shown in both general and gerontological research to affect attitudes (Zajonc, 1968), interpersonal behavior (Miller & Turnbull, 1986), residential change (Hunt & Roll, 1987), and service utilization (Regnier, 1975). Although the nature and extent of one's future agenda are certainly linked to life course considerations, planfulness is an important aspect of P-E transactions. This is reflected empirically in work on residential mobility and migration patterns among the elderly (e.g., Wiseman, 1980) and on the effect of advance planning in ameliorating relocation trauma among frail elderly (Schulz & Brenner, 1977). Conceptually, Lawton's revision of his environmental docility hypothesis (1982, 1989) to include proactivity—older people's actively shaping their physical surroundings to suit their own needs and tastes—directly acknowledges planfulness and future orientation in P-E transactions. It would be highly desirable to integrate these literatures in research on residential environments in late life, incorporating both past experiences and goals and expectations for the future as influences on the present situation.

A good example of this sort of analysis is Cuba's (1992) demonstration among migrants to a resort community of how perceptions of the present environment are shaped simultaneously by reasons for migration, past experience with the community, current activities and social integration, and expectations for one's own and the community's future. The role of past and future in the present life space is further illustrated by recent studies of the meaning of personal possessions for older persons. The work of Rubinstein (1987), E. Sherman (1991), Wapner, Demick, and Redondo (1990), and others (see Kamptner, 1989) clearly illustrates the primary role of cherished objects and even the home itself as repositories of memories of past times and people who remain deeply important to the elderly individual. Although valued possessions are idiosyncratic (one person may cherish a piece of jewelry, another a photo album or ceramic figurine), their function is clearly universal, as a tie to the past. Wapner and colleagues' recent study of nursing home entrants further highlights the important transitional function of cherished possessions in providing a sense of connection between past and present, comfort in the transition from home to institution, and a sense of belonging in the new residential milieu. In a very different vein, Rosner and her colleagues (1990) have shown how a display of familiar, personally meaningful items can serve as a way-finding aid for Alzheimer's patients.

Thus, in many ways, both the past and the future shape the present, and people actively manipulate their own life spaces. Direct exploration of this phenomenon may yield some interesting insights into the temporal dynamic of P-E transactions in late life. Again, the possible applications are numerous, but whatever the substantive focus, it may well be enhanced by explicitly assessing historical factors that shape the present life space.

SUMMARY AND CONCLUSIONS

We are making excellent progress toward a truly transactional view of aging and environment. Over the past few years, there have been noteworthy empirical and conceptual gains in acknowledging social factors as aspects of environment and influences on transactions of persons with the physical world; in recognizing the importance of personal meaning and experience in P-E relationships; and in appreciating time and change in P-E systems in an enhanced fashion. Nonetheless, several substantive and methodological tacks might prove helpful in continued development of a truly transactional view.

A first dictum of the issues reviewed in this chapter is that we must include social processes as an integral element of P-E transactions. The notion here is not to blur the distinction between interpersonal and environmental processes but simply to acknowledge that social status, roles, relationships, and transactions affect and are affected by P-E transactions. It was suggested earlier, regarding social ties among residents of special housing for older people, that we must examine interpersonal processes in environmental context in order to understand fully why and how persons make and maintain social contacts. Conversely, it may be useful to examine P-E relationships in social context. For example, older persons' desire for and use of space in the home is likely linked to their current family and friendship structures in terms not just of coresidents but also of having space available for visiting children and grandchildren. As another example, Stephens and colleagues' research (1986), cited earlier, indicates a territorial hierarchy in nursing homes that reflects status relationships among residents; without knowing that, one would be hard put to explain some of her findings. Thus, we need, in studying the living spaces and territorial ranges of older persons, to take into account their social networks and close relationships and how those relationships shape and are shaped by person-environment transactions.

One great step toward this goal would be synthesis of existing knowledge of environmental and interpersonal processes into large-scale studies. We as researchers tend to shy away from replication as somehow second-rate. But as it stands today, the field of gerontology in general, and environmental gerontology in particular, suffers from a lack of integration of existing data. As a result, although the left hand may know what the right is doing, it doesn't always recognize or incorporate that information as relevant to its own pursuits. It would be very helpful to see replication and extension of existing work on, for example, social network formation in congregate housing to examine several very different kinds of sites at once. Aside from substantiating previous findings, this contextual orientation, as recommended by Stokols (1987), would permit some analysis of the role of environmental design and meaning in shaping social relationships.

Second, environmental gerontology should overtly acknowledge and examine cultural influences on P-E transactions. This chapter has argued that cultural factors shape not only person-environment relations in late life but our conceptualizations of and research on them. Three tactics might help in beginning to understand and, hence, to overcome the ethnocentricity that has characterized environmental gerontology thus far. First, we should be seeking out and reading literature on environment and aging from and in other cultures. A first benefit of an "internationalization" of environmental gerontology would be simply to learn how generalizable our findings are: Are we observing culturally universal behavior patterns that are intrinsic to spatial behavior in late life or simply the effects of being old and North American? In addition, we need to begin to examine overtly cultural and subcultural influences on P-E transactions in old age. For example, generalizing from Lauman and House's (1970) classic study on class differences in living room decor and Werner and colleagues' work (reviewed in Werner, Altman, & Brown, 1992) on holiday decoration and neighborhood cohesiveness, I would be intrigued to see a study of a well-known urban Philadelphian phenomenon: decoration of one's living room windows for the aesthetic benefit of passers-by on the street. My own naive observations suggest that this behavior is influenced by factors as diverse as life course, ethnicity, religious affiliation, socioeconomic status, location, and house design, but how these interact remains a mystery. Similarly, it would be interesting to understand finally why a sizable proportion of northern Jews migrate south in old age, whereas midwestern Lutherans tend to stay put.

As a third step toward embedding P-E relations in cultural context, we need to begin examining how our own cultural values and biases shape research and theory on housing for the elderly. Earlier discussion noted that our value of individual autonomy is strongly reflected in current thinking about aging and environment; there are likely other, more subtle influences as well. We are beginning to make strides in this respect. For example, the predominantly white, middle-class research community has tended to presume that multigenerational households are an aberration and therefore problematic for older persons and their families. Only since we have begun to examine this phenomenon in cultural context directly (e.g., Mitchell & Register, 1984) have we discovered the ethnocentricity of that view.

Lewin's dictates on the nature of psychological "reality" recommend that we incorporate subjective/phenomenological factors into theory and research. The implications of this directive are primarily methodological. Current, largely quantitative methods are generally inadequate to capture the breadth and depth of individual cases that Lewin felt was necessary truly to understand the general laws that govern them. Thus, it would be helpful to follow the lead of much recent research cited throughout this chapter in frequently using qualitative methods to explore and highlight the importance of individual environmental meanings. This is not to say that we can or should return to the kind of case-by-case analysis that guided much of Lewin's theorizing. But as an adjunct to quantitative analyses, qualitative methods may be an excellent means of identifying relevant aspects of the life space, in terms of which our quantitative measures may be most useful. It would also be helpful to continue following the lead of O'Bryant (1982) and others in developing quantifiable measures of affective and phenomenological orientations to the physical environment, for example, attachment to place or social insideness as Rowles (1983, 1984) conceptualized it.

Finally, research on housing for the elderly should acknowledge Lewin's diffuse temporal perspective by more overtly recognizing time and change as integral elements of the life space. Here, two issues seem relevant. First, and most straightforwardly, we need directly to incorporate time into our models of P-E transactions by taking a more long-term focus. Most immediately apparent is the need for continued longitudinal research on a broad range of phenomena to explicate the processes by which observed cross-sectional effects occur. In addition, we have noted the need to assess and explore individuals' life histories and past experiences as influences upon P-E transactions—to include variables representing individuals' life situations as well as their momentary situations as predictors of environmental behavior. The effects of future orientation and expectations upon P-E transactions are also a fertile area for exploration, in terms both of environmental change (e.g., relocation) and of ongoing person-environment processes.

It would also be useful to begin to take a more life span approach to P-E transactions, integrating gerontological research with general research on environmental behavior to explore how (or if) life stage affects P-E transactions. Lewin's emphasis on developmental influences on the complexity of the life space has been translated in copious research on how the life space (e.g., living situations, territorial range, design needs, etc.) in late life differs from earlier life stages. However, little attention has been given differential processes involved in P-E transactions at different stages of life. This again represents a fertile area for conceptual development, as well as a strong potential influence on planning and design of housing for the elderly.

In summary, the richness of Kurt Lewin's thinking about the relationship between persons and their psychological environments offers much to the study of housing for the elderly. By integrating his concept of life space as a total, temporally diffuse, and subjective merger of person and environment, we may well begin to develop newer, more complete views of how the lives of older persons shape and are shaped by their homes and neighborhoods.

NOTES

1. To be sure, Lewin acknowledged varying levels of analysis of the psychological field, depending on the phenomenon under study. Thus, for example, he suggested that

to understand the dynamic of a marriage it is insufficient to examine the life space of each partner. Although such individual analysis is necessary, he argued, it is equally crucial to describe the life space of the couple, that is, the shared psychological field of the dyad. His only admonition was that one must use methods appropriate to the level of analysis (see Lewin, 1951, p. 244).

2. As Lewin pointed out, because the life space is an open system, external conditions that are usually psychologically irrelevant can intrude upon the life space and thus affect behavior. Thus, continuing our example, the public transit system does become a part of the life space of the automobile driver who gets stuck behind a slow-moving bus. However, research and design of housing for the elderly have tended to focus on environmental characteristics that are more or less stable, in terms of their constant presence/absence or consistent change trends (e.g., gentrification). Here, Lewin would argue strongly that objective characteristics of the housing site should be considered part of the life space only insofar as they are relevant to the individual, that is, part of the psychological field that affects behavior.

REFERENCES

Altman, I. (1976). Environmental psychology and social psychology. *Personality and Social Psychology Bulletin, 2*, 96–113.

Altman, I., & Gauvain, M. (1981). A cross-cultural and dialectic analysis of homes. In L. Liben, A. Patterson, & N. Newcombe (Eds.), *Spatial representation and behavior across the life span* (pp. 283–320). New York: Academic.

Altman, I., & Rogoff, B. (1987). World views in psychology: Trait, interactional, organismic, and transactional perspectives. In D. Stokols & I. Altman (Eds.), *Handbook of environmental psychology* (Vol. 1, pp. 7–40). New York: Wiley.

Brennan, P. L., Moos, R. H., & Lemke, S. (1988). Preferences of older adults and experts for physical and architectural features of group living facilities. *Gerontologist, 28*, 84–90.

Brett, J. M. (1980). The effect of job transfer on employees and their families. In C. L. Cooper & R. Payne (Eds.), *Current concerns in occupational stress* (pp. 99–136). New York: Wiley.

Brunswik, E. (1956). *Perception and the representative design of experiments*. Berkeley: University of California Press.

Cantor, M. H. (1979). Neighbors and friends: An overlooked resource in the informal support system. *Research on Aging, 1*, 434–463.

Carp, F. M. (1975). Impact of improved housing on morale and life satisfaction. *Gerontologist, 15*, 511–515.

Carp, F. M., & Carp, A. (1980). Person-environment congruence and sociability. *Research on Aging, 2*, 395–415.

Carp, F. M., & Carp, A. (1982). A role for technical environmental assessment in perceptions of environmental quality and well-being. *Journal of Environmental Psychology, 2*, 171–191.

Carp, F. M., & Carp, A. (1984). A complementarity/congruence model of well-being or mental health for the community elderly. In I. Altman, M. P. Lawton, & J. Wohlwill (Eds.), *Elderly people and the environment* (pp. 279–336). New York: Plenum.

Carp, F. M., & Christensen, D. L. (1986). Older women living alone: Technical environmental assessment predictors of psychological well-being. *Research on Aging, 8,* 407–425.

Carstens, D. Y. (1985). *Site planning and design for the elderly.* New York: Van Nostrand Reinhold.

Cuba, L. (1992). Aging places: Perspectives on change in a Cape Cod community. *Journal of Applied Gerontology, 11,* 64–83.

Duffy, M., Bailey, S., Beck, B., & Barker, D. G. (1986). Preferences in nursing home design: A comparison of residents, administrators, and designers. *Environment and Behavior, 18,* 246–257.

Epstein, Y. M. (1976). Comment on environmental psychology and social psychology. *Personality and Social Psychology Bulletin, 2,* 346–349.

Festinger, L. S., Schachter, S., & Back, K. (1950). *Social pressures in informal groups: A study of human factors in housing.* New York: Harper.

Gauvain, M., Altman, I., & Fakim, H. (1983). Home and social change: A cross-cultural analysis. In N. R. Feimer & E. S. Geller (Eds.), *Environmental psychology: Directions and perspectives.* New York: Praeger.

Gibson, J. J. (1960). The concept of the stimulus in psychology. *American Psychologist, 15,* 694–703.

Hiatt, L. (1991). *Nursing home renovation designed for reform.* Boston: Butterworth Architecture.

Hochschilds, A. R. (1973). *The unexpected community.* Englewood Cliffs, NJ: Prentice-Hall.

Hunt, M. D., & Roll, M. K. (1987). Simulation in familiarizing older people with an unknown building. *Gerontologist, 27,* 169–175.

Jacobi, M., & Stokols, D. (1983). The role of tradition in group-environment relations. In N. R. Feimer & E. S. Geller (Eds.), *Environmental psychology: Directions and perspectives* (pp. 157–179). New York: Praeger.

Jessor, R., & Jessor, S. L. (1973). The perceived environment in behavioral science: Some conceptual issues and some illustrative data. *American Behavioral Scientist, 16,* 801–828.

Kalymun, M. (1985, April). *The intergenerational ecology of households.* Paper presented at the annual meeting of the Environmental Design Research Association, Atlanta, GA.

Kamptner, N. L. (1989). Personal possessions and their meanings in old age. In S. Spacapan & S. Oskamp (Eds.), *The social psychology of aging* (pp. 165–196). Beverly Hills, CA: Sage.

Kaye, L. W., & Monk, A. (1987, November). *Social network reciprocity in enriched housing for the aged.* Paper presented at the annual meeting of the Gerontological Society of America, Washington, DC.

Lane, T. S., & Feins, J. D. (1985). Are the elderly overhoused? Definitions of space utilization and policy implications. *Gerontologist, 25,* 243–250.

Lauman, E. O., & House, J. (1970). Living room styles and social attributes: The patterning of material artifacts in a modern urban community. *Sociology and Social Research, 54,* 321–342.

Lawton, M. P. (1982). Competence, environmental press, and the adaptation of older people. In M. P. Lawton, P. G. Windley, & T. O. Byerts (Eds.), *Aging and the environment: Theoretical approaches* (pp. 33–59). New York: Springer.

Lawton, M. P. (1989). Behavior-relevant ecological factors. In K. W. Schaie & C. Schooler (Eds.), *Social structure and aging: Psychological processes* (pp. 57–78). Hillsdale, NJ: Erlbaum.

Lawton, M. P., & Hoover, S. L. (1979). *Housing and neighborhood: Objective and subjective quality.* Philadelphia: Philadelphia Geriatric Center.

Lawton, M. P., Moss, M., & Grimes, M. (1985). The changing service needs of older tenants in planned housing. *Gerontologist, 25,* 258–264.

Lawton, M. P., Moss, M., & Moles, E. (1984). The suprapersonal neighborhood context of older people: Age heterogeneity and well-being. *Environment and Behavior, 16,* 89–109.

Lawton, M. P., & Nahemow, L. (1973). Ecology and the aging process. In C. Eisdorfer & M. P. Lawton (Eds.), *Psychology of adult development and aging* (pp. 619–674). Washington, DC: American Psychological Association.

Lawton, M. P., & Simon, B. (1968). The ecology of social relationships in housing for the elderly. *Gerontologist, 8,* 108–115.

Lemke, S., & Moos, R. H. (1989). Personal and environmental determinants of activity involvement among elderly residents of congregate facilities. *Journal of Gerontology, 44,* S139–S148.

Lewin, K. (1931). The conflict between Aristotelian and Galilean modes of thought in contemporary psychology. *Journal of General Psychology, 5,* 141–177.

Lewin, K. (1935). *A dynamic theory of personality.* New York: McGraw-Hill.

Lewin, K. (1936). *Principles of topological psychology.* New York: McGraw-Hill.

Lewin, K. (1951). *Field theory in social science.* New York: Harper.

Mathews, S. H. (1979). *The social world of older women.* Beverly Hills, CA: Sage.

Miller, D. T., & Turnbull, W. (1986). Expectancies and interpersonal processes. *Annual Review of Psychology, 37,* 233–256.

Mitchell, J. S., & Register, J. C. (1984). An exploration of family interaction with the elderly by race, socioeconomic status and residence. *Gerontologist, 24,* 48–54.

Moos, R. H., & Lemke, S. (1985). Specialized living environments for older people. In J. E. Birren & K. W. Schaie (Eds.), *Handbook of the psychology of aging* (2nd ed., pp. 864–899). New York: Van Nostrand Reinhold.

Moos, R. H., Lemke, S., & David, T. G. (1987). Priorities for design and management in residential settings for the elderly. In V. Regnier & J. Pynoos (Eds.), *Housing the aged: Design directives and policy considerations* (pp. 179–205). New York: Elsevier.

Nahemow, L., & Lawton, M. P. (1975). Similarity and propinquity in friendship formation. *Journal of Personality and Social Psychology, 32,* 205–213.

Noelker, L. S., & Poulshock, S. W. (1980, August). *Intimacy: Factors affecting its development among members of a home for the aged.* Paper presented at the annual meeting of the American Sociological Association, New York.

Novak, D., & Lerner, M. J. (1968). Rejection as a consequence of perceived similarity. *Journal of Personality and Social Psychology, 9,* 147–152.

O'Bryant, S. (1982). The value of home to older persons: Relationship to housing satisfaction. *Research on Aging, 2,* 349–363.

Parmelee, P. A., & Lawton, M. P. (1990). Design of special environments for the elderly. In J. E. Birren & K. W. Schaie (Eds.), *Handbook of psychology and aging* (3rd ed., pp. 464–487). New York: Academic Press.

Piper, A. I., & Langer, E. J. (1986). Aging and mindful control. In M. M. Baltes &

P. B. Baltes (Eds.), *The psychology of control and aging* (pp. 71–89). Hillsdale, NJ: Erlbaum.

Pynoos, J., Cohen, E., Davis, L. G., & Bernhardt, S. (1987). Home modifications: Improvements that extend independence. In V. Regnier & J. Pynoos (Eds.), *Housing the aged: Design directives and policy considerations* (pp. 277–303). New York: Elsevier.

Pynoos, J., Hamburger, L., & June, A. (1990). Supportive relationships in shared housing. *Journal of Housing for the Elderly, 6,* 1–24.

Regnier, V. (1975). Matching older person's cognition with their use of neighborhood areas. In D. Carson (Ed.), *Man-environment interactions: Evaluations and applications* (pp. 19–40). Stroudsburg, PA: Dowden, Hutchinson, and Ross.

Regnier, V., & Pynoos, J. (1987). *Housing the aged: Design directives and policy considerations.* New York: Elsevier.

Rosenberg, G. S. (1970). *The worker grows old.* San Francisco: Jossey-Bass.

Rosner, T., Namazi, K. H., Calkins, M., & Grotke, L. (1990, August). *Environmental impact on Alzheimer residents of long-term care facility.* Paper presented at the annual meeting of the American Psychological Association, Boston.

Rosow, I. (1967). *Social integration of the aged.* New York: Free Press.

Rowles, G. D. (1983). Geographical dimensions of social support in rural Appalachia. In G. D. Rowles & R. J. Ohta (Eds.), *Aging and milieu: Environmental perspectives on growing old* (pp. 111–130). New York: Academic Press.

Rowles, G. D. (1984). Aging in rural environments. In I. Altman, M. P. Lawton, & J. F. Wohlwill (Eds.), *Elderly people and the environment* (pp. 129–157). New York: Plenum.

Rubinstein, R. L. (1987). The significance of personal objects to older people. *Journal of Aging Studies, 1,* 226–238.

Rubinstein, R. L. (1989). The home environments of older people: A description of psychosocial processes linking person to place. *Journal of Gerontology, 44,* S45–S53.

Rubinstein, R. L. (1990). Personal identity and environmental meaning in later life. *Journal of Aging Studies, 4,* 131–148.

Rubinstein, R. L., & Parmelee, P. A. (1992). Attachment to place and the representation of the life course by the elderly. In I. Altman & S. Low (Eds.), *Human behavior and environment: Advances in theory and research: Vol. 12, Place attachment* (pp. 139–163). New York: Plenum.

Sampson, E. E. (1977). Psychology and the American ideal. *Journal of Personality and Social Psychology, 35,* 767–782.

Schulz, R., & Brenner, G. (1977). Relocation of the aged: A review and theoretical analysis. *Journal of Gerontology, 32,* 323–333.

Sheehan, N. W. (1986). Informal support among the elderly in public senior housing. *Gerontologist, 26,* 171–175.

Sherman, E. (1991). Reminiscentia: Cherished objects as memorabilia in late-life reminiscence. *International Journal of Aging and Human Development, 33,* 89–100.

Sherman, S. R. (1975). Patterns of contact for residents of age-segregated and age-integrated housing. *Journal of Gerontology, 30,* 103–107.

Shields, R. R. (1988). *Uneasy endings: Daily life in an American nursing home.* Ithaca, NY: Cornell University Press.

Singer, J. E., & Baum, A. (1981). *Environmental psychology is applied social psychol-*

ogy. Paper presented at Colloquium toward a Social Psychology of the Environment, Paris.

Stephens, M. A. P., Kinney, J. M., & McNeer, A. E. (1986). Accommodative housing: Social integration of residents with physical limitations. *Gerontologist, 25*, 403–409.

Stevens, C., & Cvetkovich, G. (undated). *Residential mobility and childhood development: A review and meta-analysis*. Mimeograph, Western Washington University.

Stokols, D. (1987). Conceptual strategies of environmental psychology. In D. Stokols & I. Altman (Eds.), *Handbook of environmental psychology* (Vol. 1, pp. 41–70). New York: Wiley.

Streib, G. F., Folts, N. E., & LaGreca, A. J. (1985). Autonomy, power, and decision-making in 36 retirement communities. *Gerontologist, 25*, 403–409.

Sullivan, D. A. (1986). Informal support systems in a planned retirement community: Availability, proximity, and willingness to utilize. *Research on Aging, 8*, 249–268.

Teaff, J. D., Lawton, M. P., Nahemow, L., & Carlson, D. (1978). Impoact of age integration on the well-being of elderly tenants in public housing. *Journal of Gerontology, 33*, 126–133.

Tesch, S., & Whitbourne, S. (1981). Friendship, social interaction and subjective well-being of older men in an institutional setting. *International Journal of Aging and Human Development, 13*, 317–327.

Tesser, A., & Campbell, J. (1980). Self-definition: The impact of the relative performance and similarity of others. *Social Psychology Quarterly, 43*, 341–347.

Usui, W. M., & Keil, T. J. (1987). Life satisfaction and age concentration of the local area. *Psychology and Aging, 2*, 30–35.

Wapner, S., Demick, J., & Redondo, J. P. (1990). Cherished possessions and adaptation of older people to nursing homes. *International Journal of Aging and Human Development, 31*, 219–235.

Werner, C. M., Altman, I., & Brown, B. B. (1992). A transactional approach to interpersonal relations: Physical environment, social context and temporal qualities. *Journal of Social and Personal Relationships, 9*, 297–323.

Wiseman, R. F. (1980). Why older people move: Theoretical issues. *Research on Aging, 2*, 141–154.

Wohlwill, J. F. (1975). The environment is not in the head! In W. F. Preiser (Ed.), *Environmental design research: Vol 2, Symposia and workshops. Proceedings of the 4th annual Environmental Design Research Association Conference* (pp. 166–181). Stroudburg, PA: Dowden, Hutchinson, & Ross.

Zajonc, R. B. (1968). Attitudinal effects of mere exposure. *Journal of Personality and Social Psychology Monograph Supplement, 9* (2, Pt. 2), 2–27.

Index

Activation, system, 9–10

Adaptation, 5–6, 115–116; competence-press model and, 3; coping and, 54–55; level, 3–4, 6; relocation and, 77–78; well-being, 7. *See also* Outcomes

Affect: environment and, 10–12, 22; neuropsychology and, 12; positive and negative, 11

Anthropology: concern with social action, 91–92; cultural and personal interpretation, 91; of experience, 90; life histories, 90–91; study of ritual, 91

Arousal: neuropsychological level, 9–12; system, 9–10

Barker, Roger, 44–46, 141–156

Behavior circuits: conceptualizing changes in, 45–46; defined, 44–45; observer-defined changes in, 44–45; resident-appraised changes in, 47; taxonomy of, 45

Behavior settings, 25–26; autonomy and, 152–153; availability, 150–151; behavioral focus points and, 154–155; boundaries, 154; circuits, 44–46; as cultural phenomena, 149–150; defined, 143; design interventions and, 153–156; diversity, 150–151; dynamics, 146–147; focus, 150–151; housing applications, 150–153; illustrated, 142–143; optimizing size of, 155–156; participation and, 151–152; pressure, 151–152; standing patterns of behavior and, 25–26; survey, 144–145; taxonomic applications, 147–149; temporal stages of, 144; therapy, 25. *See also* Behavior circuits

Big Five, 14–15, 19–20

Carp, Abraham, 7–8

Carp, Francis, 7–8, 168

Change: environmental, 25–26; gender and, 77–80; persons and, 24–25

Cognitive-attentional mechanisms, 9–10; environmental cognition and, 9–10

Cohort: change, 25; issues, 74–75

Competence-press model, 2–4, 92–93, 126–127

Complementary/congruence model, 7–8

Congruence model, 4–5

Contextualism, 162–163

Control: autonomy and, 152–153; locus of, 20

Coping, theory, 72

Costa, Paul, 13–15

Culture: person-environment transactions

and, 90–92, 100–103, 179; time use
and, 68

Design: behavior setting theory and, 153–
156; feminist practice of, 81–82; informed by MEAP, 130; reframing
gender in, 81–82
Diversity, environmental, 24

Ecology, of aging, 35
Environmental: change, 25, 36; choice
and control, 123; discrepancy hypothesis, 34–35; dispositions, 6; diversity,
24; docility hypothesis, 16, 35, 127;
evaluation, 117–134; "experience"
model, 35; matching, 133–134; phenomenology, 89–103; press, 2–3;
proactivity hypothesis, 4, 7, 35; selection, 23–24; taxonomy, 42–45, 147–
149
Evaluation: pre-occupancy, 131; post-
occupany, 131
Extroversion, 13–15
Eysenck, Hans, 13

Feminist theory: diversity of, 66; housing
and, 65–76
Field theory: concept of life and, 163–
166; housing applications, 178–181
Functionally-relevant environment, 42–43

Gender: disadvantages and, 66–69; environmental design and, 81–82; expanding bounds of, 76–82; life cycles and,
71–76; leadership and, 78–80; relocation and, 77–78; social context and,
69–71
Golant, S., 23

Habituation, 9–10; and ritual, 95; theory
of, 94–95
Hallowell, A., 90
Home: distinct from housing, 92; experiential links with, 102–103
Household, intergenerational issues, 62–
63, 75–76
Housing: access, 80–81; environmental
theory and, 22–26; feminist theories,

65–76; government support for, 69–71;
HUD, 71; selection, 23–24; subsidized,
63

Insidedness, 5–6
Interactional approach, 165
Introversion, 13–15

Kahana, Eva, 4–5, 35

Lawton, M. Powell, 2–4
Leisure, activity, 21–22; science of, 21;
theory, 16
Lewin, Kurt, 1, 161–181
Life space: defined, 163–166; life situation and, 174; life stage and, 180; phenomenology and, 171–174; research
methods and, 179–180; social aspects,
166–171; time and, 174–178
Loss, relocation and, 77–78

McCrae, Robert, 13–15
Methods, environmental research and, 95–
96
Moos, Rudolf, 43–44, 141–156, 167–168;
compensatory model, 129
Motivation, 8–9
Multiphasic Environmental Assessment
Procedure (MEAP): components, 117–
120; housing applications, 131–134;
practical uses, 131; theoretical and research uses, 121–129

Nahemow, Lucille, 2–4
Needs, 4; "alpha" press, 5; "beta"
press, 5; Murray-defined, 7
Neuroticism, 13–14, 51; negative affect
and, 13

Observer: conceptualization of shelter and
care settings, 40; defined changes in
environmental context, 42
Openness to experience, 18
Outcomes: personal and environmental,
36–54; personal state, 56–57; resident-
experienced, 40–41, temporal context,
36–38

Person: changeable aspects of, 19; changing, 24–25; missing components of construct, 8–12. *See also* Affect; Cognitive-attentional mechanisms; Motivation

Person-environment congruence model, 4–5

Person-environment matching, 126–129, 149–150

Personality, 8; preferences and, 15–22; states and traits, 19–20; style, 52; temperament and, 12–22

Phenomenology: environmental, 100–103; experiential links between person and home, 102–103; illustrative case study, 96–100; life space and, 171–174; meanings, 89–92; methodology and, 95–96; theory and, 92–95

Physical and Architectural Features (PAF) Checklist, 118, 123

Place: aging in, 25, 34, 93, 133–134; attachment to, 73, 94–95; self, society, and, 100–103; therapy of, 25

Policy and Program Information Form (POLIF), 118–119

Positive affect, 3; environment and, 3, 22; leisure activity and, 21–22

"Power of Place" project, 79–80

Preferences, 15–16, 20–21; "demands" versus "desires," 15–16

Press: environmental, 2–4; strength of stimulus, 18

Relocation: environmental discrepancy hypothesis and, 34; illustration, 62–63; psychologically represented environments and, 133–134; residential, 33–34; symbolic meaning, 34; theories, 34–36

Resident, stability and change, 115–116

Resident Staff and Information Form (RESIF), 119; illustrative use, 127–128

Resources: coping and, 54–55; ego, 55; personal, 47–55; situational, 55–56

Rowles, Graham, 5–6

Schooler, Kermit, 5, 35

Schutz, Alfred, 90

Self: as-is, 100; as-was, 10; society and, 100–103

Shelter and care settings: changing, 33–57; new model, 38–57; temporal context, 36–40

Sheltered Care Environment Scale (SCES), 119–120

Sherman, Susan, "threshold" model, 128–129

Social climate, 116; determinants, 121–126; illustrative research on, 121–126; intervention and, typology, 125–126; resident characteristics and, 126

Social ecology: features, 113–114; integrative framework, 115–117; origins, 112–113

Social Security system, 70–71

Stress-Theoretical Model, 5

Taxonomy: behavior circuit, 45; behavior setting theory and, 147–149; organizational, 43; physical, 43; social, 43. *See also* Environmental

Temperament, 12–22; "Big Five," 14–15; personality, 12–22; preferences, 15–16, 20–21; theories of, 17–20; types, 13–15

Theoretical frameworks: early, 2–6; shortcomings, 35

Time use, 68

Traits, 12–22; environmental, 22; personal needs and, 4; preferences and, 20–21; temperament and, 17–20. *See also* Personality

Transactionalism, 5–6, 133–134, 162–163, 175–176

Well-being, 7

"Whole-person" perspective, 23, 38

Women: developmental factors, 74; disadvantages and age, 66–69; leadership and, 80; "multiple lives," 73; work and, 75–76

About the Contributors

STEPHEN M. GOLANT, a gerontologist and geographer, is a professor in the Department of Geography at the University of Florida at Gainesville. A prolific contributor to research on environment and aging, his current interests focus on the strengths and weaknesses of alternative shelter and care options occupied by both active and frail elderly.

M. POWELL LAWTON was director of research at the Philadelphia Geriatric Center for 30 years and is now a senior research scientist. He has done research on the environmental psychology of later life, assessment of the aged, the psychological well-being and quality of life of older people, caregiving stress, and evaluative studies of programs for the aged and for the mentally ill.

DOLORES E. McCARTHY is a clinical social worker and a Ph.D. candidate in environmental psychology at City University of New York. She has a private practice in psychotherapy, teaches at Fordham University Graduate School of Social Work, and has research interests in the effects of relocation upon place attachment at different points in the life cycle.

CAROLYN NORRIS-BAKER is the director of the Center for Aging and a professor in the Department of Architecture at Kansas State University in Manhattan, Kansas. A social psychologist and an architect, her research interests have focused on environment-aging interests, including aging in place, contexts of rural aging, rural housing and long-term care, and the well-being of older rural residents.

PATRICIA A. PARMELEE is an associate professor in the Center for Clinical Epidemiology and Biostatistics at the University of Pennsylvania School of Medicine in Philadelphia. Her substantive interests center on psychosocial influences on physical health in late life. Her background in environment and aging includes theory and research on privacy regulation, place attachment, and the design of special residential environments for frail older persons.

ROBERT L. RUBINSTEIN is a cultural anthropologist. He is director of the Polisher Research Institute of the Philadelphia Geriatric Center and research professor of psychiatry at Temple University School of Medicine. He has conducted research on aging in the United States and in Vanuatu (South Pacific).

SUSAN SAEGERT is the director of the Center for Human Environments and professor of environmental psychology at the City University of New York (CUNY) Graduate School. The founding director of the Center for the Study of Women and Society at CUNY, her research interests include the relationship of housing to individual development, small group processes, and community life, as well as issues related to gender and the environment.

RICK J. SCHEIDT is a professor of life span human development in the School of Family Studies and Human Services at Kansas State University in Manhattan, Kansas. His environment-aging interests include aging in rural environments, rural culture, and the impact of deculturation on mental health.

PAUL G. WINDLEY currently serves as dean of the College of Art and Architecture at the University of Idaho. He holds undergraduate degrees in architecture from Idaho State University and the University of Colorado, and graduate degrees from the University of Michigan, where he was affiliated with the Institute of Gerontology. He has published in the area of environment and aging and consulted with architects and planners on housing and long-term care facilities for the elderly.

ISBN 0-313-28389-3

90000>

EAN

9 780313 283895

HARDCOVER BAR CODE